To Zosia and Lucy

About the Author

Greg Holden has written more than 35 books and many articles in the past decade, many of which discuss new hardware and software, as well as cutting-edge technologies. Many of Greg's books address business issues connected with the Internet and eBay. His book *How to Do Everything with Your eBay Business* recently went into its second edition. Previous books for McGraw-Hill include *Secrets of the eBay Millionaires* and *Fundraising with eBay*. Greg is a columnist for AuctionBytes (www.auctionbytes.com) and he has written for such publications as *Entrepreneur* and *Inc.* magazine.

How to Do *Everything* with

Microsoft® Office Live

Greg Holden

McGraw Hill

New York   Chicago   San Francisco   Lisbon
London   Madrid   Mexico City   Milan   New Delhi
San Juan   Seoul   Singapore   Sydney   Toronto

The McGraw·Hill Companies

Cataloging-in-Publication Data is on file with the Library of Congress

McGraw-Hill books are available at special quantity discounts to use as premiums and sales promotions, or for use in corporate training programs. For more information, please write to the Director of Special Sales, Professional Publishing, McGraw-Hill, Two Penn Plaza, New York, NY 10121-2298. Or contact your local bookstore.

How to Do Everything with Microsoft® Office Live

1234567890 DOC DOC 01987

ISBN-13: 978-0-07-148560-9
ISBN-10:   0-07-148560-0

Sponsoring Editor
Roger Stewart

Editorial Supervisor
Patty Mon

Project Manager
Vasundhara Sawhney,
International Typesetting
and Composition

Acquisitions Coordinator
Carly Stapleton

Technical Editor
Jenn Kettell

Copy Editor
Marcia Baker

Proofreader
Binodini Banerjei

Indexer
Broccoli Information
Management

Production Supervisor
George Anderson

Composition
International Typesetting
and Composition

Illustration
International Typesetting
and Composition

Art Director, Cover
Jeff Weeks

Cover Designer
Pattie Lee

Cover Illustration
Jacey

Contents

V

Acknowledgments

Office Live is designed to give both beginning web publishers and experienced businesspeople a sophisticated presence online. A number of people helped me to establish my own connection to Office Live. Roger Stewart of McGraw-Hill got the ball rolling. My agents Lynn Haller and Neil Salkind of Studio B continue to help move my career in positive directions. Jay Kim of Microsoft helped with setting up SharePoint Designer. Thanks also go to Ma Charina Brooks and Kendle Marra for sharing details about their own web sites. I also gratefully acknowledge Ann Lindner for her continuing help and support, and my daughters Zosia and Lucy for inspiring me.

Introduction

It often seems like everyone has a web site—especially to those who haven't created one and to those who don't have e-mail. But, the fact is, lots of businesspeople who are adventurous and courageous in the business world need a place where they could strike out on their own, stake a claim, open their own storefront, and start to do business for the first time. As far as e-commerce on the Web is concerned, the bloom is off the rose, but eBay remains a thriving destination for anyone who wants to make a few extra bucks or even start a new career as an auction seller.

With Office Live, Microsoft has taken a big step toward making e-commerce and e-mail accessible to anyone. Among its most notable features, Office Live lets anyone create a web site and get an e-mail address—free. Those two features aren't unique. What is unique *is* Office Live makes a custom domain name available to anyone at no charge. As long as your site is hosted on Office Live, you can use a domain name that takes the form mybusiness.com. The same domain name becomes part of your e-mail address—not only your address, but those of the employees or business colleagues who work with you and who also use Office Live.

Office Live makes creating a web site, and sending and receiving e-mail a user-friendly experience. But the wealth of options available to anyone who wants to use the service complicates the choices and processes you need to follow. This book is especially for individuals who are new to the Web and to e-mail, and who need to choose the version of Office Live that fits their needs. Office Live comes in three versions—Basics, Essentials, and Premium. The latter two versions include business applications and workspaces that help members of a workgroup share information and do scheduling. Premium, in particular, gives businesses access to the sorts of productivity tools that usually cost thousands of dollars per user. (Some of those tools, such as Exchange, come from Microsoft itself.) For less than $40 per month, they are able to record business contact and account information, collaborate on schedules, and maintain libraries of documents. Office Live relieves businesses from having to set up costly and complicated application servers. It's particularly useful for small businesses that don't have dedicated IT staff who can perform the setup and maintenance of such services.

Throughout this book, you examine all of Office Lives features, from the simple to the complex. You also work with some applications that aren't technically part of the Office Live suite, including SharePoint Designer and Office Live Accounting 2007. Part I, "The Basics: Getting Your Home Office in Order" starts at the beginning— deciding what you want to accomplish with an Office Live site, choosing the version of Office Live that's right for you, and creating your first web site. You also get suggestions for using Office Live to communicate with others on the Internet.

Part II, "Collaborating and Communicating with Business Partners," guides you through the process of creating workspaces where you can collaborate with your coworkers and other business colleagues, such as contractors, suppliers, and partners.

Part III, "Working with Business Applications," goes in depth to explore one of Office Live's most advanced features in detail. Business applications are preconfigured online services designed to help you handle common business tasks. You learn how to use Project Manager to manage projects, track inventory, and work with datasheets. You also learn how to create a custom application and edit your Office Live site using SharePoint Designer.

In Part IV, "Boosting Your Sales and Productivity," you learn how to use Office Live to sell products and services. You learn how to create a sales catalog and present sales collateral and create document libraries. You also learn how to create an Office Live site that can support an eBay sales business.

Part V, "Ramping Up Your Business Processes," delves into features that can help a business run more smoothly. These include gathering estimates or Requests for Proposals (RFPs) and tracking business contact data. One chapter explores Office Live Accounting 2007, a free tool related to the Office Live family that can help you maintain your company's financial information. A final chapter discusses tools that can help your company be more productive.

I didn't write this book thinking you would read it from beginning to end, as you would read a novel. Like the Web itself, you should be able to skip around from chapter to chapter to find the information you need to know immediately. Plus, you can find special elements to help you get the most out of the book:

- **How to...**   These special boxes explain, in a nutshell, how to accomplish key tasks. Read them to discover key points covered in each chapter.

- **Notes**   These provide information that's often important to gain understanding of a particular topic.

- **Tips**   These tell you how to do something smarter or faster.

- **Cautions**   These point out potential pitfalls you need to steer around, so you can keep operating smoothly.

- **Sidebars**   Here, I address topics related to the subject at hand, that illuminate the topic in a new way.

Within the text, you also find words in special formatting. New terms are in italics, while specific commands you need to choose or type yourself are in boldface.

I wish you success using Office Live to improve your business collaboration. Relax, have fun, and enjoy your new online presence. Tell me your own experiences and whether this book has helped you by dropping me a line at greg@gregholden.com.

Part I

The Basics: Getting Your Home Office in Order

Chapter 1

Establishing Business Objectives for Moving to Office Live

How to...

- Set goals for moving your business operations to Office Live
- Use Office Live to create a commercial web site
- Envision shared workspaces where coworkers can plan, schedule, and track jobs
- Move from fax and phone to web-based shared data and images
- Improve communication through Office Live's e-mail and time management functions

A series currently on TV is called *The Office.* The show's opening credits play over scenes of conventional office life: pencils being sharpened, calculators being tapped, and water coolers gurgling. For many of us, this is what offices are like.

But there's a new kind of office, one that just opened for business. You might think of it as a virtual office building—a place where many different businesses can set up shop. But its address is a Uniform Resource Locator (URL), rather than a street number. And this new kind of office is called *Office Live*—it gives business owners, managers, and sole proprietors alike the capability to create a web site and establish a workspace where employees can collaborate on projects on the Web.

Office Live isn't the same as the set of software programs known as Microsoft Office. It's much more. Along with software that helps you crunch numbers and send messages, you gain the capability to create your own web site and a custom domain name (one that takes the user-friendly form www.mybusiness.com). You also get software that helps you collaborate and communicate, but it's not software you install on your computer. It resides on the Web. This software is called "software as a service." Instead of installing a program on your desktop computer and using it locally, you access it online. The *software as a service* you can access through Office Live is provided through the Essentials and Premium subscription packages. The *Premium version* has the full selection. You might find it well worth paying a monthly fee for Premium if you want to streamline basic business practices, such as:

- Recording business contacts, assigning contacts to sales representatives, and automatically sending e- mail alerts to those representatives.
- Keeping track of schedules and deadlines for multiple projects.

- Creating team workspaces where coworkers can access business applications and collaborate on projects.

- Assembling libraries full of Word documents and other files you and your colleagues can access from any computer connected to the Internet.

- Giving your business partners and suppliers access to shared workspaces where they can track orders and connect with you electronically.

This book explains how Microsoft Office Live can help small businesses be more productive and cost-effective by shifting many management and communications functions online. The first step is to identify the kinds of services your business needs and determine how Office Live can help you streamline operations and meet your goals effectively. As you probably know already, setting objectives and drawing up some plans is always a good idea when you undertake business projects. This first chapter describes the ways in which Office Live can help your enterprise, so you can choose the version that's best for you.

NOTE   *Office Live is related to a set of shared applications called SharePoint Technologies.* SharePoint *enables multiple individuals to collaborate via a centralized web site. But SharePoint requires you to either install special server software or sign up with a hosting service that supports this technology. Office Live is designed for small offices that don't want to run the web server software or climb the technical learning curve needed to take advantage of SharePoint.*

Office Live: The Big Picture

A few years ago, I wrote about PJHM Architects, a California-based firm that plans and designs public school facilities. PJHM has offices in California and Utah, and its employees work in many different locations. The firm has dozens, if not hundreds, of projects going on at any one time. Before the Web, the architects and other staffers recorded their time on Excel spreadsheets and had an administrative person tally them all on another Excel spreadsheet. Because some employees only came into the office once a week, getting up-to-the-minute data was difficult. When PJHM moved to a web-based timesheet service, those workers gained the capability to enter their timesheet information online from any location. "The web hosting solution is perfect for all our needs," a company representative told me.

These days, many companies use contractors who might be located across the street, across the country, or around the world. Everyone in an organization needs to share information. Office Live is also designed to help small businesses centralize communications and data, as well as to give them online capabilities that are either too expensive or too technically complex for them to establish and maintain. This is all part of what's being called *Web 2.0,* which emphasizes collaboration and openness of information to enable groups of individuals to share information and accomplish common goals. With Office Live, companies as small as ten employees or less can establish an online presence; automate key internal and external business tasks; and collaborate with employees, partners, and customers.

When you are planning business objectives to move some of your processes to the Web, you might benefit from the articles included as part of another Microsoft resource, the Small Business Center, *at (http://www.microsoft .com/smallbusiness/hub.mspx).*

Why Do You Need "Software as a Service?"

When you're establishing the goals you need to accomplish with Office Live, think about the many tedious and boring business processes you and your employees have to perform. Think of any repetitive processes or information you need to communicate on a periodic basis. Also, consider any meetings that require you to be in the same room, or that require tele- or videoconferencing. Don't necessarily conclude you have to create your own technological solution, either. Instead of assuming you have to purchase your own computer equipment, network it, and maintain it, for instance, think about the advantages of "renting" software and service for a monthly fee. These advantages include:

- **Ease of installation** Usually, there's no need for installation with software you access on a web site. You may need to upgrade your browser and you may need a particular version of a browser. With Office Live, you need Internet Explorer (IE) 5.5 or later.

- **No need for maintenance** When you "rent" software online, the software provider makes sure the programs work correctly and handles updates. You don't have to periodically buy and install a new version of a spreadsheet or other program every time an update is released.

- **A reduced learning curve** Because you are using your web browser, you don't need to learn a new software program.

■ **Access from anywhere**   You don't need to be at your own computer in your office. You can access your business software and shared information from home or while you're traveling.

> NOTE
>
> *To use Office Live, you need, at minimum, an Internet connection, IE 5.5 with Service Pack 4 (SP4) or later, running on Windows XP, or Windows Server 2003. Some functions of Office Live also require you to have Microsoft Office running on your system.*

As you can see, Software as a service means that, instead of installing software on your computer and using it only on your local machine, you access that software through your web browser from any location. Where do you find software to rent? Shopping around to various companies that provide hosted applications is a time-consuming process. That process typically involves a number of steps:

1. You have to shop around and compare programs.

2. You sign a contract for services, whether this is a month-to-month arrangement, or for a year or two-year period. The fees you pay may vary, depending on the number of employees who will use the service. Each subscription package varies, but with Essentials and Premium, you have to pay extra if the number of employees who access Office Live goes over a certain amount (see Chapter 2 for specifics).

3. You need to research, or at least ask about, the level of security the company will provide. No matter what assurances you hear, you always have to exercise a measure of trust that they are going to handle your information securely.

Office Live alleviates many of these steps. Although shopping around is always good, with Office Live, you can access a variety of services in a single location, and all for a single monthly fee. The fact that Office Live combines everything you need in a single package and eliminates the need for you to shop around is a big advantage.

And, when it comes to trust, you have the reputation of one of the biggest software companies anywhere behind you and your information. Because Microsoft is so security-conscious, it has the expertise to protect its customers' information. Your data is also somewhat safer with Microsoft than with smaller organizations. Because Microsoft has such a high profile, it can't afford to have its Office Live customers' data stolen, so it is likely to do everything possible to provide security.

Why Should I Consider Moving My Office Online?

Right now, you probably have two "offices." One is the office with a front door, one or more desks, computer equipment, wires and plugs, and at least one employee. The other is the software on the computers in the physical office that keeps information flowing. Most likely, you're probably using a version of Microsoft's own office suite of applications. These include the popular programs Word, Excel, PowerPoint, and Access. You might also be using another type of office software, such as Sun Microsystems' open source set of applications, called OpenOffice.org (http://www .openoffice.org).

Having spent a considerable amount of money purchasing the programs, and a considerable amount of time installing them and learning how to use them, you're probably asking yourself why you should consider moving your entire office software system to Office Live. The first answer is you don't have to move *all* your word processing, spreadsheet, and other software to the Office Live site. (In fact, some features, especially those that enable you to export data or make links between your Office Live data and your local computer, require you to have Office 2000 or later installed.) Both Office Live and "not-Live" can coexist on the Web and on your computer. The second answer is working online gives you lots of benefits. One that's already been mentioned is its capability to enable far-flung coworkers to collaborate and communicate. Here are some others:

- Lower up-front capital costs
- Reduce hardware costs
- Need little or no maintenance
- Improve access to information

You do, of course, have to pay a monthly fee to use the more souped-up versions of Office Live. But, you don't necessarily have to keep updating your current version of Microsoft Office every time a new version comes out. You can keep a basic version on your computer and gradually move the business functions described in the following sections over to Office Live.

What Does Your Business Need?

Do an inventory. Think of the kinds of needs your office has right now. Don't focus on all the services offered online—at least not yet. You'll run through those later in this book (particularly in Chapter 2). At this stage you're simply evaluating which version of Office Live you want, so think about what your office needs. For instance:

- Do you need an affordable web site and e-mail?

- Do you lack accounting help?

- Do you have employees in several different branch offices?

- Do you have trouble tracking customer-related data, such as which salespeople have contacted customers in the past or when the last call took place?

Some of Office Live's most useful features are that it includes web hosting, e-mail, and web site design tools, in addition to a suite of business applications. Another is that, while anyone with a web browser can gain access to your web site, the files you store on Office Live are restricted only to those to whom you have specifically granted access.

Creating a Business Web Presence

One of the primary goals behind Office Live is its capability to give a small business an Internet presence. We're in the twenty-first century and, if you have any type of business at all, it's commonly assumed you need at least a simple web site. On the one hand, you want your site to be simple and straightforward, and you want it to provide prospective clients and customers with basic information about what you do. But, on the other hand, you need to realize that thousands, if not millions, of other web sites are out there in cyberspace covering the same ground you are. Unless it's going to be a well-designed, professional-looking site that will catch people's attention and give your business credibility, there's simply no point in creating a site.

When you're planning this aspect of your Office Live presence, having a model to follow can be helpful. Accordingly, this section presents examples of businesses that set up shop with Office Live and have instituted the kinds of web site features you can use to your own advantage.

Your External Web Site

The good news is you have more options than ever before from which to choose when it comes to creating a public face for your business on the Web. The bad news is you have all those options to choose from. Small business owners can get confused determining where to get the best deals when registering domain names or finding a web site and e-mail host. They often have to turn to different service providers to assemble what they need, which can take a lot of time and effort. Office Live gives you a free domain and a free web space, no matter what version you sign up for.

Of course, the audience for an external web site isn't just external. It's a resource for the people within your company, too. A web site can be much more than a place to publish your name, phone number, or e-mail address. The following describes some of the ways in which web sites were created on Office Live—and some of them just might surprise you.

Streamlining Routine Questions and Paperwork

Every business receptionist knows the majority of questions are ones that come up on a repeated basis: How much are the fees? Where are you located? What are your hours? and so on. For a medical office, the questions are more substantive, but no less routine: What insurance programs do you accept? Do I need to arrive early for a particular kind of procedure? Do you accept credit cards?

Northwest Chiropractic Center, created on Office Live, provides visitors with the answers to basic questions online. The home page shown in Figure 1-1 points potential clients to areas where they can decide whether they want to become patients.

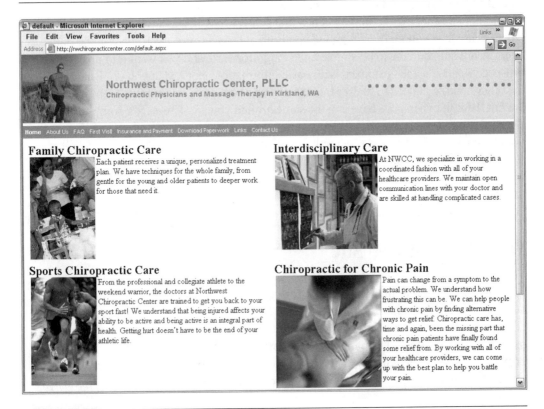

FIGURE 1-1   This company uses Office Live to sell its professional services.

Not only that, but it gives patients the capability to download and print their paperwork, so it can be filled out in advance, rather than taking up valuable office time. Customer Resources on the company's web site (http://nwchiropracticcenter .com) includes:

- A Frequently Asked Questions page with a photo of the entire staff (this personalizes the business) and general information about the field of chiropractic care.

- An insurance page with brief information about discounts and copays.

- A First Visit page, which encourages new patients to download and complete forms ahead of time and suggests what they should wear or bring to the office.

- A page full of downloadable forms presented in Adobe's popular Portable Document Format (PDF). These forms not only ask for patient information but they also provide easy-to-follow directions to the facility, saving phone calls and time spent giving directions (see Figure 1-2).

Showing Off Your Work

In many service industries, prospective customers are forced to ask around for recommendations when they are looking to hire someone. For the service provider, simply being able to display their work, as well as explain qualifications and experience can make all the difference. At its most basic level, a web site gives a professional a place to display photos of completed work. Additionally, the business owner, such as Dynabuild Construction (http://dynabuildconstruction.com, shown in Figure 1-3), can provide an online client list, a history of the company, and a description of the kind of work it has done.

Simply having a presentation on the Web, which a client can visit and observe at their convenience, can distinguish your company from your competition. Putting the customer in control, and giving them the ability to consider hiring you, after weighing the introductory information you provide on your Office Live site, can make the difference between being hired or being passed over. Creating a simple web-based showcase puts you "in the game" and gives you a chance to sell your services 24/7.

Communicating with a Group

Nonprofit organizations and clubs can benefit from Office Live web sites the same way commercial organizations can. The Port Townsend Sailing Association uses

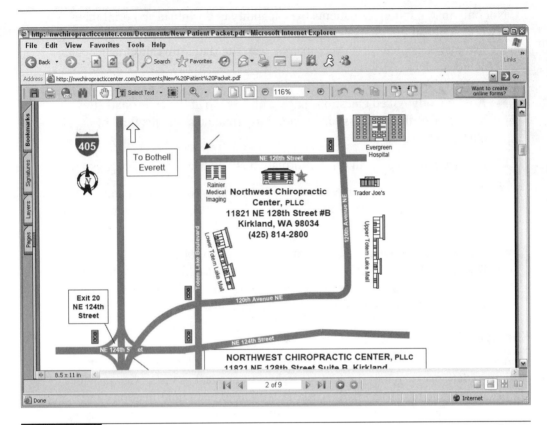

its web site for announcements and sharing information about its races. Members can go to the site (http://ptsail.org) to get results of past races and dates for upcoming events. Members can put out a call for crew they need. And everyone can view photos taken of the events (see Figure 1-4).

The kinds of information shared on the web site would be of interest to a for-profit, as well as a nonprofit organization. Along with the race photos, members can access a newsletter, a set of rules and regulations, and a form, which prospective members can fill out to join the group. And, the site has a commercial aspect—it contains a link to the Webmaster's photography business site, where they advertise their services as wedding and portrait photographers.

The Web is well into its second decade, and the reasons for creating a personal web site should be clear: this site gives you a chance to publish information about yourself, and to connect with family, friends, and other people who share your interests.

FIGURE 1-3 This construction company uses Office Live to sell its services online.

But, some benefits of creating a business web site aren't always obvious. The obvious ones are, of course, that a web site gives prospective clients a way to find out more about who you are and what your qualifications are. But, more than that, a web site created with Office Live can help you create long-term relationships, which are key to any business's success. A web site is a surprisingly personal venue for communications and ideal for one-to-one connections. An Office Live site works to develop relationships with customers over time. And, an Office Live site encourages involvement and two-way communications, providing valuable data or expertise while requesting and capturing visitor information in return.

NOTE *You can find out more about how to create a business web site in Chapter 3. And, you learn how to foster long-term business relationships through collaboration of the sort described in Chapters 5 and 7.*

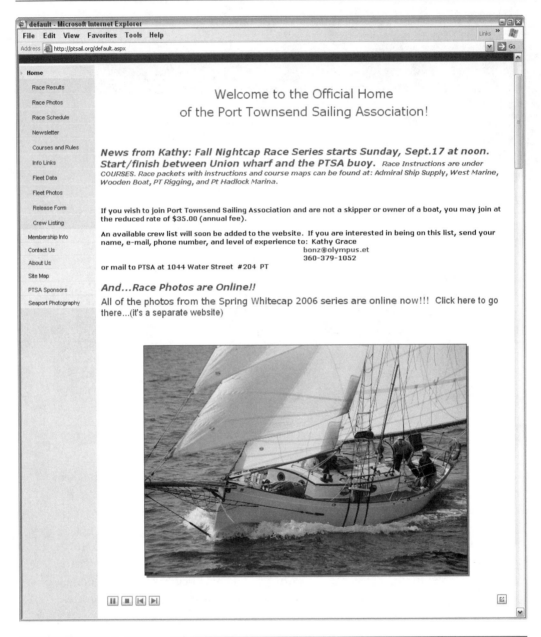

Going Live with E-Mail

E-mail is as popular as any application on the Internet (if not more), and chances are you already have experience with it as a tool for person-to-person communications. The Basic service gives you a Hotmail-like e-mail application that displays advertisements for MSN and other organizations along with messages (see Figure 1-5). The Premium service is a true Outlook-type client.

What advantages are there for signing up for e-mail through Office Live? First is security: Microsoft contracted with the highly regarded security software provider Trend Micro to provide virus scanning for the messages you receive. And, any e-mail received from someone who is not on your Allowed Senders or Contacts list produces a warning: all attachments and images contained with the messages are blocked until you allow the message through. Extensive junk e-mail settings are designed to minimize the amount of spam you receive.

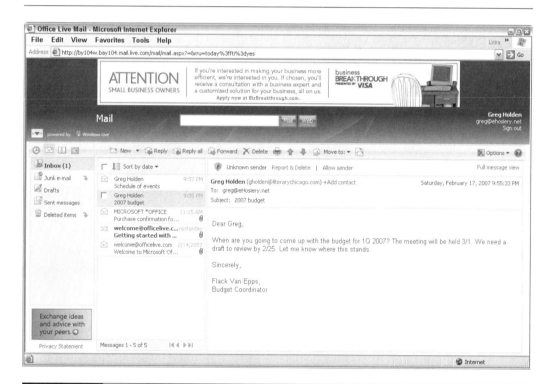

FIGURE 1-5   The e-mail interface for Outlook Live Basic is the same as Microsoft's Hotmail e-mail program.

Second, the e-mail interface is easy-to-use. You get 2GB of space and features like filters, which are found under the Options link. You learn more about e-mail in Chapter 2.

You have the capability to access your Office Live mail from your mobile device—as long as that device supports Windows Mobile technology. Other applications, such as the Blackberry, aren't supported at this time.

Creating Shared Workspaces

Small businesses frequently use hosted applications that enable them to communicate directly with vendors, customers, and business partners. They may want to provide technical support to customers. They may also want to give vendors direct access to their recent records of completed jobs. Office Live Premium, in fact, gives small business four separate designations for shared workspaces:

- **Customer workspace**   This isn't necessarily a space where customers can view their own data. Instead, it's set up so members of your own work force can keep up with company events and schedule upcoming meetings (see Figure 1-6).

- **Team workspace**   This workspace, like the others in Office Live consists of a calendar, a space for announcements, and an area for shared documents. The goal is to give workers a space where they can work together on shared projects.

- **Basic meeting workspace**   This enables a group of coworkers to communicate and share information.

- **Wiki workspace**   This area enables anyone who has access to the space to contribute to a shared repository of information, such as a diary or newsletter. See the well-known site Wikipedia (www.wikipedia.com) for an example.

The Shared Documents area of any one of the workspaces is particularly powerful: it enables designers to demonstrate their work, employees to share product descriptions with vendors, or coworkers to view one another's layouts and drafts. It can also be used for technical support: For many small businesses, the quickest way to get a problem solved is to have the customer show you what the problem is, and then show them how to accomplish the solution. You can use this area to exchange screen captures or other images that save time spent contriving complex explanations.

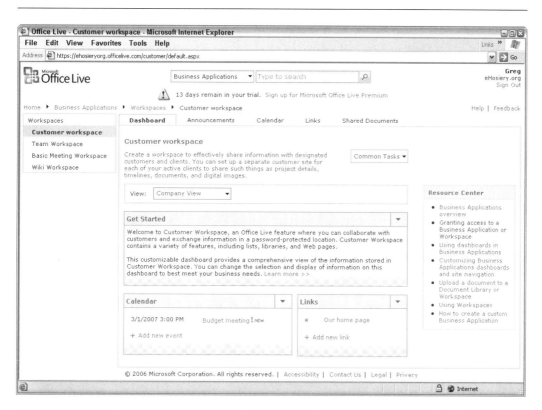

FIGURE 1-6   This workspace provides employees with a shared record of customer contacts.

Collaborating on Projects

When you think of collaborating, you usually think of employees or partners working together. But the projects on which you collaborate with an application service provider, such as Office Live, don't always have to be with other employees. They can also be with prospective clients. CMstat Corporation, a configuration management company with 20 employees based in San Diego, provides enterprise information management software to businesses around the world. Demos are essential for clients to decide if they want to make a purchase. In the past, CMstat would send a team of employees to visit each prospective customer one or more times. The trips totaled more than $10,000 per month in travel expenses. By doing demos on the Web, the company could lower expenses and shorten its sales cycle.

Better Communication Between Employees

The Users & Accounts section of Office Live gives you the capability to set up separate accounts for each of your employees. Each account can have a different level of access: Administrator, Editor, or Reader.

In addition, the Administration category within Office Live's Business Applications contains an Employee Directory, which you can populate with contact information for everyone in your company. (This list can also be linked to your Outlook mailing list.)

Other applications let you create estimates, track expenses, or set up To Do lists you can share with your fellow employees. What you do with these applications is up to you. Once you set up the system, a good idea is to invite suggestions from individual staff people, who are likely to come up with uses you never thought of before. Sometimes, you might be communicating about high-level projects. Other times, you are communicating about mundane daily tasks that are important, nonetheless. Either way, managing your time well or saving time in some way or another is the key. By giving your employees the capability to share information by using a web-based application, you encourage them to work collaboratively. You might find they decide to work together more closely for the sake of trying out the new technological tools they've been given.

For example, consider the simple task of entering time and expenses. In a traditional (that is, non-"e-") business environment, time is usually recorded the old-fashioned way. Staff people enter their time into a database or send a message by e-mail or (shudder) paper to the accounting staff. In any case, the data goes to a single point in a sort of information funnel: The burden of recording time falls to a financial administrator. No matter what job title this person goes by—bookkeeper, accountant, or fiscal assistant—this person has a lot of work to do. He/She has to crunch the timesheet data, and then print out invoices, reports, or paychecks, depending on the data being calculated.

By allowing employees to record the information in a simple web-based form they access through Office Live, you gain several advantages:

- Employees submit data from wherever they are, whenever they need to. They don't have an excuse for "losing" printed timesheets.

- Timesheet data can be entered using a web browser, rather than proprietary software.

- Using a timesheet service frees your fiscal person for other duties.

- Administrators can access timesheet data easily from any location (not just the local area network) to see not only how much time has been spent, but also how much of the project is complete.

This doesn't put your accountants or bookkeepers out of business, of course. They still have to calculate pay, do billing, or track the progress of individual jobs. This still has to be done in-house—but they'll also get the job done more quickly and more accurately.

Scheduling Improvements

One of the biggest sources of misunderstandings among coworkers in an office environment involves scheduling. Someone forgets an appointment; someone gets a time wrong. You can use Office Live to put your schedules online and get on the same page—web page, that is.

You don't have to be in a high-tech business to take advantage of online collaboration. I once wrote about a massage therapy company (BetterBodyTherapy) that was overworked from having to drive from one Colorado company to another, helping harried high-tech employees relax. It seemed only natural to move to a web-based scheduling system. Clients who have web access can immediately check for openings in the businessperson's schedule. They can then choose an available time and instantly confirm the appointment is scheduled.

Each Office Live business application includes a scheduling function in the form of a familiar-looking calendar. You can either view the calendar in a month's worth of days or in a single day (see Figure 1-7).

With Office Live, you can use the Project Manager (shown in Figure 1-8) to view not only the start and end times for a job, but also a designation of how urgent the job is and how much of the job is done. (You learn more about Project Management in Chapter 10.)

Improved Collaboration with Business Partners

I never thought I'd hear e-mail and fax technology described as being too slow. But if you're an anxious vendor or supplier who is waiting to see if you have received the supplies that were shipped, or if you have shipped the items that were purchased, a few minutes can seem like an eternity. By allowing partners direct access to the information on your Office Live site that pertains to their company, you can not only fend off some anxious phone calls, but also keep your business partners in the loop.

Giving Outsiders Access to Your Network

Chances are your business (or your home business) already has a connection to the Internet, which you use for e-mail, research, and other essential functions. If you have a small office where employees share information about projects

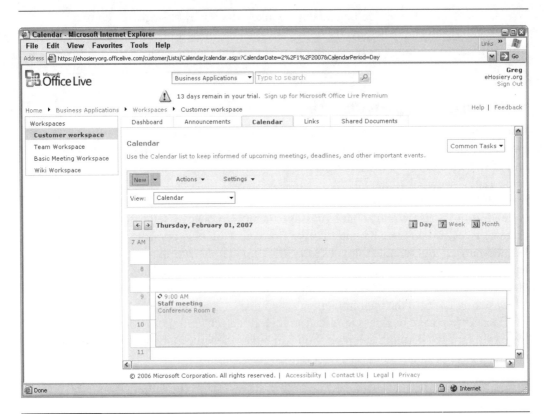

FIGURE 1-7 Shared calendars help team members meet deadlines and manage projects.

they're working on, you also have an internal network. Many businesses provide information to their individual employees by means of an internal web server. This gives them the capability to browse their internal network and share files.

Many businesses go a step further: they give their business partners and customers access to their internal network. By issuing partners and customers a password, businesses allow only approved users to access the site. Not only that, but they are able to restrict access to the company files, so a business partner only sees the data sheets that apply to their company. When a company gives external users the capability to access internally networked information, they are said to have created an extranet. An *extranet* is a network that runs on Internet-based software, but that gives external users secure access.

Setting up an extranet is a technically demanding prospect. It requires you to have at least one IT staffer on board who can configure and maintain a web server and other servers. You also need to set up a password protection system for the files you want to share. Office Live saves you the trouble of having to create an

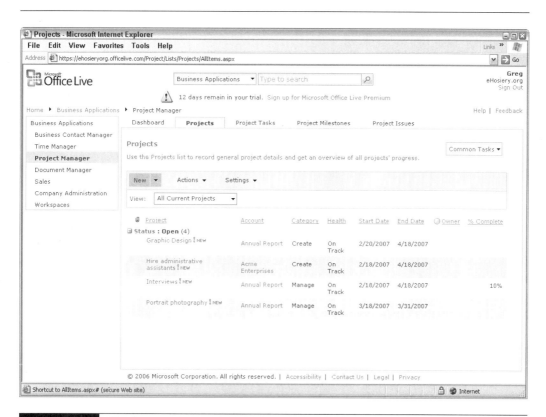

FIGURE 1-8 You have no excuse for missing a deadline or forgetting a job, thanks to Project Manager.

extranet of your own. It doesn't use the fancy word "extranet," but it allows you to give password-protected access to your live workspace on the Web to employees, suppliers, business partners, and other customers.

Why consider giving external clients access to part of your Office Live space? Here are some ways in which an extranet can help:

- Shared calendars can help you keep on time and meet deadlines.

- Phone bills are decreased and time spent communicating by telephone is saved.

- A centralized "paper trail" you and your clients can refer to is provided. This eliminates communication errors and decreases the risk of lawsuits.

- Staff people can set up a shared site where they can post blueprints, designs, or other images to get client approval.

Giving outsiders the capability to look into some your files and, possibly, even to make changes to them is quite a step forward for many businesses. But, by taking that step, you not only improve relations with your clients by giving them a measure of control, but you can also save your own staff time and effort, and streamline critical business processes. Rather than having the client call your sales representatives to ask about the status of an order or a shipment, they can log into your network and see where the shipment is. They can even make changes to the shipment on a timely basis.

Several years ago, I wrote about a company called Corrugated Supplies Company (CSC), a manufacturer of boxes and other corrugated products, in Chicago. This company regularly ships large numbers of boxes and other materials to retail stores around the Chicago area. Often, shipments go out several days a week. By giving clients the capability to log into their own pages on the CSC network (http://www .csclive.com), they can see when shipments are going out and adjust quantities as needed. But, this is not an Office Live shared site. Setting up this internal network required a huge amount of work, and maintaining it also requires considerable technical expertise. Office Live provides the same sorts of functions to businesses as the aforementioned Northwest Chiropractic Center, but without the need to hire programmers or Webmasters.

Creating a user account for someone outside your immediate circle of employees is as easy as assigning them an e-mail address in your domain and a password, and then assigning them the right level of permissions in the Users & Accounts area of Business Applications. With the Essentials version of Office Live, you have the capability to create as many as 50 separate e-mail addresses. By designating one of your clients or business partners as a Reader in a particular Shared Site, you give that person the capability to read information, but not to change it. If a client needs to make changes, you can have him/her speak to one of your sales representatives in person.

Giving Customers the Information They Need

Do you really want to give customers access to your company records through the Web? Not exactly. You don't want them looking over your books or your full employee phone directory. But, some of the best web sites are giving customers a way to contribute their own content in the form of reviews. Comments posted on a message board can give prospective customers more information about items in which they're interested and, I hope, help them make the decision to purchase. Simply making it clear to customers that you care about their questions and concerns, and you have taken steps to address their needs by providing information on the Web, builds trust in you and your products.

The Business Applications section of Office Live includes a Customer Support area. This is divided into two tabs: an FAQ (Frequently Asked Questions) and an Inquiries area. On the FAQ area, you can either enter questions you have received from customers, along with your corresponding answers, or questions you and your staff create that are likely to be asked at some point. The Inquiries tab is more for your staff's own reference than that of the public. The Inquiries tab serves as a common "message board" where your employees can see which customers have asked questions and which issues are resolved.

At this initial planning stage, the important thing to remember is you don't need to keep information, such as customer phone numbers or the status of inquiries, on a piece of paper sitting on an individual employee's desk or on one person's computer. Instead, you can store this information in your Office Live workspace where everyone can access it at any time. Office Live, in other words, gives your small business a new way to think about information: it opens access, and emphasizes sharing and working together, instead of working in relative isolation.

Where to Find It

■ **Microsoft Office Live**

http://officelive.microsoft.com

The home page for the Microsoft Office site, where you can find out more about product offerings and sign up to test the software.

■ **Microsoft Office Live Comparison Chart**

http://officelive.microsoft.com/WebHosting.aspx

A chart that compares the features included in the Basic, Collaboration, and Essentials versions of Office Live.

■ **Openoffice.org**

http://www.openoffice.org

A set of desktop spreadsheet, word processing, and other office applications provided by Sun Microsystems.

■ **Customer Stories**

http://officelive.microsoft.com/Misc/Links.aspx?linkId=customerstories

Profiles of small businesses and how they have used Office Live to improve both their internal and external communications.

■ **Tips for Outsourcing Your Small Business Needs**

http://www.microsoft.com/smallbusiness/resources/management/ recruiting_staffing/tips_for_outsourcing_your_small_business_needs .mspx

An article on the Microsoft Small Business Center web site, which presents some points to consider before you sign with an outside firm to handle some of your business needs (this includes Microsoft and Office Live, of course).

Chapter 2

Choosing the Office Live Version That's Right for You

How to...

- Establish the groundwork for your Office Live business presence

- Set up a web site with Office Live Basics

- Create a Shared Site with Office Live Essentials

- Access Business Applications with Office Live Premium

- Make sure you have the computer setup you need

Small business managers have a tough job. They need to accomplish everything with limited resources. They need to be as productive as larger competitors with far fewer employees. They need to keep track of multiple projects and not get mixed up, calling the wrong client for the wrong job. They need end-to-end solutions with only a single vendor providing them. At the same time, they don't want to make lots of service calls to technical professionals.

Office Live enables you to achieve these goals with the three versions of its service. But which version is right for you, and what do you need to get started? One potentially confusing aspect of the service's three packages is that some overlap occurs as far as features they contain. The difference between the packages is partly one of the number of features, and partly one of disk space and computing power. In a nutshell, the versions break down like this:

- Basics lets you create a web site and includes e-mail service for 25 accounts.

- Essentials also includes a web site, but it has e-mail service for 50 accounts. Along with using Office Live's Site Designer tool to create the site, you can upload an existing site to your space. You also gain the capability to use third-party web design tools, such as Microsoft FrontPage. And you gain access to one business application: Business Contact Manager. Ten users can access this application, as well as the workspaces you get with Essentials.

- Premium lets you create a web site, and it has all the collaboration features included in Essentials. You get 2GB of web storage space with Premium (compared with 1GB for Essentials and 500MB with Basics). One of the biggest differences between Premium and Essentials, though, is the number of business applications you get with Premium. These include a wide variety of applications for managing projects, employees, and documents. Twenty users can access the applications and workspaces.

Customers today are bombarded with information and advertising, and they are in a hurry. Increasingly, more of them are looking for what they want online. Yet, research indicates that only about half of all small businesses have a web site up and running. You need to be on the Web, or you're in danger of being invisible.

With Office Live, you get a big head start on web site design work and shared applications. All you need to do is focus on your business, develop your business identity, and reach your customers. The following sections explain how the different versions work, so you can let Microsoft Office Live take care of the rest. You can get a quick comparison of the three subscription packages at http://office.microsoft. com/en-us/officelive/FX101925601033.aspx. If you only want a quick overview, however, you can scan the comparison presented in the next section.

You may well need to build a case for moving to Office Live. You may need to convince the stakeholders in your organization why it's a good idea to sign on with Microsoft as your web host and business software provider. You may need to come up with a list in which you match the features offered by Office Live to the business functions you need to perform. Table 2-1 lists some of the business goals you might need to achieve and briefly describes how Office Live can meet them.

At press time, you could move "up" from Basics to Essentials or from Essentials to Premium. But you couldn't move down: you had to end your Essentials or Premium account, and then move "down" to a Basics account.

Before You Sign Up

Choosing the right version of Office Live is important, but it's not the first thing you should worry about. In fact, you shouldn't worry about the choice at all: you can decide to end one level of service or start another at any time. Rather than focusing on what version to choose, you need to get your business plans and infrastructure in order. Then, you can make a smooth transition, no matter what program you choose.

What's in a Name? Plenty!

You can start with your mission statement, your goals, your target audience, or any number of high-level objectives. But when you're preparing to sign up for Office Live, you might start with a simple question: what is the name of your business? Why start with your name, you ask? Ideally, your business name should be the same as your domain name—the part of the URL that includes .com or other domain suffix. As mentioned in Chapter 1, your Office Live Basics or Essentials account includes a web site and a domain name. Is a domain name available that matches the business name you want to use? The dot-com domain is the best known and most desirable,

If You Need...	Scenario	Office Live Versions with this Feature	Features Included
A web site	You need a simple web presence, so potential customers can find out about you online, but you can't afford a web designer.	Basic (free), Essentials ($19.95 per month)	Web-based Site Designer tool helps you create simple web pages. In addition, with Essentials, you can upload an existing web site.
A domain name for your web address	You need to find an easy-to-remember domain name for your web site URL.	Basic, Essentials	Office Live helps you locate and register a domain name for no extra cost—a service that costs $9 to $20 per year at other sites.
Web server storage space	You need a place to post web page text, images, transfer layouts, and files from one person to another.	Basic (500MB), Essentials (1GB), Premium (2GB)	All versions give you lots of storage space. In addition, you get 10GB per month of data transfer with Basics, 15GB with Essentials, and 20GB with Premium.
E-mail	You need to communicate by e-mail with other employees as well as with suppliers and clients.	Basic: 25 e-mail accounts Essentials, Premium: 50 e-mail accounts	Office Live Mail is included with all three versions of the service.
Streamlined Human Resources (HR) functions	You need to set up password-protected payroll and HR management.	Essentials, Premium	Shared Sites, such as an HR workspace, let you track sensitive payroll and timesheet date securely.
Training and new hire information	You need to convey standard new hire orientation instructions.	Essentials, Premium	You can post the training information and new hire forms and data sheets in an online training area.
Manage projects	You need to track progress and share information.	Premium	Project management functions let coworkers view the progress of shared projects from any computer on the Internet.

TABLE 2-1   Meeting Business Goals with Office Live Features

because it's what people look for when they think of a commercial entity that has a presence on the Internet. They naturally think of a "dot-com" company when they think of an online business.

I'm suggesting, then, that you do a search for a domain name that matches your ideal business name. Go to the Office Live home page (http://officelive.microsoft.com), type the domain name you want in the search box labeled Get a domain name, and then click Go. The Find a domain page appears with the results of your search. If the name you're looking for is unavailable, you can choose one of three options from the drop-down list shown in Figure 2-1. These are three of the most popular domains:

- ■ **.com**   This is intended for commercial businesses

- ■ **.org**   This was originally intended for nonprofit organizations. In reality, this is often used by commercial entities that either can't find their preferred domain name in the .com domain, or that want to register their preferred name in more than one domain to avoid confusion.

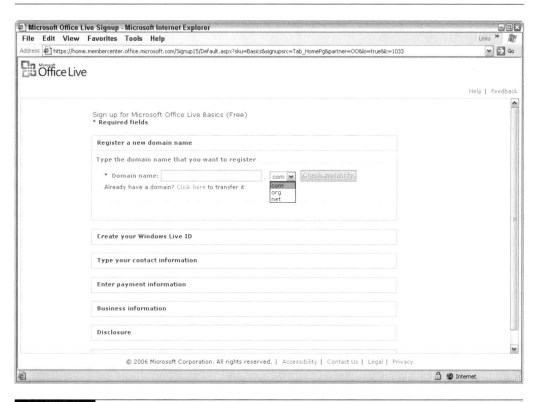

FIGURE 2-1   Begin by doing a search for the domain name, which should match your business name.

■ **.net** This domain was originally set aside for use by network service providers (for example, earthlink.net, which is used by the popular Internet service provider (ISP) Earthlink). It, too, is often used by individuals and commercial businesses.

Currently, you can only use Office Live's domain name registration service to secure names in one of these three domains. If someone else has already registered the name you want, you can't use it; only one entity at a time can own a domain name. If more than one person had the same domain name and URL, you can imagine the chaos that would result on the Internet.

You have to get creative about the domain name you want. For instance, a common domain name, such as nailart.com, is likely to be taken. But, if you add your own name, you increase your chances of finding something no one else has used. For instance, Kendle Marra used her nickname, Keni, to come with the domain name kenisnailart.com. This is also the name of her business: Keni's Nail Art. It doesn't matter whether you come up with the domain name or the English name first. The important thing is to find a name that is:

■ Short and uncomplicated, so the average person can type it without making mistakes. (By short, I mean anywhere from 2 to 12 or 15 characters long, though longer names are fine as long as they are easy to remember.)

■ Ideally, identical to the business name you want. Although if your business name is Acme Enterprises LLC and your domain name is acmeenterprises. com, that's fine.

■ Says something about the kind of products and services you sell.

Your domain name, in other words, is the first chance you have to promote your business, so it's important to choose a name that doesn't sacrifice a professional demeanor for being easy to remember. Don't get too frivolous or silly. The advantage of using Office Live is it gives you credibility for your operation. Don't undo that credibility by choosing a domain name/business name that doesn't reflect well on you as a professional.

Putting the "Tact" in Contact

Contact information is an essential part of any business web site. After all, you want the people who learn about your products and services online to be able to get back to you with inquiries and feedback, not to mention purchases.

The site you create with Office Live lets you get more than a simple e-mail message from interested visitors. By default, you present them with a form that gathers their name, e-mail address, and other information. You can design this page so it matches the look and feel of the rest of your site. The page that appears when you click the Contact Us link on the Keni's Nail Art site has even been "dressed up" with photos (see Figure 2-2).

The standard contact page that comes with an Office Live web site is a *web page form*—a page with a few text boxes the visitor fills out and a SUBMIT button that sends the information to you. Because the contact information is part of a form, you don't communicate with the individual directly by e-mail. Conceivably, they can enter an incorrect e-mail address in the text box supplied by the form. As an alternative, many Office Live sellers include their e-mail address on the Contact Us page. This enables someone to send you a message using their e-mail program, rather than filling out a form.

FIGURE 2-2   You can design your contact page to resemble the rest of your web site.

Because even the Basics level of Office Live includes multiple e-mail accounts, you may want to give some thought to creating multiple e-mail addresses for different purposes. This enables you to sort your e-mail and prioritize it more easily. Many merchants create e-mail addresses like these:

- info@mybusiness.com for general inquiries

- customerservice@mybusiness.com for existing customers who need support with items they already purchased

- webmaster@mybusiness.com for questions or problems regarding your web site

- [yourname]@mybusiness.com for people who want to reach you directly

By providing potential customers with a variety of ways to reach you, you give them a way to use their preferred method of communication. In other words, you should feel free to customize your contact page with different contact options (you find out how to do this in Chapter 7). Even in the early planning stages, you should decide whether you want contact options, such as phone numbers, on your Contact Us page. Some businesses include toll-free phone numbers to encourage people to make inquiries. You might also want to include a fax number. Signing up for a toll-free number and purchasing a fax machine (and possibly paying an extra monthly fee for a dedicated business phone number) are both things you can be doing when you establish your business parameters.

TIP *Plenty of services are available on the Web to help businesspeople obtain their own toll-free phone numbers. One I am personally familiar with is at http://www.billquimby.com. You have to pay a fee to obtain the number, and then you pay the tolls for the phone calls you receive—plus, you have to transfer the number to an existing phone service. You might also have to obtain a land line, so you can assign the toll-free number to it. But, many businesspeople are happy to have the phone ring more often and consider such a phone number worth the expense. If you want to obtain a generic toll-free number for as little as $2.85 per minute, look into 800numbers. com (http://www.800numbers.com/).*

Minding Your Legal Ps and Qs

Before you go online, give some thought to the legal considerations of starting up and running a business. My brother was exceptionally careful to consult with an attorney and protect himself before he started his audio restoration business (http://www.lp2cdsolutions.com). Why? He makes copies of old LP records, cleans them up digitally, and re-creates them as CDs. He didn't want to run afoul of record industry executives who have been coming down hard on people who distribute music through file-sharing sites. He's careful to make only one copy of a recording, and then return it and the original to the owner after the work is done. On his site, he has a lengthy Terms of Use page (http://www.lp2cdsolutions.com/terms-of-use.html), which identifies his attorney as his Copyright Agent. He has also incorporated his company, which shields him to some extent from full liability in case of lawsuits.

You don't have to go to these lengths to "cover yourself" legally, although it's a good idea to take some protection to prevent problems from cropping up. But, at the very least, you probably need to register your business with your state as a sole proprietorship—a business run by a single individual. You might have to obtain a business license from your municipality, so you can work within the city limits. By observing such requirements, you aren't just protecting yourself from getting into trouble. When you run your own business, you also get tax benefits: you can deduct your business expenses, for instance, or obtain a business checking account.

You can find a set of links to articles about legal requirements for small businesses on the Entrepreneur.com web site, http://www.entrepreneur.com/startupbasics/legalissues/archive116046.html. The U.S. Small Business Administration's guide to legal and tax requirements for small businesses is at http://www.sba.gov/starting_business.

Getting the Business Equipment You Need

Office Live can do a lot, but you can't expect it to solve all your problems. You probably need to purchase hardware, such as a telephone answering machine for your office, a fax machine, or a multifunction machine that also produces photocopies.

Another type of hardware you might need to shop for at this early stage is a digital camera. I explain this in greater detail in the section "Capturing Images of Your Products."

If you're going to ship out merchandise to customers who purchase it from you online, you need a variety of shipping supplies. These include:

■ **Boxes**   U.S. Postal Service Priority Mail boxes are free and you can order them shipped to you from the USPS web site (http://www.usps.com). Otherwise, you need clean boxes to hold your merchandise. (These boxes don't need to be new, but they do need to be clean.)

- **Shipping tape**   The USPS requires you to use shipping tape, not duct tape. If you ship a lot, a packing tape dispenser you hold in your hand can save you a lot of time.

- **A postal scale**   You can print your own postage as long as you weigh your packages carefully. It's worth investing in a good digital scale upfront. You can find affordable ones on eBay (http://www.ebay.com).

Where are you planning to store your inventory before you need to ship it out? Set your storage area up beforehand and stock it with lots of shelves. If you work from your house, your family members will appreciate it if you can keep your inventory from taking over your living space. This is a common occurrence with eBay sellers and a subject with which I have personal experience.

Building a Graphic Identity

One thing I notice when I scan the different web sites created with Office Live (many of which are profiled in this book) is their owners "get it" when it comes to the need to establish a graphic identity. Consider the two sites profiled in this chapter. Simply SoyNaturals has a green banner across its home page (see Figure 2-3). The green fits perfectly with the natural ingredients used in the products being sold on the site. In contrast, Keni's Nail Art uses bright colors that suggest the colorful nails you can create with the products being sold there. I'm not going to go into great detail on creating a graphic look and feel for your site in this chapter. But at this early stage, when you are assembling the ingredients you need to create your site, you should give some thought to creating a logo and choosing colors and typefaces that will create a good impression on the customers you want.

Creating a Logo

If you already have a brick-and-mortar business and are considering the move to Office Live as a way to expand your reach to the Web, you probably already have a head start on a graphic identity. Your store might have a sign. You probably have a business card. You might also have business stationery. Each of these publications can and should make use of a business logo: a single visual image that represents who you are and what you do.

If you already have an existing logo, you can simply scan it and save it as a Graphics Interchange Format (GIF) image. Once you have the GIF image on your computer, you can easily add it when you start building your site with

FIGURE 2-3   Artwork that comes with Office Live helps you create banners and other graphics.

Office Live. If you don't have a logo yet, take heart. You have two options from which to choose:

- Hire a graphic designer to create one for you. This can cost a few hundred dollars, but it pays off in the long run because you can use your logo for years to come. You can find designers on sites such as Elance (http://www .elanceonline.com).

- Do it yourself. Some web sites, such as Cool Text (http://cooltext.com), lead you through the process of creating a simple text design that can serve as a banner or a logo. The clip art made available to you with Office Live gives you a big head start toward creating your own logo.

The Viva Dance Company site, which was one of the sites being showcased by Microsoft at press time, includes a simple, yet effective, logo in the conventional location—the upper left-hand corner of the site's home page (see Figure 2-4).

FIGURE 2-4   A simple text logo can help establish your site's—and your business's—visual identity.

NOTE   *You can find more about designing your web site in Chapter 3.*

Capturing Images of Your Products

If you need an Office Live site to sell goods and services, then you probably need to take photos of them to post on your web site. The best and most convenient way to capture digital images—images that consist of digital information and can be stored on a computer—is with a digital camera. If you don't already have a digital camera for your personal use, consider buying one, so you can take web site photos, as well as your own personal photos. The two uses require a far different set of qualities, though. Personal photos you might print on photographic paper need to be high quality. Web photos don't need fine resolution because of the medium on which they appear. Most computer screens can only display 72 dots per inch,

FIGURE 2-5   You don't need the latest and greatest model to take photos for your web site.

which is a coarse resolution (the low resolution also keeps file sizes low, which allows images to appear on web pages more quickly).

When I take photos for the Web, I take them at the lowest resolution available on my 5-megapixel camera: 640×480. If you're only going to take photos for a web site, you can look for a camera with the capability to capture 2 or 3 megapixels worth of data. These days, that's low resolution, so you should be able to purchase a camera for a bargain price. I purchased the Sony CyberShot DSC S600, shown in Figure 2-5, for my daughter. This digital camera has 6 megapixels and, as you can see, you could purchase it on eBay for the good price of $149.99. (You learn more about adding images in Chapter 3.)

NOTE   *I said you "probably" need a digital camera because some Office Live customers, such as the owner of Simply SoyNatural, http://www .simplysoynatural.com, uses her Office Live site to sell as an affiliate, and the manufacturers provide her with product images to post on the site.*

Why Host Any Site with Office Live?

By now, I've probably made it clear why *I* think Office Live is a good choice for hosting your business web site. You don't have to take it from me, however. In the following, I listed some comments from people I interviewed and people who have commented on the Office Live message boards:

- ■ It's free.

- ■ It's easy to use.

- ■ It "looks professional."

- ■ You don't have to hire a designer.

Having examined some of the groundwork you need to cover before you choose the version of Office Live that fits your needs, the rest of this chapter discusses the three flavors of the service available to help you: Basics, Collaboration, and Essentials. One way to get started is to follow the "decision chart," shown in Figure 2-6.

Office Live Basics

If you've been "living" on the Web, as I have, for any length of time, you are aware of services that give people a place to create their own web pages. Sites such as Yahoo! GeoCities (http://geocities.yahoo.com) still do this: they give you the resources to create a simple web site for the first time, without having to know HyperText Markup Language (HTML), one of the languages used to format the contents of web pages, so web browsers can display them as the designer intended.

Office Live Basics falls into this same general category. This is a place where people who want to create their first web page or to start a small business can do so—free—and without having to know HTML. In return, Microsoft places advertisements on the web pages you create (and on the Office Live site itself). But, Office Live takes a step or two beyond sites like Yahoo! GeoCities. Both Office Live and GeoCities include free web site hosting options. But only Office Live gives you a free domain name.

Easy Web Design

These days, you have lots of options for designing a professional-looking web page. You don't have to know a line of HTML, Extensible Markup Language (XML), or JavaScript, because you're bound to find software that formats web page contents by

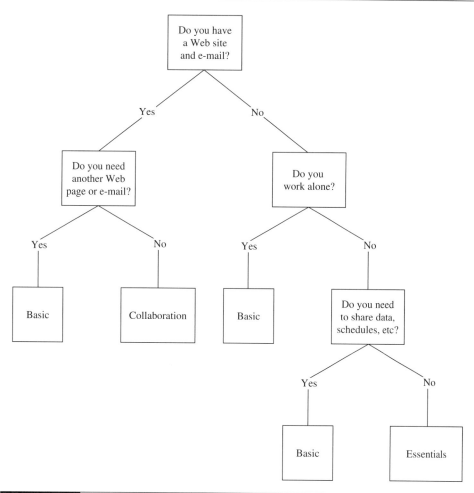

FIGURE 2-6   An Office Live "decision chart"

clicking toolbar buttons or entering options in dialog boxes. These tools (described in Chapter 3) enable you to do anything you want with a web page.

The problem is consumers don't necessarily *want* avant-garde designs. Think about how you surf the Web. Which sites seem to you to be the most user-friendly? Are they the ones with Flash animations, background sounds, and unusual colors? Speaking personally, for me they are the ones where information is easiest and quickest to find. There isn't anything wrong with sites that are functional and not flashy. These are just the kinds of sites you can build with Office Live. To some

Nail Art Seller Finds the "Easy Button"

Kendle Marra knows people are always in need of an "Easy Button"—something to help them save time and money, no matter what they want to do. That applies to expensive nail art, as well as creating web sites.

Marra, age 25, who lives in Tri-Cities, Washington, sells nail-stamping kits that let anyone place eye-catching, colorful designs on their fingernails or toenails. "They allow the user to create an airbrushed look without the hassle or cost of going to a salon and getting it done," Marra explains.

When Marra started her new business (which happened only a few months after I contacted her), she sold at weekend fairs, birthday parties, and home parties. As a user of Microsoft's Hotmail e-mail service, she received an e-mail about Office Live, and knew immediately it could be her "Easy Button" to taking her business online.

"In this day and age, you really need to have a web site up and running," Marra says. "I've already had several people asking me, 'Where is your web site?' or 'Don't you have a web site?' Having started my own business, I already have so much debt that I really don't need to add to it by hiring a designer."

Marra also has a full-time job and sells her nail kits on her own time, so she needed a solution that didn't have a big learning curve and would get her online quickly. "I did everything myself, and I really like the feeling of accomplishment. It makes me feel fantastic." Marra says. One of the most notable features of the site—the "Buy" buttons described in Chapter 3—were obtained as a "hack" from another web site.

Marra doesn't run every other aspect of her business on her own, however. It's a real family affair: "My mom is my bookkeeper, advisor, and moral support. My dad is my investor, advisor, and moral support. My best friend, Traci, helps me sell at shows and has helped me maintain inventory. My cousin, who loves my product, also helps me sell. Without all of these people there to help me out, I would be lost."

Marra used Office Live Basics to create her web site. In the few months her site has been online, traffic has doubled. "I have big dreams that can be achieved through this product," she says. "I can see this product taking off fairly quickly."

extent, they look the same—typically, a banner is at the top, links along the side, and a second set of links at the bottom of each page. But they look professional, and that's what counts, especially when you're just starting a new business and need to develop credibility. And, keeping your web site simple makes it easier for shoppers to find what they want, so they can make a purchase.

Setting Up E-Mail Accounts

E-mail is just as popular as the Web, if not more. The capability to set up five separate e-mail addresses is one of Basic's best features, in fact. E-mail, even more than phone numbers, is the quickest and easiest way to establish contact with potential customers or clients, or anyone in particular who wants to find out more about you.

When you're setting up a business, appearance counts. And, on the Web, little things, such as your e-mail address, count. Other services, such as Yahoo! and Google's Gmail, enable you to send and receive e-mail free. Office Live isn't the only game in town, as far as free e-mail service goes. But all free e-mail services are not created equal. If your business name is Acme Sprockets, which of the following has the better e-mail address for your company?

- acme@gmail.com

- sprocket-info@yahoo.com

- acmesprockets@internetaccess.com

- info@acmesprockets.com

The last option is the best because it looks the most businesslike. The domain name part of the e-mail address is the same as the company name. Experienced web surfers know that e-mail addresses ending in aol.com, yahoo.com, or gmail.com (or even Microsoft's Hotmail.com) are fine for individuals, but they don't have the cachet of legitimate business addresses. With Office Live, you gain e-mail addresses that take the same form as your web site's domain name. To get this feature free is a benefit unique to Office Live. See Chapter 3 for more about Office Live's e-mail features and how to implement them.

Data Storage Space

Your Office Live Basics account comes with 500MB of storage space. You also get daily backups of your data. Why would you want to store your data on a web server owned and operated by a company as large as Microsoft? For one thing, you need some storage space just for the files that make up your web site. The image and text files have to go somewhere if they are to appear on the Web. Other reasons include:

- **Data transfer** It's always good to have a place on the Web where you can transfer files from one office or individual to another—or from one of your own computers to another one or to a laptop, if you're on the road. If you work collaboratively with other professionals or with suppliers or partners in other offices, being able to send and retrieve files via your Office Live data storage space is invaluable.

- **Backups** Some files are so important that losing them would be a disaster. When I'm working on an important project, I make a backup on my Office Live storage area. That way, if my laptop is lost or damaged, I still have a copy I can retrieve.

- **Storage** The average web site only contains a few megabytes worth of data. With 500MB available to you, you have lots of space left over to store files that would eat up valuable hard disk space on your local file system.

Storing your files on a remote web site has pros and cons, of course. The Office Live site is secure, but you shouldn't depend solely on it. You should keep backups of important data—your customers' credit card numbers and contact information—on your local computer, so you also have a secure copy.

Analyzing Web Site Traffic

Look at the Office Live message boards, and you discover that Office Live Basics customers are concerned not only with whether their sites look professional, but also whether they are getting noticed by the general public. Kendle Marra was able to recognize that the number of visitors to her web site had doubled since she first took her business online. She was able to do so by taking advantage of Office Live's web site tracking features, which enable you to track which pages on your site are the most popular. Not only that, but you can track which visitors return to your site, and where visitors enter and exit your site. Such features aren't unique to Office Live. They're the kinds of things any web host should provide. But, to be able to access such a rich array of features is part of what makes the Basics package exceptional. (See Chapter 3 for more about tracking your web site visitors.)

Essentials

Is it Office Live Basic on steroids or is it Premium Lite? At first glance, it's easy to see where Essentials fits in Office Live's big picture. Essentials costs half as much as Premium, and you get approximately half the features. If you sign up for this service, you pay $19.95 per month for up to 10 users, compared to 20 users with Premium, for instance. Ten more business application or workspace users is also ten more than you get with Basics service, which pretty much only includes web site and e-mail-related services.

Essentials is for small business owners who have less than ten employees, who need a web site, and who have a moderate need to share business information. With Essentials, you get one business application, Business Contact manager. It helps you manage your customers and account information. Essentials alleviates the need for your company to make the substantial investment in money and time to set up application servers for your office network, deploy the applications to your employees' desktops, and train your staff on how to use them. Small businesses don't have the access to the networking expertise, hardware, and software required. Essentials fills the gap.

Setting Up Workspaces

Another challenge for small companies is that information tends to accumulate on many different computers in different locations. Worker *A* has information about one group of customers or clients. Worker *B* has different information pertaining to their own customers. The accountant keeps information about which customers have paid and which invoices are outstanding. You, the manager, maintain all the scheduling information.

By establishing a workspace as part of the Essentials package, you invite authorized individuals to come and work with you on a password-protected basis. They can share scheduling, contact, and deadline information using standard Office Live tools, such as the Dashboard. Because different shared sites can be set up for different projects, you can create a distinct set of permissions levels for each one, so you protect your information, while allowing access to colleagues who need it. In Chapter 5, you learn more about creating workspaces Shared Sites for customers, vendors, HR professionals, and accountants.

Premium

You're probably familiar with Swiss Army Knives, those red pocket knives that are equipped with screwdrivers, can openers, and lots of other attachments. *Essentials* is like the biggest and most well-equipped of the Swiss Army Knives for your business, the one with the magnifying glass, miniature saw, and other specialized tools. The most robust and full-featured offering, *Premium* gives you all the features in both Basics and Essentials. You also get:

- 2GB of web site storage space instead of the 1GB offered by Essentials

- The capability to transfer 20GB worth of data each month, instead of the 15GB provided by Basics

- Support for Microsoft Expression web features, such as forms, discussion boards, and more

- Fifty e-mail accounts, instead of only five

- The capability to grow by adding on "user packs"

Basics, in other words, may be just right for someone who's starting out with a brand new business, or an office of up to five individuals that needs to establish an Internet presence. But, for organizations of 10, 20, 30, or more people who need to get online, who need to share information, and who expect to grow with the help of their web presence, Essentials is the tool of choice.

NOTE   *The precise amount of storage space and other specific features offered by Basics, Essentials, and Premium may have changed by the time you read this. Check them for yourself by viewing the handy comparison chart at http://officelive.microsoft.com/WebHosting.aspx.*

Accessing Business Applications

If you often travel on business and you need to access up-to-date business data while you're on the road, you have several options. The oldest and simplest way is to take your data with you: save it to a CD or hard disk. Another option, that's a little more high-tech, is to synchronize your desktop computer in your office with the laptop you carry on the road.

It's not secure to take the data with you. This involves security risks. And, any work you do on the road needs to be synchronized with your business when you return to the office. The Remote Desktop feature on Windows XP also lets you access your data on the road.

A small business server, which is an e-mail system, is a preferred method. This gives you better security because you aren't carrying your data with you. Things like Exchange Server require you to have an IT professional set up the system for you. As stated earlier, Office Live Premium gives you a full set of business applications, along with a sizeable storage idea where you can store information. But, often, the information won't do you any good if you're on the road and you lack the application to view it or work with it. That's where shared business applications come in.

What You Need to Get Started

The process of planning your business's move to Office Live includes having the hardware and software you need. No matter which version you choose, you need to make sure your hardware and software are robust enough that collaboration is made easy and the process of creating web sites goes smoothly.

Hardware Considerations

One of the biggest advantages of a service like Office Live is that you don't need extra memory, special software, or tons of computer storage space—at least, not to use the web site, e-mail, Shared Sites, or even Business Applications features. You "rent" software online to cut back on overhead and maintenance. The service handles those needs, so you don't have to.

The only real requirement for Office Live, as far as hardware goes, is to have access to a computer with either a dial-up or "always on" (DSL, cable modem, or faster) an Internet connection, and a Super VGA monitor that can display at least 600 × 800 pixels of digital information.

On the other hand, storing information on your own local file system, as well as on Office Live, is always a good idea. You probably want to export information to Excel and Office, as described in subsequent chapters of this book. You might need to store digital images you take of your merchandise. The point is, when you start to use your computer for business, as well as for personal purposes, you need to make sure it's up to the mark in terms of memory and speed. At the very least, you should strongly consider purchasing a portable hard disk you can use to back up your files: these disks are becoming inexpensive and they hold multiple gigabytes worth of data.

Software Requirements

The operating system (OS) and application requirements to use Office Live are a bit more extensive than the hardware requirements. The single biggest one is this: the Office Live Collaboration and Essentials shared applications, as well as Shared Sites, can only be accessed on a computer running Windows XP or Windows Server 2003. At press time, Macintosh and Linux users are out of the picture, as well as Windows Me or 98 users.

The second biggest requirement: you need to use Internet Explorer 5.5 or later to log into Office Live and use any of the features, including the Basics Site Designer. Firefox, Netscape, and Opera users are out of the picture, at least at press time. Even though you're limited to one browser, you can use that browser on Windows, Macintosh, and Linux OSs. You still have lots of flexibility in how you access your Office Live site.

You might see grumblings on the Internet about features that require Microsoft Office 2000 or later to be installed on your computer. Why, the pundits say, does Office Live require you to have Office installed beforehand? What's the point of using Office Live if you already have Office on your computer? The fact is, you don't *need* to have Office installed to use Office Live. You only need Office if you plan to export the business data you gather with Office Live's shared applications to Excel, Outlook, or other applications, as listed in Table 2-2.

Choosing the Business Data You Want to Share

Once you have your software and hardware needs resolved, one of the last things you need to decide before you choose among Basics, Collaboration, and Essentials is how "open" you want to be with your business information. A good idea is to sit down with your staff or advisors and determine what you want to share online.

If you want to give customers the capability to track jobs and change contact information, for instance, you need Collaboration or Essentials, so you can create a Shared Workspace for them. If you want everyone to enter their timesheet information online, you should set up the business application that lets you track work hours. A good idea is to be cautious with the amount of information you

You need...	If you plan to...
Microsoft Office 2003 (*not* 2000)	Use the Edit in Datasheet feature that is part of Business Applications and Shared Sites.
Microsoft Office 2000, XP, or 2003	Export contact information to Business Contact Manager.
Microsoft Office XP or 2003	Import contact information from Microsoft Office Outlook to Office Live.
Microsoft Office XP or 2003	Link your Office Live contacts to Microsoft Office Outlook.

TABLE 2-2   Microsoft Office Requirements for Using Office Live

post online. Be restrictive in the beginning and give yourself and your employees time to get used to the idea of working in a collaborative web environment. Your contact information, hours worked, and customer data are all among your most important assets and you need to manage them wisely.

 This is a book about Office Live, but when you're at the planning stage it's good to be aware that a number of competitors are out there, all seeking to take business away from Microsoft's online business application. The big one is Google Apps for Your Domain (http://www.google.com/a), which includes the popular Gmail e-mail application, as well as an instant messaging (IM) tool, calendar, and web page creator. BlueTie (http://www.bluetie.com) includes e-mail and collaboration tools, but no web site hosting.

Where to Find It

- **Microsoft Office Live Community**

  http://officelivecommunity.com/default.aspx

  The message boards, described in more detail in Chapter 4, give you a place to talk with other users, ask questions, and get reactions to your site.

- **U.S. Small Business Administration's guide to legal and tax requirements**

  http://www.sba.gov/starting_business

  Links to helpful articles designed especially for new businesspeople starting their own companies.

- **Legal Issues**

  http://www.entrepreneur.com/startupbasics/legalissues/archive116046.html

  A page full of links to articles about legal issues facing startups and other businesses.

- **Cool Text**

  http://cooltext.com

  A service that enables nondesigners to create simple textual logos they can use on their web pages.

Chapter 3

Creating a Fully Functional Business Web Site

How to...

- Drawing a plan for your web site
- Identifying your goals and targeting your customers
- Obtaining or transferring your domain name
- Designing the look and feel of your web site
- Creating your site with the Page Editor and Site Designer
- Marketing your site so it can be found on search engines

These days, creating a web site is a big step, as well as a necessary one, for individuals and businesses alike. As owner or manager of your business, you have big hopes and dreams. Perhaps you want to take your first commercial enterprise online. Or, maybe you want to give your existing small business a new presence on the Internet and the chance to reach a whole new customer base. You have an idea what you want to accomplish, but you lack some technical expertise. Office Live is there to fill the gap, so you can focus on making your dream a reality.

Getting a head start with Microsoft Office Live isn't just a matter of saving time. It also helps you make your business look good. You know from experience that following the crowd and taking a "copy-cat" approach to creating a business venture doesn't work. You want to put your heart and soul into your venture and place your personal stamp on it. Office Live fills the bill: it streamlines the technical aspects of creating web sites, while giving you the freedom to be creative and present your products or services exactly the way you want.

 *This chapter focuses on setting up a web site with Office Live. Another important aspect of setting up a business site, creating and managing e-mail accounts, is discussed in Chapter 4.*

Drawing Up a Plan for Success

Even though you've probably surfed the Web yourself for a while and you're comfortable with the Internet, your goal in signing up with Office Live is not to break new technical ground. You want to share your knowledge of your field of interest by marketing the goods and services you've developed. Today, web sites—particularly commercial web ventures—need to be planned out and sophisticated. Today's online shoppers demand well-designed content that appears quickly in their web browser and is easy to navigate. The following sections lead you through the planning process so, when you begin to put your site together, you know what you want to do to achieve your goals.

What Do You Want to Do?

You're probably in a big hurry to start creating your web site. But take a moment to step back, and set your goals and strategies. Office Live makes the mechanics of setting up a basic e-commerce site relatively easy: the hard part is deciding what you want to do. This means focusing on your target market and coming up with a plan for your business and web site as described throughout the rest of this chapter.

"Making money on the Web" doesn't only mean selling products or services online. You can also create a site that functions as an online resource and attracts enough visitors that other businesses will pay to advertise with you. Some of the most common goals for a business-oriented web site are listed in the following sections.

Selling Your Own Goods and Services

When they think about setting up a profitable online business, most people plan on conducting sales of products. Office Live isn't specifically set up for this purpose. If it were, you would be provided with standard pages called "Catalog," as well as a shopping cart, a utility that enables shoppers to save their selections until they are ready to pay for them. A link to a payment service to complete the transaction would also be provided.

At press time, those pages aren't available directly through Office Live (although you can set them up by linking to other services), but don't let that be an obstacle. Some enterprising web site owners have configured their own product catalogs with Office Live by taking advantage of some "workarounds." You follow the process in more detail in Chapter 12. You can also link to someone else's product catalog, as Ma Charina Brooks did with her Simply SoyNaturals site on Office Live.

Selling Someone Else's Products

An *affiliate* is someone who earns a fee by selling products produced by a manufacturer. Ma Charina Brooks does this through her Simply SoyNatural

FIGURE 3-1 You can sell on behalf of other companies and make money as an affiliate.

web site (http://www.simplysoynatural.com), which was created with Office Live Basic. As you can see from Figure 3-1, Brooks has loaded the links on the left side of her site's web pages with pages that sell products of all sorts. She can do that because she's not only listing her descriptions on her Office Live site, but also linking to pages on other sites where shoppers can make selections and pay for what they purchase.

Making Money from Advertising

If you have a strong customer base and consistently attract visitors to your site, you may be able to offer advertising to other businesses that want to reach your customers. These days, with the popularity of online web-based diaries called

Office Live as a Business "Landing Page"

As Ma Charina Brooks knows, businesses don't have a single "front door." In the traditional, brick-and-mortar business world, customers find out about companies through signs on the street, ads in the local paper, listings in the phone book, and word-of-mouth. Web sites work the same way: the most successful ones present their target audience with links, directory listings, advertisements, and multiple "landing pages," all of which direct people to the pages where they sell their products and services.

Brooks, a resident of North Carolina, uses her Office Live site not for direct sales, but for *indirect* selling. Her site is a "landing page" that presents her products and her business, as well as leads visitors to other sites where they can complete transactions. Not only that, but Brooks sells as an affiliate on behalf of various health- and beauty-product manufacturers.

"For now, I am using Office Live as a landing site for my Direct Sales business, with the intention of redirecting them to my affiliate site," Brooks says. "I am thinking of upgrading my account with Office Live in the future. By then, I will have more options and get more features, so my site will be used for direct sales," she adds.

Simply SoyNatural isn't Brooks's first or only web site. She also created both a personal web site and one for her church. The big advantage of selling as an affiliate is the capability to get started instantly. The manufacturer provides the products and, often, photos you can add to your web site. You don't need to reinvent the wheel. Brooks is pleased with the response so far, and says it is "more than what I expected."

Brooks isn't an artist, but she was able to create her site's logo with the images incorporated into Office Live's graphic web page "themes." In fact, Brooks was surprised by how easy Office Live Basics is to use. "Office Live looks very professional," she explains. "At first, I was worried that I might not be able to figure out how to create a site on Office Live, but I was wrong. It is so easy to use, user-friendly (at least for me), and for something that is free (at least with the Basics service), it is well worth the time and effort."

blogs, you have more ways than ever to develop a following and earn some advertising revenue. Once you get lots of visitors, you can earn money by placing ads. Advertising services, such as *blogads* (http://www.blogads.com), specialize in finding popular blogs on which merchants can place advertisements.

Finding More Buyers for Your Existing Products

Owners of traditional stores—one with real street addresses and a physical front door that customers can actually walk through—can turn to Office Live to create a new doorway for visitors on the Web. Operating a web site in tandem with a real physical facility gives you a number of advantages:

- You're not starting from ground zero. You can build on distribution, fulfillment, sales, and marketing techniques already working in your physical location.

- You can share the wealth . . . and the problems. You can distribute profits and losses over more than one channel to even out your financial situation.

- You can do cross-channel selling. You can use your web site to point people to deals and promotions available at your physical location. You can also put your web site name on your receipts and on signage at your store, and create promotions that point visitors to your online offerings.

A web site that supplements your company's existing presence in the "brick-and-mortar" business world adds considerable value to a company's products and services. On the Web, you can put customer service data online, provide your address and hours of business, give contact information, or spell out your policies on returns and exchanges. If your web site generates sales, so much the better. Rather than generating revenue, it generates customer loyalty, which leads directly to sales.

Ideally, your web site and your physical store should work together. But, remember, products that sell well in the brick-and-mortar business world don't necessarily sell well online. Couches, heavy appliances, tractors, and other heavy equipment can be sold online; but, in general, products sold on the Web need to be easy to ship and easy to photograph, or easy to describe.

TIP

It's perfectly OK to use your web site as a front-end advertisement for your brick-and-mortar operation, rather than as a location where sales are conducted. Use the web site as a customer service resource to help people learn about you and your products; publish your store hours, postal and e-mail addresses, and data sheets about your products or white papers about your services. Let the Web publicize your business around the clock, but leave the selling to your physical store. You can encourage customers to phone or fax in their orders. When you're ready, you can add a "buy" button, so customers can also make purchases online.

Who Do You Want to Reach?

You might think your Office Live site is all about you. But, if you think this, you're missing the point. Many web sites are personal in orientation and they exist to give their owners a forum for promoting themselves or spreading their views and opinions. Office Live can be used for personal web sites, but it's primarily intended for business web site owners. Commercial web sites aren't about their owners—they're all about addressing the needs and desires of specific clients or customers. Identifying the people you want to reach is an essential part of making a web site successful. The following gives you some suggestions.

Reaching Out to Your "Ideal Customers"

Identify the customers who want and need what you have to offer by searching through discussion groups and web sites where they congregate. You won't be able to identify them by name on such sites, but message board and discussion group comments can, at least, let you know what they want and are concerned about. Let their needs and habits drive the process of developing compelling sales content. Keeping your audience and what *they* want in the forefront of your thoughts increases the chances your site will become a truly useful resource for your customer —a place on the Web they'll visit not just once, but on a regular basis. Remember, most online shoppers are:

■ **In a big hurry**   Web surfers can and do shop at any time—in the office during "coffee breaks," in the airport waiting for their flight, or in the brief interval between dinner and the children's bedtime. They want to find things fast, and they want web sites to be available whenever they're ready to visit.

■ **On the move**   Consumers and business people aren't necessarily tied to a computer network to shop the Web. You have to keep your information simple and straightforward because it's increasingly likely your shoppers are using handheld devices or web-enabled phones in addition to "traditional" web browsers.

■ **Looking for convenience**   Innovation is important when it comes to software, but it isn't the most important thing to individual consumers. Convenience and strong content rank higher than technical gimmicks and frills, such as animations or video clips.

Write a description of the kind of customer you want to reach. Be as specific as possible. Focus on one or two individuals, rather than a generic shopper. Give each a name, age, and hometown. Describe what they wear and what they do for a living. Keep these people in mind as you create your site.

As previously stated, you can find out a lot about your customers by browsing through the thousands of discussion groups that make up an area of the Internet called Usenet. *Discussion groups give individuals with similar interests the chance to "converse" by typing messages to one another. Find groups that fit your own area of business, and then "eavesdrop" on what they have to say. Once you get a feel for the group's concerns, you can post your own newsgroup messages. You can read or post messages with the help of newsgroup software or by visiting Google Groups (http://groups.google.com).*

You Want To Reach Other Businesses

A growing and increasingly lucrative segment of e-commerce is trade that occurs between businesses. Business-to-Business (B2B) e-commerce works because one online business needs to obtain specific commodities from other online businesses to stay in business. A company that regularly needs cleaning supplies establishes an account with an online cleaning supply house, so authorized employees can buy cleanser by clicking a button. A company that needs new employees can search the résumé database of a personnel agency and avoid the hassle of placing newspaper advertisements.

The Jordan Machine Company's web site (http://www.jordanmachine.com), for example, was created by the owner of a machine tool manufacturing and assembly company. Its products aren't intended to reach individual consumers but, instead, to reach businesses that need precision parts and design services.

Include the "Must-Have" Pages

When you obtain an Office Live account and domain name, you automatically get a web site with a core set of four web pages. For most commercial web sites, four pages isn't enough. You need to make sure you have the essentials. What are the "must-have" features every e-commerce web site needs? The following lists the basics:

- **Welcome page**   Every customer wants to enter a store feeling welcome, feeling it's a place where they want to spend some time. Brick-and-mortar stores sometimes do this by placing a receptionist or greeter near the front of the store. You can do it with a welcoming first page.

■ **Photos**   In a real store, you can see and touch what you're shopping for. You can't do that when you're shopping online. Photos are essential to help people get acquainted with the products they're thinking of buying. You need to purchase a digital camera or scanner and get some experience capturing images for the Web.

■ **An "About Me" or "About Us" page**   Such a page describes who you are, why you started your online business, and what your goals are for helping your shoppers.

■ **A customer contact page**   This is included in the core Office Live pages along with About Us, Home, and Site Map. But make sure the contact page contains all the options available for letting shoppers get in touch with you.

■ **A description of your goods or services**   A web catalog is far less expensive to produce than a printed catalog. You can update an online catalog at any time and, if you're doing the work yourself, the only cost is the time involved in capturing images, writing product descriptions, and publishing the information to your site.

■ **A way to make purchases**   You want to close the deal. You want your customer to mail in that check, phone in that order, or fill out that online form and click the SUBMIT button. You can't force shoppers to do this. Instead, you can provide a comforting environment for shoppers by addressing safety concerns, providing safe payment options, and making the check out process as friendly as possible.

■ **Navigational aids**   In a physical store, aisles are positioned to guide the shopper around the store in a particular way. You do something akin to this online by providing links and featuring items you want shoppers to see first. Suggest pages for shoppers to visit in your online store.

Follow the Web Site Checklist

You have a lot to think about when it comes to creating an online business web site. Office Live gives you the framework for that site, but it's still up to you to make sure you have all the information you and your customers need. To create a welcoming environment for shopping, following a list of the essentials you need can be helpful. Such a list, which also tracks where each topic is discussed in this book, is provided in Table 3-1.

Step	Comments	Chapter
Choose the right version of Office Live	Remember, you can start with the free Basics service and move up to Essentials.	2
Choose a domain name	Makes your site easy to find through its URL and creates easy-to-remember e-mail addresses.	2
Design your web site	Use Office Live's template or customize it to fit your needs.	3
Set up e-mail service	You may want to add your e-mail address to your contact page.	4
Market your site	Make sure your site turns up prominently in search engine results.	3
Create a sales catalog and offer products for sale	If you are interested in selling products through a catalog, you can do so through Office Live.	12
Build trust by adding sales material to your site	Testimonials, case studies, and fact sheets can provide customers with the information they need to make a purchase from you.	13
Promote your professional services on your site	Even if you don't provide professional services, promoting your qualifications and background is always a good idea.	15

TABLE 3-1   E-Commerce Web Site Essentials

Signing Up with Office Live

You've assembled the basic tools described in Chapter 2 and identified the purpose of your web site, as well as the customers you want to reach. Once you have the building blocks in order, you can get started with Office Live. Go to the site's home page (http://officelive.microsoft.com). Click one of the Sign Up Now buttons. Your browser (which must be Internet Explorer (IE); other browsers won't work) goes to find a domain page. Before you even put your name, address, and other personal information on the "dotted line," you need to find a domain name for your site.

Getting a Domain Name

The post office gets mail to you by means of your street address and a ZIP code. On the Web, addresses, such as officelive.microsoft.com and www.mybusiness. com, get visitors to your online "home." The microsoft.com or mybusiness.com part of the address is called a *domain name.* Domain names were introduced in Chapter 2. In this chapter, you learn what makes a good domain name and how to transfer an already existing domain name to your Office Live site.

The important thing is to pick a domain name for your business that customers can remember immediately without having to write it down and that fits your organization's identity. Also, keep it short (ideally, no more than six to eight letters) and easy to spell. And be sure the name is clearly different from those of your competitors. Take a page from the world of psychology and do some free association. Ask customers and colleagues: what's the first thing you think about when you think of our company? Write down the answers and try to get domain names that correspond. Then make sure no one else already has the name you want—it's as easy as typing www.*[thenameyouwant].*com into your web browser's address box. If the name is not taken, a registrar's site appears. The domain name registrars make it easy for you to search for available names.

Once you find a domain name, a page appears, prompting you either to apply for a Microsoft Passport account or enter a Passport user name and password if you already have one. Passport, Microsoft's user identification system, is used for the Hotmail e-mail service, as well as other Microsoft services. Click the button that applies to you (I have an account, or I want to apply for an account), and then click Next.

Follow the sign in or application process. After you enter your personal information, you're prompted to enter your credit card information. You are asked for a credit card number even if you plan to sign up for the free Basics service. Microsoft explains: the information is needed to verify your identity and to pay for services you might purchase at a later date. After entering your information, click Next. Read the terms of service, "sign" your name by typing it at the bottom of the service agreement form, and click I accept. You can then begin to create your web site and set up your e-mail addresses.

CAUTION

Be cautious when choosing a domain name. You don't want to infringe on someone else's trademark or cause confusion by choosing a name that's too close to someone else's name (for instance, Lindows.com versus Windows.com, which led to a lawsuit). Do a thorough search with the domain name registrar of your choice to make sure other names that are close to the one you want don't already exist. You might also even want to discuss trade name registration and trademark issues with a knowledgeable attorney, so you don't lose your domain name because it's already taken.

Transferring an Existing Domain Name

Purchasing the ownership rights to your ideal domain name makes sense, even before you begin to create your web site. Locking down your domain name as soon as you find it prevents domain name "squatters" (companies that buy up domain names in bulk and attempt to make money selling them when companies express an interest in them) from buying them.

If you already have a domain name in the .com, .org, or .net domains registered with an inexpensive registrar, such as GoDaddy (http://www.godaddy.com), you can transfer it to your Office Live site. When you connect to the Find a Domain Name page early in the process of signing up with Office Live, click the button labeled Transfer current domain name and follow the instructions on subsequent screens to switch to Office Live.

NOTE *Microsoft uses an Australian domain name registrar, Melbourne IT, to hold its domain name registrations. You are the owner of this domain name, not Microsoft. If you cancel the Office Live service, you maintain control of your domain name through the web site of Melbourne IT (http://www .melbourneit.com.au). However, you cannot transfer your domain name to another registrar for 60 days after signing up with Office Live. Note, once you cancel your Office Live subscription, you are responsible for paying the annual registration fee for the domain name. Melbourne IT's domain name packages start at $35 per year.*

Designing Your Web Site

Lucky you, you don't have to worry about how best to sell your products and services *and* how to organize the products into a web site. The Microsoft folks who create Office Live have already developed a site framework that draws on research and experience about the basic requirements a small business needs to present itself in a professional way on the Web. When you use one of Office Live's complete web site templates, in minutes, you get a set of pages into which you put your words and images.

A *template* is a web page or a web site designed by a professional that contains "dummy" content you replace with your own headings, words, and images. Office Live comes with a standard set of multiple linked pages. You can stick with the set of pages you're given, or use it as a starting point to create a customized presentation. Both options are described in the following sections.

3

Office Live's Default Site Map

A *site map* is a visual representation of the pages within a web site and how they link to one another. Ideally, a web site should contain different products and multiple levels of information. Sites that feature lots of areas to explore and multiple links on which to click give those visitors a reason to stay on the site longer.

A site map functions like a Table of Contents for your web site. The purpose of developing a visual guide to your web site is to help you focus on translating your customers' needs and preferred methods of absorbing information into individual web pages. By mapping out your site, you can keep track of everything you want to do. You can organize the site in a way that makes sense and helps customers move from the home page to wherever you want them to go—the contact us area or the checkout area, for instance. What does the generic, typical Office Live Basics web site look like? You see it when you connect to your home page—you might not realize it, but you have one the moment your domain name is registered and you sign up with Office Live. You can view this page in one of two ways:

- Go to the Office Live home page, click Log in to your Office Live account, and then click Web Site on the Member Center page. This takes you to the Page manager page for your site. You see a list of the four standard pages already created as part of your site.

- Go directly to the URL for your new site: [mydomainname]/default.aspx.

I registered the domain name newcorgroup.com, so my home page has the URL http://newcorgroup.com/default.aspx. Figure 3-2 shows the generic home page that appeared when I first connected to this URL.

As you can easily see, there are a number of generic features that you need to customize. The title bar simply reads home page; it should be changed to your business name or something specific to your web site's contents. The contents of the home page should also be changed. Initially, you are given four pages: Home, Contact Us, About Us, and Site Map. The Site Map page itself only lists these three pages. A graphical representation of this simple site map is shown in Figure 3-3.

Nothing is wrong with this site map's simplicity. One of the tips I frequently give for creating web sites is to start out small and build your web site gradually. You may just want to begin with revising these four pages. Once you have them set, you can expand your site and draw a new site map.

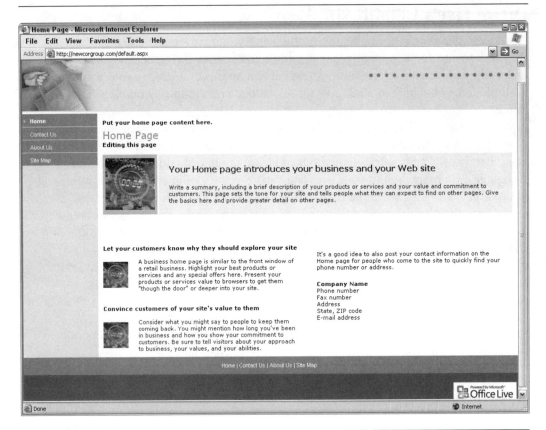

As soon as your domain name is registered, you have a generic home page you can customize.

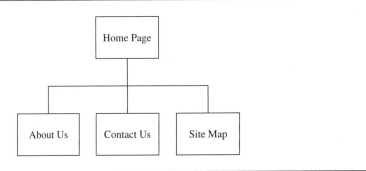

Just the basics: your site starts out with only four pages.

Drawing Your Own Site Map

You're in charge of your Office Live site. The Page Editor and Site Designer described in the sections "Working With the Page Editor" and "Choosing a Look and Feel with the Site Designer" put you in complete control. The four-page site map you are given when you sign up is only a starting point. Feel free to make a list and add pages that suit your site's needs, as well as those of your customers.

When it comes to organizing an e-commerce site, your goal is to lead your visitors in, make it easy for them to find what they want, and guide them to the check out area. The average Office Live site is intended more for presentation of services, rather than selling consumer goods. To enrich this site, consider adding these common types of web pages that aren't included in the initial four-page version:

- **Customer Service**   Explain how your products work, where they come from, and how to get them repaired or replaced.

- **Services**   Describe your professional services and qualifications.

- **Links**   Direct visitors to sites other than yours. Nothing is wrong with this, and it positions you as a resource. You can add a set of links to sites with products or services that complement your own by clicking the Links option in the list of Web Parts (see the section "Moving Web Parts").

A typical site map is shown in Figure 3-4.

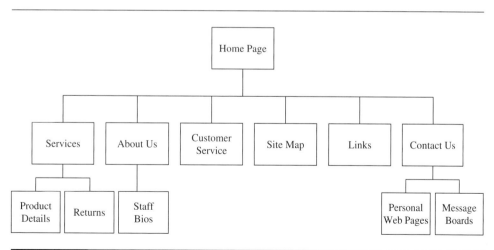

FIGURE 3-4   A more full-featured site map.

Working with the Page Editor

When you're ready to start creating your page, click the Page Editor link in the Member Center. Your default home page opens in the Page Editor window. The silver bar running horizontally across the top of the Page Editor indicates it is divided into four areas:

- *Font* lets you assign font styles, sizes, and formatting to selected text

- *Paragraph* lets you create bulleted and numbered lists, as well as cut-and-paste content

- *Insert* lets you add images or other elements

- *Advanced* lets you control the overall layout or general properties of the page

You can start with any number of web site contents to edit, but I suggest you begin with the overall look and feel of your site—the way the columns are arranged, and the choice of colors, typefaces, and other graphic elements. Once you have the general appearance down. you can customize the content to fit your needs.

You don't have to edit the graphic design of your default Office Live web site. If you're happy with the default appearance, you can simply add headings and text. But then, your site will look like all the default sites on Office Live. Customizing your page can give you a look and feel that lends credibility to your business.

Picking a Layout

Web pages are frequently subdivided into separate containers that not only bring order to the page, but also boost interactivity. The default Office Live home page is divided into four subdivisions, often called *frames* (Office Live doesn't call them frames, but I do for the purposes of this chapter):

- The horizontal strip at the top is the *header* frame

- The narrow strip running horizontally at the bottom is the *footer* frame

- The frame on the left—running vertically—contains links to the web pages contained in the site (Home, About Us, Contact Us, and Site Map)

■ The largest frame, to the right of the links frame, is where the main content appears. This main area is further subdivided into one or more parts called *zones*. Clicking on a link in the links frame on the left causes a new web page to appear in the main frame.

The default arrangement used in the Office Live home page you receive initially is a common one, and it's popular because it's effective. But, lots of Office Live sites stick with this arrangement, which tends to give them a "cookie-cutter" appearance. Click the Layout button under Page tools to view a set of alternate zone arrangements within the main frame (see Figure 3-5).

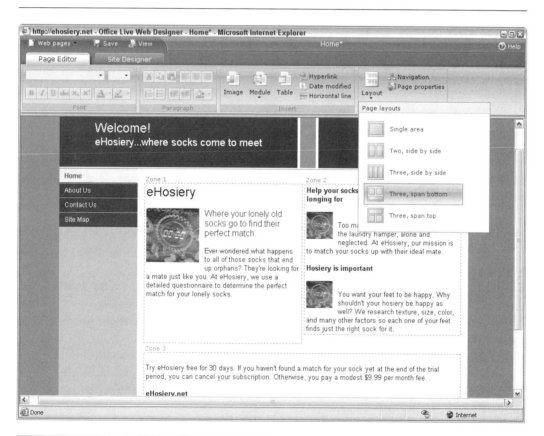

FIGURE 3-5   You don't need to stick with the default Web Zone arrangement.

 *If you want to change the arrangement of frames on a page or perform other advanced formatting, you can open your Office Live site using a special web design tool called SharePoint Designer, as described in Chapter 10.*

The design you choose should reflect the contents you want to present. For instance, if you want to present visitors with three stories, photos, or other elements that are equally important, you might choose the layout that divides the frame into three equal zones. If you're looking for something that's similar to the default layout, but still slightly different, so you don't fall into the cookie-cutter syndrome, choose the second layout from the bottom, which has two zones at the top of the frame and one zone spanning the bottom of the frame. Remember, even if you want to stay with the default layout, you can customize it by changing colors and typefaces with the help of the Site Designer.

Choosing a Look and Feel with the Site Designer

You can't personally greet each customer on a web site, so how do you make the customer feel welcome? You have to create a "look and feel" for your site through graphics and personalized content. The *Site Designer*, which you access when you click the Design tab at the top of the Page Editor, lets you select colors and typefaces your customers respond to in a positive way. If your customers are conservative, choose muted colors and use simple and easy-to-read typefaces, such as Helvetica. If, on the other hand, your customers are mainly teenagers, select bright primary colors for your web page backgrounds, headings, and graphics. The key is making the contents consistent with the characteristics and needs of the customers whose profiles you already created.

Choosing a Theme

The place to start with the Site Designer is by choosing an overall theme for your page—a combination of colors, typefaces, and graphics that gives your site a visual identity. Click Theme, and a drop-down list appears with a set of graphic themes (see Figure 3-6).

Choose a field of business from the list. Then, Click Style and browse through the sets of design elements that appear—images, layouts, and color schemes—and choose the ones you want. Whenever you make a choice, the Site Designer reloads to show you how each one looks.

Try to make choices that complement any business cards or printed material your company already uses. In the case of the site I set up, our business card had bright orange and white colors, so I choose brown to go along with them. After you make your choice, move on to one of the other tabs at the top of the Site Designer.

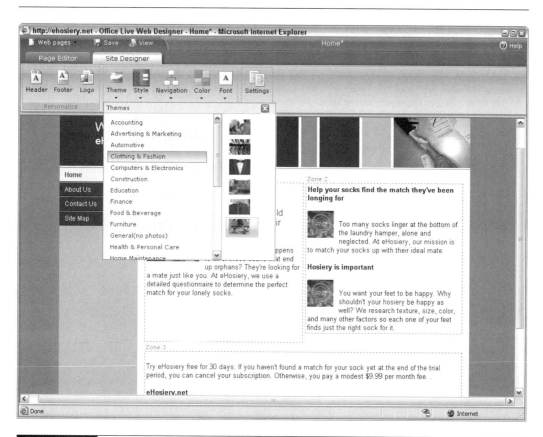

FIGURE 3-6   Site Designer helps you create a graphic appearance for your Office Live site.

CAUTION   *The problem with themes is they can look so cliché that viewers immediately think they're looking at a "Microsoft Office Live" web site, rather than your web site. This happened with the Themes that Microsoft built into its web design program FrontPage. Some of the themes became so well known and widely used, they began to look like many other sites on the Web. If you want to ensure you don't look like anyone else online, then develop your own graphic identity and stay away from Office Live's themes and styles.*

Picking a Header

A *web page header* is a narrow horizontal strip at the top of a web page. Typically, a header contains your organization's logo, name, and secondary information, such as a slogan or photos if available. If the layout you chose in the preceding section includes a header, this is the logical place for your logo. If you don't have a logo for your company, you can use one of the generic images that come with the theme you selected in the preceding section.

1. To enter the title for the web page, click Header, and then type the title in the Customize Header dialog box, as shown in Figure 3-7. I entered Welcome.

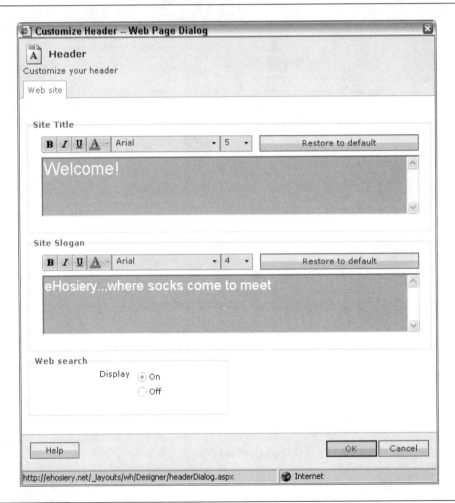

FIGURE 3-7 Enter a title and subtitle for your page here.

2. In the Tagline box, I entered a second phrase that describes what my group does: eHosiery...Where socks come to meet.

3. I clicked OK.

4. Because I have a logo for the site I'm building, I add it by clicking the Logo button at the top of Site Designer.

3

5. I clicked Upload Pictures. A new window entitled Image Uploader appeared. Before it appeared in its entirety, though, a Security Warning dialog box appeared, prompting me to install software called Office Live Image Uploader. I clicked Install.

6. The software installed itself, and, in a minute or so, the window displayed the contents of the My Pictures folder on my Windows file system (see Figure 3-8).

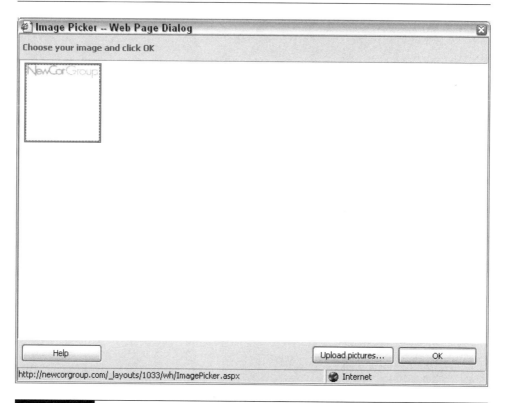

FIGURE 3-8   The Image Uploader lets you choose image files from My Pictures or another directory on your computer.

7. I navigated to the directory where the logo file was stored (not in My Pictures), selected it, and clicked Upload Now. The Image Uploader closed, and I returned to Site Designer, where the logo was visible (see Figure 3-9).

8. I selected the image and clicked OK. The Image Picker closed and the logo was added to the header of my web page (see Figure 3-10).

By default, your logo image is added to the top of your header. You also have the option of placing it next to your site's title and tagline. To change position, you could choose an option from the Position drop-down list, and then click Apply at the bottom of Site designer to see the change immediately.

 **NOTE** *Image Picker is intended to hold multiple files you want to use in your web site. You upload them at once and can add them more easily from within the Site Designer interface.*

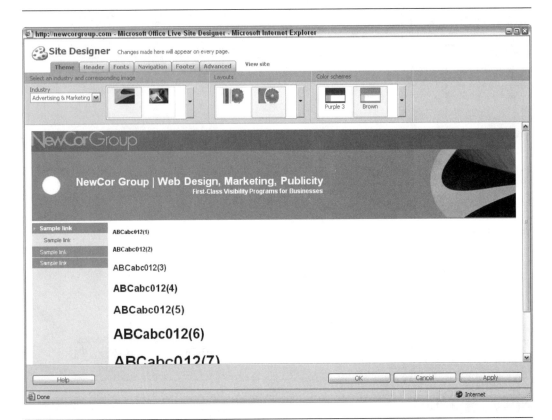

FIGURE 3-9   Use the Image Picker to store images for your site and add them to Site Designer.

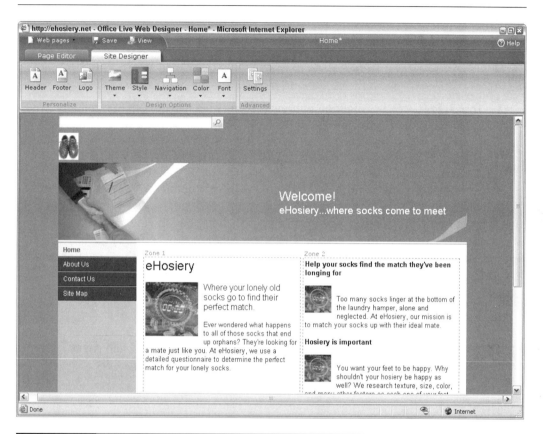

FIGURE 3-10   Your logo, title, and tagline all work together in your header.

Selecting Fonts

Typefaces are another essential part of creating your web site. *Sans serif typefaces,* such as Arial and Verdana, don't have the curly ornaments at the ends of ascenders and descenders. *Serif typefaces,* such as Times New Roman and Century Schoolbook, do have those ornaments. Sans serif typefaces have a sleek, high-tech look. Serif typefaces look more "dignified," and some editors believe they are more readable than sans-serif. But the decision is up to you.

The choices here are simple. The default typeface, Arial, is sans serif. Times and Courier are the only serif options. Click each of the other buttons along the top of the Fonts tab to view the typefaces as they would appear on your page. When you choose the one you want, click Apply and then move on to the next tab.

Adding Navigation

The *Navigation tab* lets you choose where the links to your site's main web pages appear. By default, they appear vertically along the left-hand frame. You have two other options from which to choose:

- **Top & Left** The navigation buttons for your site appear both horizontally in a narrow row across the top of the home page and on the left.

- **Top** The navigation links appear only across the top of your home page.

Because you have only four links at this point, you can probably leave them in the default position. But, if you plan to enlarge your site dramatically, you should consider the Left & Top option. Having links across both the left side and the top of a single page might seem redundant. But it's a common convention to have links in multiple places on a single web page. You don't have to put the same links in both locations, of course. You can place different links in both locations, as shown on Office Live's own Products & Solutions page (see Figure 3-11).

Adding a Footer

The footer is the horizontal strip that runs across the bottom of many web pages. Many web sites use this area to provide standard information, such as:

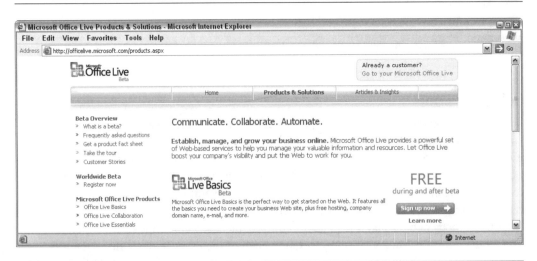

FIGURE 3-11 Placing links in two locations on your page is common.

- A copyright notice

- The date the site was last updated

- A link to the Webmaster's e-mail in case the viewer encounters problems with the site

- Links to privacy statements

- Contact information, such as an address and/or phone number

When you click the Footer button at the top of Site Designer, you are able to add such details, in fact. You can add new links, reorder the standard links to your web pages (these repeat the links along the left-hand side of the page), or add text such as copyright information in the box labeled Footer text.

Your contact information, of course, is intended to go on the page entitled Contact Us. You don't have to put it in the footer area as well. You can also include links to Customer Service areas and other essential parts of your web site. Don't immediately assume you need to put the least important information in your footer. Many visitors go to the bottom of the page immediately to find what they want— it's much like flipping through the index at the back of a book rather than looking through the Table of Contents.

Advanced Options

The Advanced section at the top of Site Designer has only one button: Settings. This probably isn't something you need to try out when you are first creating your web page. However, you might want to revisit it later when you're editing and refining your site. This tab's options include the capability to change the alignment of your page's contents and to add margins around the page by making it less than 100 percent wide.

When you're done with the Site Designer, click OK to close it and return to the Page Editor. Remember, though, you can click Design at any time to return to the Site Designer, and edit its look and feel.

Adding New Pages

Before long, you'll probably want to add web pages to your site. All the Office Live hosting packages give you plenty of room to add pages whenever you like. All you have to do is click web pages at the upper left-hand corner of either Page Editor or Site Designer and choose New Page. The Create Web page dialog box, shown in Figure 3-12, appears. Choose one of the items in the Templates box that describes what kind of page you want to create. (If you don't know what you

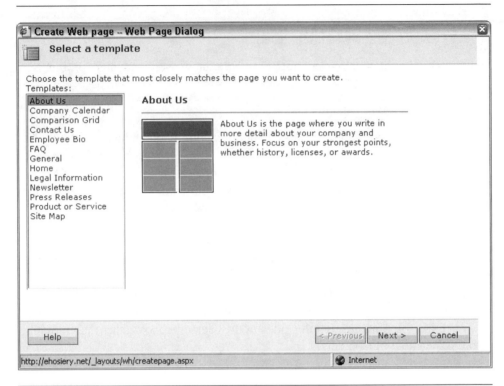

FIGURE 3-12 Office Live gives you a head start on adding a new page to your site.

want to do with your page, click General.) Then, click Next. The Choose page properties dialog box appears.

Enter a title in the Page title box. This is the title that appears in the colored bar near the top of the page.

TIP

Remember, keep your title short and clear. If possible, add a keyword or two to help people find your site more easily when they search for its content on search engines, such as Google. Consider including the name of your site in the title. For instance, if your site is called Acme Widgets, and the page is called Employee Directory, you might enter Acme Widgets | Employees in the title bar.

In the web address box, enter a short file name for the new page. If the page contains employee information, enter "employees," for instance. Don't worry about the .aspx filename extension. Office Live adds that automatically.

The Navigation section of Choose page properties determines whether the page has a link in your site's navigation bars. Whether it does or not depends on how important the page is to your site's overall structure. If you want the page to be included, leave the Add this page to the Navigation bar button clicked. Enter the name you want to appear in the navigation bar in the Navigation title box (this should be a short bit of text—no more than a word or two). In the Place page under drop-down list (see Figure 3-13), you determine whether the navigation button for this page appears beneath one of your root pages or whether it is added to the root pages. For instance, if you are creating an employee directory, you might want the navigation button for this page to be "nested" under the root page title About Us. If so, you would select About Us from the Place page under drop-down list. When you're done, click OK.

The page you created is added to your navigation structure. If you nested the page under one of your root page names, you need to click the root page name to view the new page's title. In Figure 3-14, I added a page called Staff under the About Us root page. The new page you created is not totally blank, of course. It incorporates any editing decisions you've made thus far, including your logo, colors, typeface selections, and the general page layout.

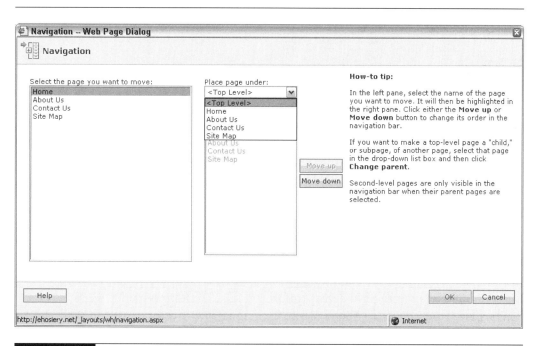

FIGURE 3-13   Be sure to add a title to your new page and add it to your navigation bar.

FIGURE 3-14 Your new page is added to your site's navigation buttons.

See the following sections for adding content to your new page. If you ever want to delete this or other pages, click DEL in the Page Editor toolbar.

> **TIP** *You can quickly switch from one page to another on your site by clicking the button directly under the Page tools heading in Page Editor. By default, this button is labeled default.aspx. When you click it, a list drops down, bearing the filenames of all the pages, including any new ones you added. The .aspx filename extension stands for Active Server Pages technology.*

Adding Content to Your Office Live Site

On most web pages, the *body text*—the text that appears on the main body of the page—as opposed to the links, titles, or headings—is one of the simplest parts of the page. The body text sits on the page, and text wraps at the end of each one. On Office Live, text is contained in boxed areas called Zones. Within each zone, you have one or more Web Parts. You need to work with these two elements to change the contents of Web pages.

Content Zones

The text area on each Office Live web page is divided into three content zones—not two, not four, but three. Each *content zone* is simply a container that can be the width of the text area or less than half the width. (The narrow-width zones can be placed side-by-side.) When you're looking at an Office Live page in the

Page Editor, the zones are represented only by the red dashed line around the edge. Everything inside the zone is another element called a *Web Part* (see the following). If you want to change the layout of zones, click the Layouts button at the top of the Page Designer and choose a different arrangement.

Modules

Content zones contain one or more types of content called Modules. A *Module* can consist of HTML markup, a map, a slideshow, or other elements that make web pages more compelling.

If you ever want to add a Module to a page, you have to do so within a zone. First, you need to position your cursor inside the zone you want to contain the part. Then, you click the down arrow beneath the Module button in Page Editor. A list drops down with a variety of modules you can add. This list is shown in Figure 3-15.

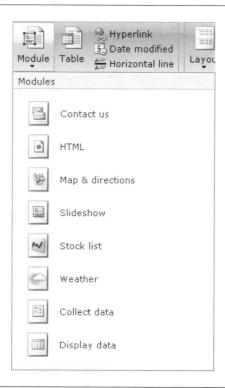

FIGURE 3-15   Modules are content units that perform specific functions on web pages.

As you might expect, each type of module listed has a specific function. For detailed information, you can read the Help files that come with Office Live (click the Help link near the top of the Page Editor or the Member Center). Brief descriptions of each module follow:

- **Contact Us** This module adds an entire contact form to a zone. This is the same form contained on your default Contact Us page. It asks a visitor for their e-mail address, provides a box for a subject line, and has another text box where the visitor can send you a message.

- **HTML** This module opens a box into which you can type or paste HTML markup to add formatting or functionality to the content in a Web Zone.

- **Map & Directions** This module lets you present a map on your web page, along with directions to a specific location. The obvious use is to direct visitors to your office.

- **Slideshow** This module presents multiple photos on a web page. The images appear one after another on the page.

- **Stock List** This module lets you add current stock quotes you might want your visitors to track. Office Live gathers the latest stock prices and presents them on the page for you.

- **Weather** This module adds the current weather conditions for your own area, or for any area, into your web page. You specify the city and ZIP code and Office Live presents the weather for that region on the page for you.

- **Collect Data** This module lets you collect data from your customers: it comes with Office Live Essentials or Premium.

- **Display Data** This module enables you to display "live" data on your web page, and is only available with Essentials or Premium.

For some of these modules, the best way to learn how to use them and what they can do is simply to add them to your web page. Insert them, save your changes, and click View to view your pages with the new content. If you don't like what you see or have second thoughts about adding it, you can always return to the Page Editor by clicking the Page Editor button in the Member center, and then clicking DEL in the Web Part you want to remove.

Moving Web Parts

The easiest way to move a Web Part from one zone to another is to click-and-drag it. Drag it atop the zone where you want it to appear, and then release your mouse button. If the Web Part isn't in quite the right place in relation to the other parts already in the zone, you can drag it to another position.

 *Make sure you save changes before you move to another Web Part or to another page.*

Making Hyperlinks

Too many web sites include links or buttons that give the visitor little or no information about what they will gain by clicking them. (The classic example is the link contained in the phrase "Click <u>here</u> to find out more.") Make sure your own links are specific and customer oriented. Enter some text in a Web Part that describes the destination of your link. Highlight the text you want to serve as the link. (You can also select an image and turn it into a link.) Then, click the Insert link box in the Add Content dialog box for the part in which the link is contained. When the Type the link dialog box, shown in Figure 3-16, appears, click the button that describes the kind of link you want to make. Enter the URL in the Link box, and then click ENTER to create the link.

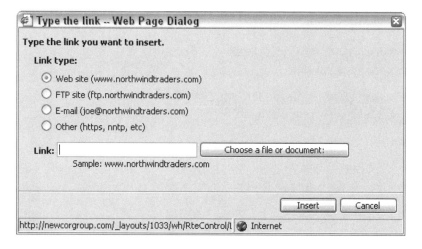

FIGURE 3-16   You can link to web pages, e-mail addresses, or files on your web site.

Where to Find It

■ **Melbourne IT**

http://www.melbourneit.com.au

The company that functions as domain name registrar for Office Live sites.

■ **Blogads**

http://www.blogads.com

An advertising service especially for blogs. It places ads on well-traveled blogs and generates revenue for the operators.

■ **Google Groups**

http://groups.google.com

A web-based interface to the thousands of discussion groups on Usenet. You can search for groups related to your area of business and get an idea of what your potential customers are looking for.

Chapter 4

Communicating with the Outside World

How to...

- Establish e-mail accounts for yourself and your colleagues

- Use Microsoft Outlook to access and manage your Office Live mail

- Participate and solve problems with the Office Live community

- Spread the word about your site via search engine optimization

- Using adManager to publicize your site on Windows Live Search

Office Live is meant to enable you to communicate—with your coworkers, your colleagues, your customers, or anyone else who is interested in what you do or what you sell. The moment you go on the Web with your own web page, some level of communication with the outside world is inevitable. But Office Live exists to give you many ways to connect with the people you need to make your business thrive. You can spread the word through optimizing your site for top appearance on search engines, as well as through other types of advertising.

Once you learn how to use each of these communications methods, you can get in touch with all your important constituents—your customers, suppliers, and colleagues—so you can keep in touch when you need to and get the help you need. This chapter shows you how to make the best business use of the tools Office Live gives you, so you can maximize your results.

Creating an E-Mail Address

E-mail is no longer a novelty—it's a necessity for both business and personal communication. Not only is e-mail an essential way to stay connected, but it's also now ubiquitous enough to be tailored to your needs. Virtually any Internet service provider (ISP) account you get gives you the capability to set up multiple e-mail addresses for yourself, your family, or your business colleagues. Other free e-mail services enable you to set up "disposable" addresses you can use to subscribe to newsletters or other services. With so many e-mail services, such as Hotmail, Google's Gmail, and Yahoo! Mail around, what can Microsoft Office Live give you that they don't?

The answer is simple: Office Live gives you a business e-mail address that contains your own domain name—the same domain name you selected for your Office Live web site. If your domain name is worldwidewickets.com, for instance, you can have the e-mail address marty@worldwidewickets.com. How is this different from marty@gmail.com or marty@earthlink.net? The difference is a subtle one, but with an address from your own domain, you are saying to people,

"Here is my business, and here is my business identity. I take what I do seriously, and you can trust me." The following sections describe how to configure and take full advantage of the e-mail accounts that come with your Office Live account.

Configuring E-Mail Service for Your Organization

You have two ways to access your Office Live e-mail: as an administrator who needs to set up and manage e-mail accounts, and as an individual user who needs to send and receive your e-mail messages. First, you need to adopt the Administrator hat and set up individual e-mail accounts and preferences for you and any coworkers who need to access e-mail through Office Live. You do that by first signing in to what you might think of as your "Administrative" e-mail address: the address you used to create your Office Live account and to sign in to the service yourself. (This is the e-mail address Microsoft uses when the company wants to communicate with *you* about your account, by the way.)

> **NOTE**   *The Administrator account used to set up Office Live is the only one that can be used to create, delete, or otherwise manage e-mail accounts. Even if you give someone in your small business Administrator privileges, that person cannot manage e-mail. If you need a backup administrator, you can give that person access with your user name and password. Be aware, though, you run a security risk for your whole office the moment you begin to share this critical account information.*

Begin by deciding how you want to handle e-mail passwords for your office. To access their Office Live e-mail, each employee must enter a distinct user name and password. You have two options: you can either create passwords for everyone and hand them out yourself, or confer with the individual users and have them create their own passwords. Personally, I suggest you give employees a generic password to use because they'll be prompted to change their passwords as soon as they attempt to sign in to their accounts the first time. You might have to explain to the employees how to enter the password themselves when they create their accounts, as described in the following steps.

Once you determine how to handle passwords, you begin by signing in to Office Live. You automatically go to the Member Center. Then follow these steps to configure e-mail:

1. In the set of links on the left-hand side of the Member Center page, click Users & Accounts under the e-mail heading. The E-Mail Accounts page appears. As you can see, you start with a clean slate: 25 e-mail accounts are available with Office Live Basic, and only one is created as yet. See Figure 4-1.

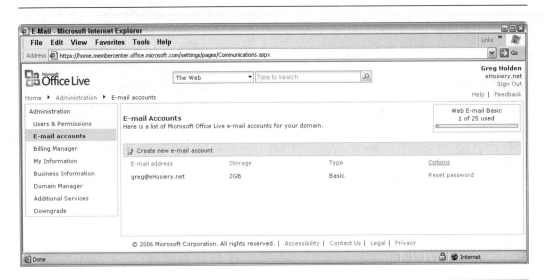

As Administrator, you need to configure e-mail accounts for your employees.

2. Click Create new e-mail account. The Create new e-mail account dialog box, shown in Figure 4-2, appears.

3. Fill out the fields in the dialog box (presumably, you have determined how you want to assign or obtain passwords for your coworkers by this point). Make sure you use the first name and last name your coworkers want to use. When you're done, click Next. A progress bar appears, notifying you the mailbox is being set up. Then, a Summary dialog box appears, telling you the address has been created.

4. Click Finish. You return to the E-mail Accounts screen, where the new account is displayed.

5. Repeat Steps 3 through 5 for each of the mailboxes you need to configure.

If you create shared sites (workspaces or shared content areas that multiple individuals can access, see Chapter 5), you need to determine what level of permissions each user will have to those sites. Click Shared Sites, and then click Users & Accounts to assign such permissions (and see Chapter 6 for more information).

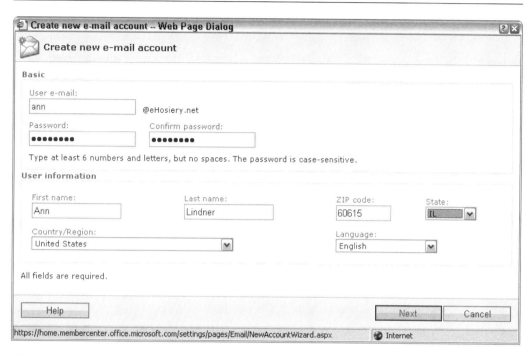

FIGURE 4-2   Use this dialog box to configure e-mail accounts and initial passwords for your colleagues.

Accessing Your Mailbox as a Client

When you're not creating or managing e-mail accounts for your small business, you simply need to retrieve and send e-mail as you do with any other service. Office Live isn't like Outlook Express, Eudora, or another conventional e-mail application, however. It's a web-based e-mail program you access with a web browser, such as Hotmail. With any web-based program, checking e-mail is a two-step process: you connect and sign in to the web site that provides your e-mail service, and then you send and receive e-mail, as needed.

Logging in Through Office Live

Once you sign in to Office Live, you retrieve your e-mail by clicking the E-mail button in the set of links on the left-hand side of the Member Center page. Under the e-mail heading, click Inbox. You go to the Office Live Mail page, shown in Figure 4-3. Click Inbox to read your mail.

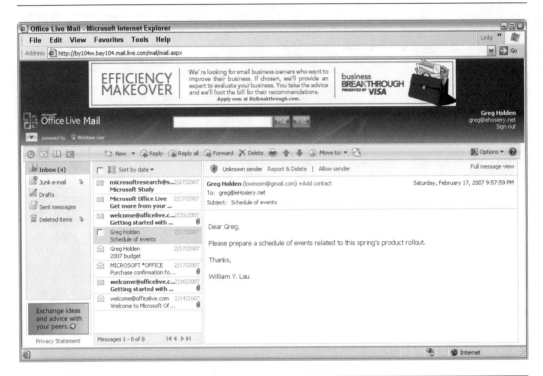

FIGURE 4-3   Once you sign in to Office Live, you can easily access your Office Live Mail account.

Customizing the Interface

The first time you log in to your e-mail account, a message appears, inviting you to switch to the Classic version of the program. You don't have to choose this option. You can always customize the way your messages are displayed. In the main Office Live Mail window you can click the option Customize your Inbox, and then choose options that determine how your Office Live e-mail interface will look. The Themes and Reading pane settings options, shown in Figure 4-4, are self-explanatory and control the visual appearance of your e-mail.

Choose More Options at the bottom of the Options list for a full set of choices. More Options opens a new browser window where you can change your account information, set up spam filters, or change how your mail is automatically handled. One option (Save sent messages) has long-term implications: generally, I think it's a good idea to save your business e-mail because it can be an invaluable record of your communications. But, Sent Mail piles up quickly and, before long, it

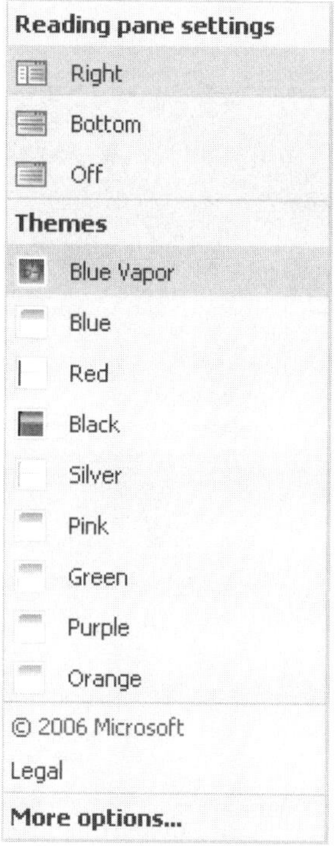

Reading pane settings

Right

Bottom

Off

Themes

Blue Vapor

Blue

Red

Black

Silver

Pink

Green

Purple

Orange

© 2006 Microsoft

Legal

More options...

FIGURE 4-4   Choose options to change the layout, as well as the visual look and feel of your page.

can consume many megabytes of disk space. If you choose Yes to save the mail you send, get in the habit of either cleaning out the old mail periodically when it becomes outdated or file it, so it doesn't consume too much disk space.

Switching to the "Light" E-Mail Interface   When you finish customizing your e-mail interface, you're left with a pretty spare and basic e-mail window that resembles the look and feel of other e-mail programs you've used. If you're on a dial-up connection or your regular connection isn't working quite right, you may want to switch to the Classic version of Office Live Mail. To my mind, the light version, shown in Figure 4-5, doesn't look that different from the regular version. But, the light version doesn't automatically open a reading pane so you can read your mail immediately in the same window as the list of messages.

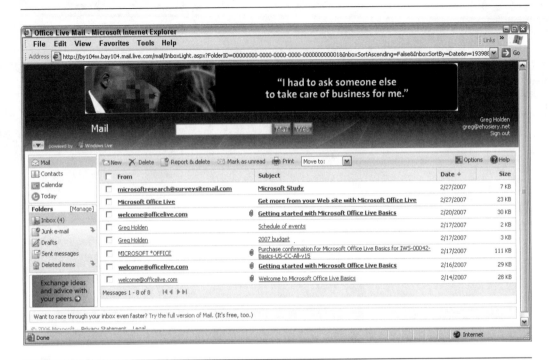

FIGURE 4-5   The light e-mail interface doesn't display as much content as the regular version.

For comparison, the regular version of the interface immediately displays your messages, along with message headers. This is a slight difference: for most users, the regular version, shown in Figure 4-6, is probably sufficient.

NOTE   *The advantage of web-based e-mail is you can access it from virtually any computer. The disadvantage is in terms of security: people in coffee shops or other public spaces can look over your shoulder and steal your password or other information. Be sure to pick a good password—one with six to eight characters, a mixture of capital and small letters, and numerals as well as characters. Think of a phrase that has meaning for you, such as "I Live at 39 River Street," and use the initials to make a hard-to-guess password: ILa39RS.*

Switching from One E-Mail Address to Another   Chances are, if you are a hard-working, lone entrepreneur, you have lots of e-mail addresses. You respond to info@mycompany.com, webmaster@mycompany.com, and Jeremy@mycompany .com. You need to be able to switch back and forth among these addresses easily. You can do so through Office Live.

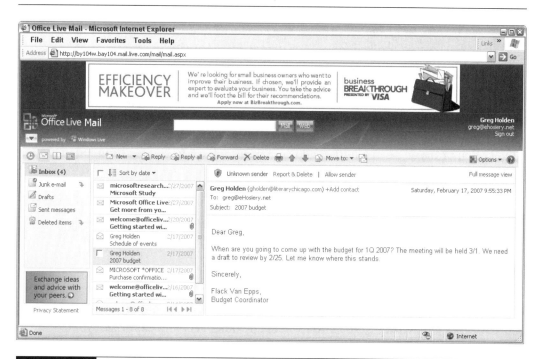

FIGURE 4-6   The standard version displays message content, along with message headers.

When you connect to the Office Live home page, the site "recognizes" you through a *cookie* (a tiny bit of digital information) it placed on your computer. It greets you with your e-mail address at the top of the Office Live home page. This doesn't mean you're signed in, however. You still need to sign in—but you don't necessarily need to use the address to log in to your e-mail. You can have multiple e-mail addresses, and switching back and forth among them is a matter of following these steps:

1. Sign out by clicking the Sign Out link near the upper right-hand corner of the Office Live screen you're viewing.

2. Click Sign in.

3. First, you need to sign in with your "main" e-mail address—the e-mail address you used when you first signed up for the service. Enter the password associated with the main e-mail address and click Sign In. You go to the Office Live Mail login page, shown earlier in this chapter.

You don't have to switch among e-mail accounts by signing in and signing out if you don't want to. Instead, you can forward e-mail from one or more addresses to a single address. See the section "Forwarding your e-mail" for more information.

Switching to the "Light" E-Mail Interface

Office Live gives you two interfaces for accessing your e-mail: a full version and a light version. By default, you get the *full version*. If you don't access your e-mail often or if you're in a hurry and don't want to have to choose from too many options, you can switch to the *light version*.

When Office Live is accessing your e-mail, a "Loading..." message appears on screen. A link appears beneath the word "loading..." that invites you to switch to the light e-mail version if the full version is taking too long to load.

Accessing E-Mail with Your Wireless Device

If you have a cell phone that sends and receives e-mail, you can use your cell phone to work with Office Live as you would any other account. Configure your phone with an account name (for instance, My Cell Phone), so you can distinguish it from other accounts you have. Enter the user name and password. From then on, you connect to your Office Live inbox, just as you would any other e-mail address.

Working with Outlook

If you have a subscription to the Essentials version of Office Live, you have the capability to access your e-mail, contact, calendar, task, note, and other information from within Microsoft Office Outlook. You need to use an application called Outlook Connector to gain access to most of these features. However, if you only want to use Outlook to connect to your Office Live e-mail, follow these steps (which don't require Outlook Connector):

1. Open Microsoft Outlook and choose E-mail Accounts from the Tools menu.

2. When the first screen of the E-mail Accounts Wizard opens, leave the Add a new e-mail account button selected, and then click Next.

3. Click Add in the next E-mail Accounts window.

4. When the window entitled Server Type appears, click HTTP, and then click Next. The Internet E-mail Settings (HTTP) window, shown in Figure 4-7, opens.

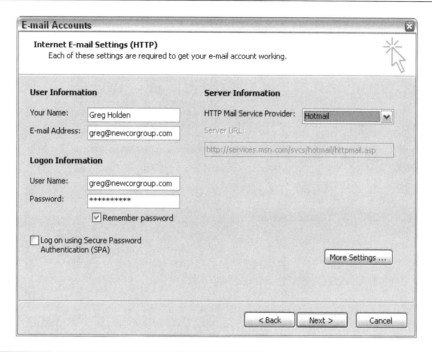

FIGURE 4-7 You can use Microsoft Outlook to access your Office Live e-mail and other information.

5. In the Your Name box, type your name as you want it to appear in your outgoing e-mail messages.

6. In the e-mail address box, type your Office Live e-mail address.

7. Leave Hotmail as the provider in the HTTP Mail Service Provider box.

8. Under Logon Information, enter the Office Live e-mail address you want to connect to and the password associated with it.

Optionally, you can click Remember password, so you won't have to type your password each time you connect to your Office Live e-mail account. When you finish, click Next. The new account is listed as Hotmail in the E-mail Accounts window. When you're done, click Finish. After a minute or so, your Office Live e-mail should appear in the Outlook window, as shown in Figure 4-8.

NOTE *The preceding steps apply to Outlook 2003. For Outlook 2007, you begin by choosing Tools | Account Settings, and then follow a slightly different set of steps.*

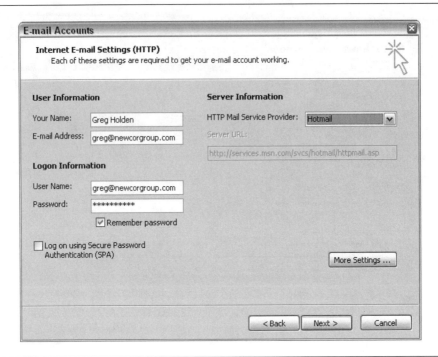

FIGURE 4-8 You can take advantage of Outlook's sorting and filtering capabilities to manage your e-mail.

If you do want Outlook to be able to access your Office Live calendar and other data, you need to use the Outlook Connector. See Chapter 6 for instructions.

Managing Your E-Mail

One advantage of using Outlook as the interface to your Office Live e-mail is you don't have to perform the elaborate login procedure previously described (log in to Office Live, Open Office Live Mail, retrieve your e-mail). You can use the familiar surroundings of Outlook to manage your correspondence.

Receive E-Mail

Once you configure Outlook as your Office Live e-mail client, you can send and receive e-mail using the controls you always use. When you receive e-mail by clicking Send/Receive in the Outlook toolbar, you receive e-mail not only from Office Live, but also from any other e-mail accounts you have set up with Outlook.

> **TIP**
>
> *By choosing Send/Receive all from the Send/Receive menu in the Outlook toolbar, you can send or receive e-mail from all your Office Live accounts and any other accounts you have set up. This is one of the biggest advantages of using Outlook for your Office Live e-mail: you can access multiple e-mail accounts instantly without having to sign out, and then sign in with another user name.*

Configure Multiple Office Live Accounts

You can set up more than one Office Live e-mail account with Outlook. The mail folders associated with each account are listed as Hotmail, Hotmail (1), Hotmail (2), and so on in Outlook's Mail column. These sorts of designations don't help you keep track of which account is which, however. You can rename accounts for clarity, but you have to follow a few steps:

1. Right-click the name of the e-mail account you want to rename—for example, Hotmail(1)—and choose Properties from the pop-up menu.

2. The Properties sheet for the account opens with the name of the account at the top, but you can't retype the name of the account in this properties sheet (try it and see). Instead, you have to click the Advanced button at the bottom of the screen.

3. The Personal Folders window opens with the name of the account at the top. Now, you can retype the name to the one you want to use (see Figure 4-9).

4. Click OK twice to close Personal Folders and Properties, and then return to the Outlook window.

> **CAUTION**
>
> *You may rename your Office Live e-mail accounts for clarity, as described in the previous section, but Outlook still calls them Hotmail, Hotmail (1), Hotmail (2), and so on. You discover this when you click Accounts in the Untitled Message window and choose the e-mail account you want to use. For instance, I don't see Greg's Great Buys or NewCorGroup, two Office Live accounts I set up. Instead, I see Hotmail and Hotmail (1). For extra clarity, you may want to append a code to your accounts to keep them straight, such as NewCorGroup (H), Greg's Great Buys (H1), and so on.*

Send E-Mail

With your Office Live account as your only e-mail account in Outlook, sending e-mail is easy: you click New, choose New Message, compose your e-mail, and click Send as usual. When you have multiple e-mail accounts set up with Outlook, sending

Rename accounts, rather than using the default Hotmail name for each one.

e-mail requires an extra step or two. Basically, you need to check first to make sure the e-mail message you compose is originating from the e-mail address you want to use. Click New, choose Mail Message, and then when the Untitled Message window opens, choose the account you want to use from the Accounts menu.

Manage Folders

In terms of capabilities, there isn't much difference between Office Live on the Web and your Microsoft Outlook program when it comes to creating folders or moving mail from one folder to another. The difference is slight—it's a difference of speed as the following describes—but it might be significant for some users.

On Office Live   To create a new folder on Office Live, follow these steps:

1. Click Manage, next to the Folders heading on the left side of the e-mail page.

2. Click New.

3. When the New Folder heading appears, type the name of the new folder, and then press ENTER.

4. To move a message from your inbox into the folder, check the box next to the name of the message, and then choose a destination from the Move to menu at the top of the screen (see Figure 4-10).

As you notice when you follow these steps, the web page you're viewing needs to refresh each time to present the new information. The speed with which the refresh occurs depends on the speed and quality of your Internet connection and the speed of your computer. It might take a second or two. Or, if your computer is tied up with other processes such as a virus scan or file download, it can take longer.

On Microsoft Outlook   On Outlook, the same number of steps are involved in creating folders or moving mail from one folder to another. For instance, to create a new folder, follow these steps:

1. Right-click the name of the account you want to edit.

2. Choose New Folder from the pop-up menu.

3. In the Create New Folder dialog box, type the name of the new folder and then click OK.

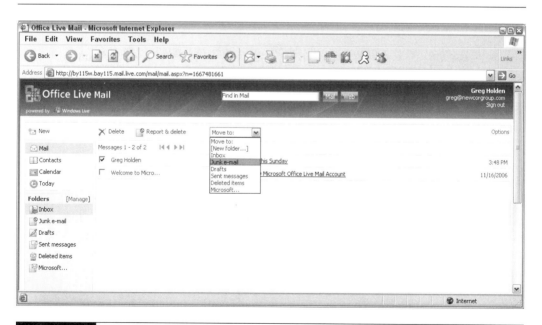

FIGURE 4-10   You can create new folders and move e-mail easily on Office Live.

Things happen slightly faster, however, because the changes are taking place only on your local computer. The Internet connection isn't involved until you want to send and receive more e-mail.

Forwarding Your E-Mail

Forwarding your e-mail from one or more accounts to a single e-mail address is easy. But, you can't forward your Office Live e-mail to another address. If you want to forward e-mail from your ISP or another service, such as Yahoo! or Google, you need to log in to that service's e-mail interface and forward your mail using their instructions.

Participating in the Office Live Community

As you probably already know from surfing on eBay or other popular web sites, the best place to get questions answered, learn from other users, or meet other people is through *community discussion boards*. Windows Live provides members and visitors alike with a lively community area that is divided into common subject areas, so you can be reasonably sure of meeting people who will welcome what you have to say. To participate on the boards, it pays to follow some useful general rules that apply to Usenet and other online discussion areas, as you learn in the next section.

NOTE   *If you have ever wondered how Microsoft generates revenue from Office Live while giving away—free—at least the Basics level of services, you get a clue the moment you start reading discussion board messages: each message page has an advertisement posted across the top of the page. Even if you are paying a monthly fee for Essentials or Premium service, you see the ads.*

Accessing the Office Live Community

Connecting to the Office Live community discussion area is so easy, there's no excuse for not trying it. You don't need special newsgroup software, and you don't even need to change your user name and password. You simply connect to the Office Live home page, and click the link Community & Blog. (Or, you can go directly to http://officelivecommunity.com/default.aspx.)

Once the Microsoft Office Live Community page opens, you can scroll down to read the selection of message boards. Each message board is intended for discussions focusing on a particular aspect of working with Office Live: the Getting Started with

Microsoft Office Live board is good when you are just starting, for instance, and the Using Office Live Mail board would be suitable for the topic of this chapter. The two icons to the left of a message board's name indicate whether new messages have been posted since your last visited or if someone has posted an answer to the original question.

Click on a message board's name to read the discussions within it. If you don't see a question or answer on one of the discussion boards, go back to the Microsoft Office Live Community page and scroll down to the bottom; the Questions and Answers board is intended for problems not covered on the other boards. In addition, the archives of the Get Started board might help with your problem.

4

TIP *Online businesspeople stand to perform better if they reach out to join communities of other online sellers and managers. If you deal in business materials, rather than consumer goods, online marketplaces like Perfect Commerce (http://www.perfect.com/home/index.html) and Verticalnet (http://www.verticalnet.com) can help you find a supplier or group of related supply companies who already provide the goods and services you are looking for. You can also join the Small Business Discussion List (http://www.talkbiz.com/bizlist/index.html) where you can share your experiences with fellow online entrepreneurs.*

Posting Messages

Reading the messages posted on a board thoroughly before you post your own message is always a good idea. Instead of starting a completely new discussion, you may find someone has already covered the same topic you want to discuss or, at least, started a discussion marginally related to it. Each board has a number of discussions within it. The discussions take the form of a thread—an original message and a series of replies to it. To reply to someone else's comment, you type your message in the box at the bottom of the page and then click SUBMIT.

If you don't see any discussions that address what you want to talk about, go to the message board's opening page. Scroll down to the bottom of the page and type your question into the box labeled Start a new discussion. You need to enter a short, but clear, title for your comment (usually, a question you want someone to answer) and the comment itself. Then click SUBMIT.

Observing Netiquette

One great thing about discussion forums on the Internet is that everyone can participate and post nearly anything they want. But discussion forums have a downside—they can easily be abused with off-topic, profane, and abusive postings. A moderator keeps discussions focused by deleting inappropriate messages. You don't see moderators in the Office Live Community, but you do see individuals who are identified by the acronym MSFT: Microsoft. Microsoft staff people monitor the boards to answer questions and help users. Click the Code of Conduct link at the bottom of any community page to find out more about rules regarding how users need to behave toward one another on the boards.

Posting to the Office Live Blog

Typically, a *blog* is a series of comments posted by one individual. But, the *Office Live Blog* is one where members of Microsoft's Office Live team post news and announcements about the service. You can't post announcements yourself, but you can post comments about any of the blog messages. It's a way to "talk back" to Microsoft and give them feedback about Office Live.

 *Also, a Suggestion Box message board is intended for customers to provide feedback on Office Live and ideas about features they want to see or problems they are encountering.*

Marketing Your Site

For everyone from presidential candidates to big-name manufacturers, the Web is fast becoming an essential place to advertise and get their messages out. But, advertising online can cost thousands of dollars if you want to place pricey banner ads and hire marketing consultants. The best way to ensure visits to your web site, as well as purchases or online orders, is simply to make your site more easily found. Office Live gives you a head start with its adManager tool. The following describes other common sense strategies.

Getting Found by the Search Engines

One of the most frequently asked questions on the Office Live discussion boards is this: now that I've created my web site, how do I get exposure for it? One of the most effective ways to direct visitors to your Office Live site is to work with search networks, such as MSN, Google, and Yahoo! Search Engine Optimization (SEO) is the name given to the process of adjusting your site's content and links, so more people can find the site and so your site appears prominently in search results. SEO isn't an exact science, and it isn't guaranteed to give you perfect results, but it is cost-effective (it's free if you do it yourself) and can give you good results.

Office adManager

Many people, when they think about publicizing their web site with a search engine, automatically think of Google. You're being short-sighted (or, should I say, short-*sited*) if you only focus on this one service, however. Google might be well known, but it's also well known as the most difficult search engine to "crack" in terms of improving your placement in search results. In my experience, MSN Search (http://search.msn.com) is much more "responsive" when it comes to spreading the word and making sure your site gets prominent placement.

Office adManager, which is included with each of the three levels of Office Live service, is designed to help you market your site on MSN Search and Windows Live Search. It's similar to Google's popular AdWords service: it enables business owners to create ads designed to appear along with search results. You can also bid on keywords that cause your ad to appear alongside search results relevant to your site's contents. For instance, if you create a site with Office Live on which you sell handcrafted Christmas tree ornaments, you would first create an ad for your site, like this:

> Unique Handcrafted
>
> Christmas Ornaments
>
> www.fredsornaments.com

You could then use adManager to bid on keywords your prospective customers would be likely to use to search for your site, such as "ornaments," "tree decorations," and the like. If your bids are higher than those of your competitors, your short ad would appear prominently in any search results that include those keywords. You pay only when someone clicks on your ad: in this pay-per-click system, you don't necessarily pay when the page is viewed but, instead, only when a viewer clicks on the ad and goes to your web site. If your ad appears 500 times a month, you bid .10 per click and you get 50 clicks; you pay $5 for that month's adManager fee.

To get started with adManager, log in to Office Live and click Advertise Online. The adManager—Beta page appears. Click Start to launch the Microsoft Office Live adManager Wizard, which leads you through the process of setting up an account for this service. See Chapter 16 for more information.

Search Engine Optimization with Google and Other Sites

SEO is quickly becoming an essential publicity strategy for businesses of all sizes, whether or not they sell tangible goods and services on the Internet. *SEO* is a set of practices designed to make a web site more easily found by consumers who conduct searches on Google, Yahoo!, MSN Search, and other web directories. SEO ensures a site appears as close to the top of the first page of search results as possible, and that it appears prominently in directory listings.

One of the best things about SEO is you don't have to pay consultants to perform SEO for you—and it doesn't have to cost thousands of dollars, either. By devoting only a few hours a week, you can improve your site's visibility and do some networking that can have other benefits for your business. By following a few simple and cost-effective techniques, you can move your site from Page 10 to Page 1 of a set of search results. You might even be able to move yourself to number 1—or at least within the top five. The following strategies describe how to improve your visibility.

Site Submissions   How do search engines scour the Web so quickly after you submit a word or phrase, and how do they gather so many results? They don't gather the results directly from the Web at the time of your search. They search through a database of web sites previously been indexed by automated programs. That's not the only way to get into the database, however. Rather than waiting for one of the automated programs to index your site, you can speed the process by submitting your site to the search network. Each of the well-known search engines, as well as many that aren't as well known, give you a way to send your site.

To submit your site, visit the following URLs:

- Google: http://www.google.com/addurl/

- Yahoo!: http://search.yahoo.com/info/submit.html

- MSN Search: http://submitit.bcentral.com/msnsubmit.htm

Simply making sure your site is included in the search engine's index goes a long way toward making your site more visible on the Web. By submitting the site yourself, you can also control exactly how the site is described, so you can be sure to emphasize the products and services you want people to know about.

TIP   *One advantage of submitting your site to a search and content network is you ensure the description reads the way you want. This is because you write the description yourself before you submit it.*

Adjusting Your Title Bar   *Google* is the most recognizable search engine around but, paradoxically, it's also the hardest to "tweak" when it comes to adjusting your placement in search results. One of the few ways to improve your placement is to

4

make every effort to include your most important keywords in the title bar of your home page and as many other pages as possible.

The number of words that can appear in the browser window is limited. If the viewer who has connected to your site happens to have their web browser open to a narrow space (say, three inches), then only a few words appear. But, the program automatically indexing the page can "see" more than those few words because it is scanning the underlying HTML code. If you can add your keywords to the title bar, then your page appears more often in Google search results. One problem is web site owners want to keep their title bars relatively "clean" and uncluttered, such as this example:

```
Feathered Friends Bird Store
```

If, however, you can create a page with the attributes described here, you can get better search results. Your page won't look as "clean," of course, and it will seem as if you are blatantly trying to publish your keywords (which you are, of course). But, for many web site owners, the search results are worth the price of a much longer and more cluttered-looking title bar, such as this one:

```
Feathered Friends | Bird Seed | Bird Grooming | Cages | Parrots |
Clipping | Bird Toys
```

 *A title bar like the previous one improves placement in search engines, but it also might turn visitors off because it looks cumbersome. This is especially true when someone adds the page to their Favorites list.*

Keeping Your Content Fresh   As stated earlier, by updating your text on a regular basis, you give visitors a reason to come to your site on a regular basis. You also improve your search results on Google, which gives higher ranking to "active" pages, the content of which is updated frequently, as opposed to pages that grow "cobwebs" and sit idle for weeks at a time. Ideally, you can create new articles or pages on a regular basis. Even if you simply change your headings and, occasionally, a few words in your text, you benefit because your page is then reindexed by the search engines.

Adding Keywords to Your Page Headings and Text   Generally, people agree that Google scans not only title text, but headings and the first 50 or so words of text on a web page. Your job is to improve your search ranking on Google by adding your most important keywords—the keywords people are most likely to enter when they search for your site—in your headings and in the first paragraph or two of text.

How do you find keywords? Look to a service called Wordtracker (http://www.wordtracker.com), which lets you conduct a free search for keywords related to your web site.

Adding Keywords to Your Web Page Code A *meta tag* is a line of web page code that begins with the META command. One of the meta tags enables you to add a set of relevant keywords to the underlying code for each of your pages. Your viewers won't see such code in their web browser windows. But, it will be "read" by the automated programs that are used by search engines to index web page contents. You can add such keywords in one of two ways:

- Open your web site in the Page Editor, then open the page you want to edit by clicking the link you made to it, and then click the Properties button.

- Open Page Manager and click the Properties link next to the page you want to edit.

In either case, the Choose page properties—Web Page Dialog window opens with the Page Settings tab in front. Make sure you type a title for your page in the Page Title box. Then, click the Search Engine Optimization tab. Next, enter a series of words or phrases related to your site—words or phrases you think people might enter in a search engine when they're looking for your site, or for a site like yours—in the Keyword Metatags box. Separate each keyword by a comma, like this:

```
bird,feathers,seed,cage,toys,grooming,beak,parrot,finch,macaw
```

In the box labeled Description Metatag, enter a brief description of your web site, like this:

```
An online bird store devoted to the food, supplies, and loving care
our feathered friends need.
```

An example is shown in Figure 4-11.

Metatags are oversold as SEO tools. They work with some search engines (notably, MSN), but not with Google. They should be a part of your publicity campaign for your web site, but don't make them the whole effort.

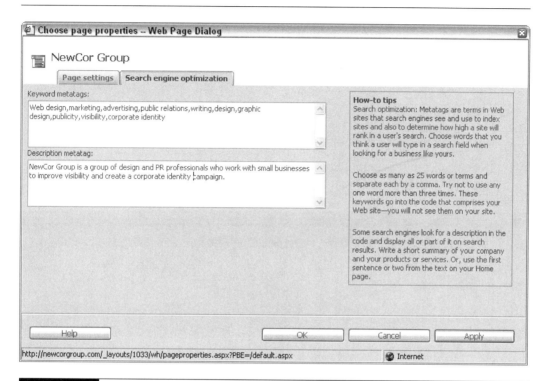

FIGURE 4-11   Enter metatags for your web site, so search engines can be sure to find it.

Where to Find It

- **Office Live Community**

  http://officelivecommunity.com/default.aspx

  The home page for the discussion area where you can communicate with other Office Live users and the Office Live team at Microsoft, either on the message boards or through the Office Live blog.

- **Small Business Discussion List**

  http://www.talkbiz.com/bizlist/index.html

  An online discussion board outside of Office Live where you can meet other small business owners and share notes about your experiences.

- **Add Your URL to Google**

  http://www.google.com/addurl/

  A page that lets anyone submit a web site for inclusion in Google's online directory.

- **Wordtracker**

  http://www.wordtracker.com

  Keywords are important to help search engines find your web site. You need to work keywords into headings, text, titles, and metatags. This service suggests popular keywords based on your site's description.

Part II

Collaborating and Communicating with Business Partners

Chapter 5

Creating Shared Workspaces

How to...

- Create workspaces for employees, customers, and colleagues
- Choose the right custom workspace template for your needs
- Adjust access levels for the workspaces you create
- Customize your workspaces by adding Web Parts
- Observe best practices for working with workspaces

The World Wide Web (WWW) is all about making connections. Rather than working or operating in isolation, you are able to communicate with other people, either across the office or across the sea. Office Live's workspaces enable you to take online collaboration to a new level. A *web site* is a place where images and web pages "live," and where people can view them. Workspaces aren't web sites of their own, and they aren't single locations on Office Live, either. Rather, *workspaces* are a way of viewing, sharing, and working with information on Office Live.

Workspaces, like web sites, can be open or restricted in terms of who can access them. Most web sites are open to anyone with an Internet connection. Some (particularly internal networks called *intranets*) are password-protected: they are available only to the individuals you need to work with. The way workspaces are presented and organized on the Office Live is hardly intuitive, however. If you're like me, the moment you start clicking around your Office Live site, you quickly become confused over the difference between workspaces and Business Applications. Is a workspace a site or an application? Or, is it a workspace? And what's the best way to access a workspace: from the Member Center, the Site Directory, or the Site Manager (or Business Applications, where many workspaces overlap with the Site Directory)? In this chapter, you get a clear picture of what workspaces are, which type of site to choose, and how to establish a site for selected individuals so you can make new connections and work more efficiently.

> **NOTE** *This chapter primarily focuses on workspace management and selection, and the use of Web Parts. It provides only brief descriptions of the specific types of sites you can create and applications you can use with them. The next two chapters discuss different types of sites in more detail: Chapter 6 discusses workspaces and Business Applications for your employees, while Chapter 7 examines workspaces you can create for customers and vendors.*

Getting Started with Workspaces

The idea behind workspaces on Office Live becomes clearer when you get at least a brief overview of a completely different technology—one that preceded Office Live—called Microsoft SharePoint. *SharePoint* enables coworkers to access shared documents and business applications in a centralized location. Rather than having that location be a web site (such as Office Live), it exists on a computer on which SharePoint Server software is installed. Although some web sites provide access to SharePoint services, the program is intended for network administrators in a workgroup to configure and install. With SharePoint, you set up sites using site templates. The main types of sites are:

- A team site, where colleagues can share information.

- A document workspace, where you collaborate on documents created in Word, Excel, or PowerPoint.

- A meeting workspace, where coworkers can schedule and track meetings.

The same sorts of SharePoint workspaces are also available to Office Live users. In both cases, each site has a home page, and each page is comprised of one or more Web Parts. A *Web Part* is a control: a small-scale application designed to present and process data for you. A SharePoint site can provide a workgroup with a library full of documents they can access from any location via the Internet, provided they are assigned a sufficient access level.

Sound familiar? It should: the same sort of technology has been carried forward to Office Live. Much of the same SharePoint terminology is used on Office Live, too. In both cases, you have the capability to configure shared areas where you and others can collaborate. In the case of Office Live, you don't need the server setup or technical expertise to do the configuration and maintenance.

NOTE *Before you start using your workspaces' space to store complete images and graphics files that consume lots of memory, make sure you know what you have to begin with. A Basics account does* not *include workspace or workgroup storage space at all. If you want to set up workspaces for collaborating, you have to move up to Essentials or Premium. An Essentials account gives you 500MB, and a Premium account gives you 1GB. You can purchase additional storage space as your site grows: at press time, the rate is $1.95 per month for 50MB. You can also add five users for $11.95 per month.*

Understanding Basic Terms and Features

As previously stated, working with workspaces is hardly as straightforward as it could be. The problem is twofold: the terminology isn't clear and considerable overlap occurs among the different features. To make things less "fuzzy," here are definitions of some basic terms to put everything in focus:

- **Workspaces**   This term can be misleading because it implies that workspaces are locations, such as web pages or directories, where you and coworkers can view information. In the world of Office Live, workspaces are more than a location. They can also be Business Applications.

- **Business Applications**   These are utilities that employees in a business environment use to manage information. Six general types of applications are available: the Dashboard, and applications for customers, projects, sales, employees, and your company.

- **Dashboard**   This lets you track events, agendas, and projects in a calendar-type format.

- **Workspaces**   These bring together two or more collaborators who need to share information.

- **Site Manager**   A list of the same workspaces as contained in the Site Directory (which is confusing). The difference is Site Manager lets you add users or change site settings.

- **Web Part**   A feature you can add to workspaces or Business Applications.

- **Web Zone**   A region on an Office Live web page that functions as a container for one or more Web Parts.

When you log in to Office Live Premium and click Workspaces, you are presented with the options shown in Figure 5-1.

Planning Shared Projects

The obvious first step in getting started with workspaces is to click the Workspaces button on the Member Center page. Before you do that, have at least a general idea of which people you want to bring together, and what you hope to accomplish. Ask yourself:

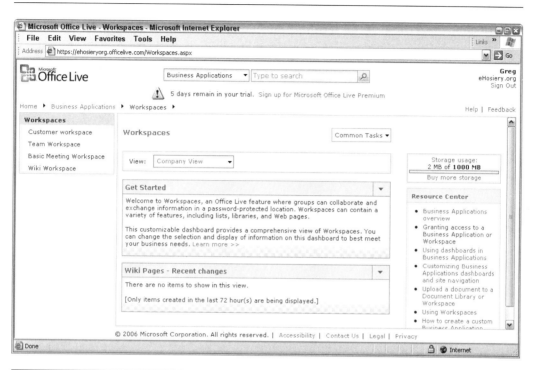

FIGURE 5-1   This Office Live page lets you get started with workspaces.

■ What's the goal of your site?

■ Who will have access to your site?

■ What kind of data do you need to share?

■ Is working online the best way to accomplish what you want?

That last question might seem a little surprising. After all, this book is intended to promote Office Live as a tool for helping a small office function more efficiently. But sometimes, the Web and the Internet are used as substitutes for traditional, face-to-face interactions. If you're going online to give people a way to work together because they don't get along in person, you might be trying to avoid a personnel problem that can be solved another way. Also, you may be trying to share information that Office Live can't present, such as page layouts constructed in applications, like Quark XPress. Getting together the old-fashioned way might be advisable—across a table, on the phone, or in a videoconference—rather than trying to make Office Live perform a function it wasn't intended to handle.

Once you have a clear idea of what you need to do, find workspaces that can accommodate it. You have a basic selection of four options from which to choose when you click workspaces. But, before you do, scroll down to the Workspaces box on the Member Center page. You see a slightly different selection of workspaces, as shown in Figure 5-2.

The Member Center, Business Applications, and Workspaces page obviously overlap. Where do you turn first, and which option do you choose? Table 5-1 gives you an overview of the choices:

NOTE   *When you first enter a workspace, these options are populated with sample data to give you an idea of what it can do. This data can be useful if the reader is simply poking around or they can delete the sample data to get right to work on their own applications.*

FIGURE 5-2   The Member Center page presents you with these workspaces' options.

Main Category	Applications/Workspaces	Lists
Business Applications	Business Contact Manager	Dashboard Accounts Contacts Opportunities Products Business Documents
	Time Manager	Dashboard Schedule and Reservations To Do Resources Manage Resources Holidays
	Project Manager	Dashboard Projects Project Tasks Project Milestones Project Issues
	Document Manager	Dashboard Document Library Picture Library
	Sales	Competition Tracker Customer Support Estimates Company Assets Inventory Manager
	Company Administration	Company Assets Employee Directory Expenses Jobs and Hiring Training Expenses Income
Workspaces	Customer Workspace	Dashboard Announcements Calendar Links Shared Documents

TABLE 5-1   Business Application and Workspace Options (*continued*)

Main Category	Applications/Workspaces	Lists
Work spaces	Team Workspace	Dashboard Announcements Calendar Links Shared Documents Tasks Team Discussion
	Basic Meeting Workspace	Dashboard Agenda Attendees Document Library Objectives
	Wiki Workspace	Dashboard Wiki Pages

TABLE 5-1   Business Application and Workspace Options

Business Applications, as you can see, presents the widest set of options. They are discussed in Chapter 6, because these tools are primarily intended for employees working within an office. The Customer Workspace is described in Chapter 7. The following sections describe how to create and configure workspaces, as well as manage them, so you can then move on to specific Business Applications.

Creating a New Workspace

Once you have a general idea of the kind of workspaces you want to create, you turn to one of Office Live's many Applications and Workspaces templates. The tricky part is you don't access all the available options from the Workspaces main page. First, you choose the general type of workspaces you want. You might want to set up meeting workspaces where you and your coworkers can share information, follow agendas, and discuss projects. To create such workspaces, follow these steps:

1. Click Workspaces, if necessary, and then click Basic Meeting Workspace.

2. Click Common Tasks, and then click Create New. The Basic Meeting Workspace—Create page form appears (see Figure 5-3).

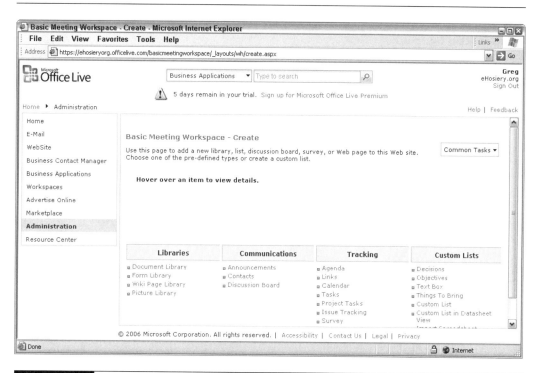

Office Live presents you with a variety of templates for workspaces.

3. Hover your mouse over each of the meeting workspace options in the bottom half of the Basic MeetingWorkspace—Create window. Each option causes an explanation to appear in the upper half of the window (see Figure 5-4). Each option has its own characteristics that help you and your colleagues share information.

4. Follow the steps on subsequent screens to create the workspaces you chose. For instance, if you click Project issues, you type the name of the workspace and a brief, but clear, name for your meeting workspace—something that indicates to your colleagues the topics to be discussed (for instance, 2007 Budget Meeting or Annual Report Planning Session).

5. In the Description box, type a brief description of your workspace, so your coworkers know its purpose.

6. Click Create to create the new workspace.

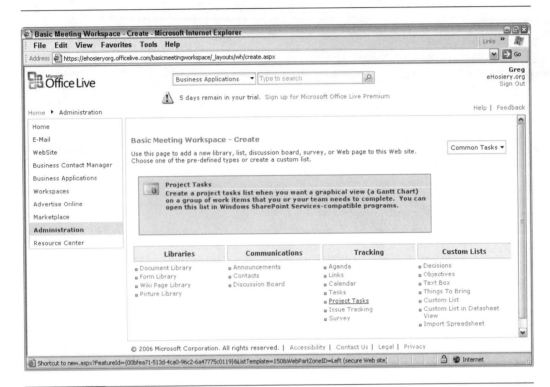

FIGURE 5-4 Read each explanation to choose the types of workspaces you want.

7. Inspect the workspace page (see Figure 5-5) to make sure it looks the way you want.

8. When you're done, click New, and then choose New Item to start adding issues or other items to the workspace.

Now that you have a workspace, you need to do two things: choose the tools you need to enable workgroup members to collaborate, and then invite users to participate. When it comes to choosing tools, you have four options, whichare described in the following sections.

NOTE *A site template is only a starting point. The site administrator can customize the template at any time to make it specific to a company's identity or needs. You can add a column or change other characteristics by choosing one of the options from the Settings drop-down list. You can also change the dashboard options available to each workspace. Also see Chapter 10 for more on customization.*

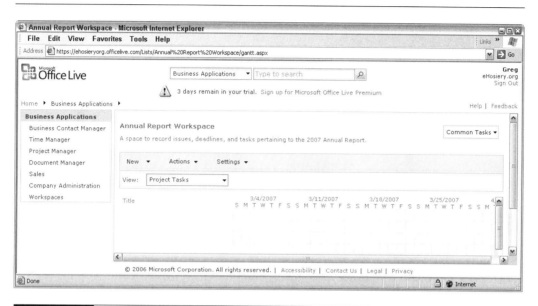

FIGURE 5-5 You can create your own workspace in a few steps.

Choosing Collaboration Tools

The easy step in setting up your own workspaces is providing them with a name and location. The challenge is to furnish your workspaces with tools that participants can use to communicate and share information. First, you need to choose the general type of workspaces you want to create (team workspaces, basic meeting workspaces, and so on). Click Common Tasks, and then click Create New. You can then choose from among five types of workspaces: libraries, communications, tracking, custom lists, and web pages.

Uploading Files to a Document Library

You're probably familiar with the handouts distributed at meetings. They provide background information to the attendees. Instead of going to the photocopier and running off multiple copies for everyone, you can upload electronic versions to your workspace's Document Library. A *Library* is a repository for files that multiple users need to access. When you open the Create Page, the first of the five types of workspace options you see is Libraries. You can create four types of libraries:

■ **Document library** This workspace enables you to create and share Microsoft Word documents.

- ■ **Form Library**   This library is specially designed for documents created using eXtensible Markup Language (XML) and designed to be viewed in web browsers.

- ■ **Wiki Library**   A *wiki* is an interconnected set of web pages that all members of your workgroup can add to collaboratively. You can upload image, text, and other files.

- ■ **Picture Library**   Although you can upload images to other workspaces, the Picture Library lets you view contents in the form of thumbnails and can present a series of images in the form of a slide show, if you choose.

To upload a document (in other words, to transfer it from your file system to Office Live), click one of the four libraries. Name the workshop, create a Description, and then click New.

At this point, the exact steps vary, depending on the type of workshop you are creating. If you are creating a document library, click New Document. When the Document Library: Upload Document screen appears, click OK. A blank Microsoft Word document opens, so you can begin typing. You can then click Save on the Word toolbar, and the file is saved on your Office Live site. The document library page refreshes and the name of the file appears (Figure 5-6).

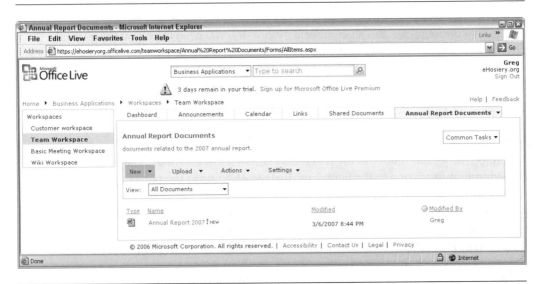

FIGURE 5-6   It's easy to save a Word file in an Office Live document library.

 *When you open a new file, a warning dialog box appears. The warning appears, depending on your security settings and the applications available on your computer. If you change your security settings, you won't see the dialog box in the figure. But, if you simply click OK, you open a new Word document (in Word 2003 or 2007).*

 If you want the file you are uploading to overwrite a file with the same name, leave the Overwrite Existing File(s) option selected.

Communicating with Attendees

Once you determine what you need to discuss at your meeting, you can use a workspace to assemble the people who are going to do the discussing. Choose one of three Communications workspaces to send out messages and announcements to your colleagues:

- **Announcements**   This workspace lets you create short notes and announcements you can share with your coworkers.

- **Contacts**   When your project involves many different individuals who need to be contacted, you can add them in a list here.

- **Discussion Group**   This is one of the most useful workspaces: a full-fledged discussion area where you or coworkers can initiate threads and add a series of responses, counterresponses, or new topics. The New item lets you initiate a new topic by filling out a subject and a message in the form shown in Figure 5-7.

Tracking Issues, Schedules, and Objectives

The third type of workgroup is a real time-saver: it enables you to perform the essential business task of setting goals and objectives for your employees. by stating up-front what you want the meeting to accomplish. You give everyone a structure, and you give them the chance to think in advance about the subject, so everyone in the meeting isn't speaking off-the-cuff.

To start, you choose the type of workspace you want to create from the Tracking list in the Create page. You have five options:

- **Links**   Use this option to create a series of links to other documents or pages.

- **Calendar**   Use this option to create a scheduling calendar.

- **Tasks**   Create a set of tasks using this workspace.

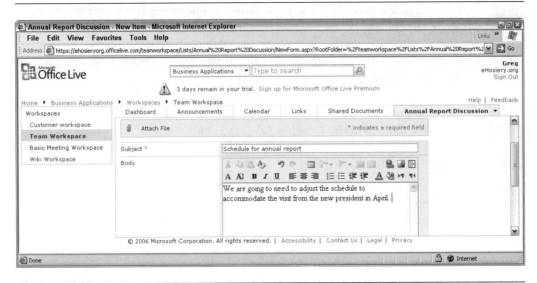

FIGURE 5-7   You can create a web-based discussion area by creating a Discussion workspace.

- **Project tasks**   This set of Tasks is more targeted toward a specific project you are working on.

- **Issue Tracking**   Establish the primary issues you need to tackle.

- **Survey**   Ask your coworkers, partners, or customers who have access to your Office Live site for their opinions about different topics.

Once you choose the workspace, specify its name and description, and then click New Item. When the New Item form appears (see Figure 5-8), type your message to your colleagues. Click OK to save your new task, issue, link, or other item.

You can either put all your objectives into a single New Item box or open a separate New Item box to enter each objective separately. You can also attach a file you want your colleagues to review in preparation for the meeting by clicking the Attach File link. When you finish, click OK to view the entire list. Any items with attachments have a special icon preceding them. You can change the order of objectives by clicking the Change Order link.

TIP   *To move from one collaborative tool to another within a workgroup (for instance, from Project Tasks to Document Library), click the Home link in the blue bar at the top of the current workspace view.*

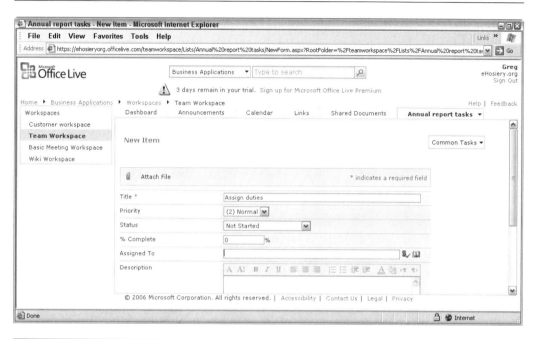

FIGURE 5-8   Listing tasks or issues beforehand keeps meetings from getting out of hand.

Managing Attendees

Once you determine what you need to discuss at your meeting, assemble the people who are going to do the discussing. Click either the Dashboard and go to the Attendees Web Part or click the Attendees tab, and then choose Manage Attendees from the View drop-down list to request the individuals who need to attend. If you need to add someone, click New Item from the New drop-down list, enter the name of the person, and then click OK.

- An e-mail address—for example, janedoe@mycompany.com

- The person's name as listed in Office Live's Users & Accounts

If you click the Address Book button next to the Name box, you get a dialog box that enables you to look up the person's user name or e-mail address, in case you can't remember it.

In the Comment box, you can add a note to the person, giving them specific instructions. From the Response drop-down list, choose an option that describes the person's response: Accepted, Tentative, or Declined. (Presumably, you will have discussed the meeting on the phone or in person with the individual beforehand.) In the Attendance box, choose whether the person's attendance is Optional, Required, or Organizer. When you finish, click the Save and Close link. When you've added all the attendees, click Go Back to List to review the names and make sure no one has been left out.

Don't forget to include yourself in the list and label yourself as Organizer. You know you are organizing the meeting, but others in your workgroup might not.

Adding an Agenda Item

The difference might not seem clear at first, but a list of objectives isn't the same as a list of agenda items for a meeting. *Objectives* are overarching goals that need to be achieved by the time the meeting is over. *Agenda items* are the individual steps the meeting participants take to meet the objectives. For instance, to meet the goal of drawing up a budget, you need to:

1. Compile a list of expenses

2. Review overall budget

3. Discuss promotional materials

Those three are agenda items. To add one for your meeting workspace, click Add New Item under the Agenda section of the Dashboard. However, you must be in the Basic Meeting Workspace to see the Agenda section; it isn't available in other workspaces. When the Agenda: New Item screen appears, fill out the boxes that appear. Subject is the subject of the item, owner is the person responsible for it, Time is the time needed to discuss it, and Notes are supplemental bits of information about it. When you finish, click OK.

Creating Custom Lists

Custom Lists are ones you create from scratch. When you click one of the three options—Custom List, Custom List in Datasheet View, or Import Spreadsheet— you name your workspace. The workspace opens with the three standard menus: New, Actions, and Settings. You can choose New Item from the New menu and add an item of your choice. But, you need to choose options from the Settings menu, such as Create Column or Create View, to customize your list.

NOTE *The Web Pages option for creating workspaces isn't all that different from the web pages discussed in Chapter 3. One option,* Web Part Page, *is a web page broken into two or more containers called Web Parts.* Web Parts *are self-contained programs that allow web users to manipulate and view information online.*

Giving Users Access to Workspaces

Each Office Live account includes access for a fixed number of users to access workspaces. With Office Live Essentials, you get access for ten users; with Premium, the limit is 20. If you ever need access for more users, you can purchase it in additional "packs" of five.

To gain access to a workspace, each user must have a user name and a password. You set up this information in the Users & Accounts screen. The permissions system for workspaces works like web sites. You can choose from three possible levels:

- **Administrator**   This level of permissions lets you set up or delete user accounts, or modify or delete data stored on workspaces.

- **Editor**   As an editor, you can add, modify, or delete data stored on workspaces, but you can't create or delete user accounts.

- **Reader**   You can only read information stored on workspaces; you can't add comments, or modify or delete information.

TIP *Your first impulse is probably to restrict administrator access to yourself alone. This is a good idea for security reasons because it prevents everyone else from being able to make changes to the site. But what happens if you go on vacation or are sick, and your coworkers need to create new user accounts or make other changes? To prevent getting anxious phone calls with such questions, give someone else administrator status as a backup.*

Creating Workspace User Accounts

You can create user accounts for the four types of workspaces—the sites you are given by default when you sign up for the service:

- Customer Workspaces

- Team Workspaces

- Basic Meeting Workspaces

- Wiki Workspaces

In addition, you can (and should) assign users to any custom sites you create, such as the meeting workspaces described in the previous section.

To create an account, log in to Office Live, and then click Workspaces. Then, follow these steps:

1. Click Common Tasks and choose Set Permissions.

2. Choose one type of site (any type) from the All sites drop-down list, shown in Figure 5-9.

It doesn't matter, initially, which type of site you select. You have the chance to assign permissions for this user for multiple workspaces later in the process. But, you should choose the workspace or business application you are working on currently.

3. Click Add User. The Add User—Web Page Dialog box opens.

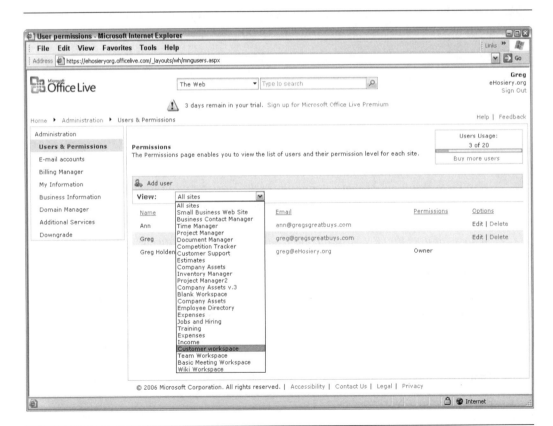

FIGURE 5-9　You can create one user account for all the workspaces you plan to use.

4. Type the individual's e-mail address (their Office Live e-mail address, that is), and then click Next.

You aren't limited to Office Live e-mail addresses when you add users to a workspace. You can enter an e-mail address outside your Office Live site and you'll send an invitation to that address. But the user needs an Office Live address to log in to the site and use the workspaces and their features.

5. In the next screen (see Figure 5-10), you assign a permissions level for this user for any or all of the workspaces you want to create. Choose a role for each one of the sites. The individual can be an editor in one site and a reader in another. If you don't plan to create one type of workspace or you don't plan to give the user access, don't choose a permissions level.

6. Click Next.

5

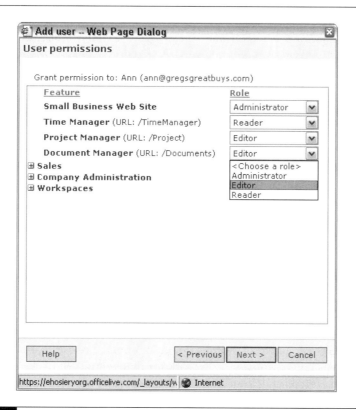

FIGURE 5-10   Each user can have different permissions levels for different workspaces.

7. In the next screen, you invite the individual to participate in the workspaces to which they are assigned. Type a short e-mail message, and then click Next.

8. After a few seconds, a Congratulations screen lets you know your message has been sent. Click Finish to close Add User. You return to the previous Office Live window, where the user is now added to the list of those who have permissions to work with your workspaces.

Modifying Accounts and Permissions

If you ever want to change a user's account information, you log into Office Live, and then click Users & Accounts. Next, click Edit or DEL next to the individual's user name.

If you want a quick glimpse at whether a user has permissions to work with, say, the Business Applications workspace, you can choose the type of site from the All Sites drop-down list. A list of registered users for that site appears.

 *When you delete a user, that permission loses access to all workspaces to which they previously had access. However, their e-mail address still exists. If that person leaves your organization, you need to delete the address from within Office Live's e-mail area.*

Sharing Information with a Document Workspace

As you learned earlier in this chapter, workspaces are set aside for people to work on a project collaboratively. Document workspaces are specially designed to help you create and circulate the Microsoft Word memos, letters, and reports that commonly circulate around many offices. You work on the document on your computer, but it resides on your Office Live site, where everyone in your group can access it.

Document workspaces aren't about conducting an online meeting. They provide an alternative to the traditional way of circulating documents, in which the document goes from person-to-person, and each person adds comments by hand. When the document (or different versions of it, each with its own edits) is eventually returned to a central point of contact, consolidating all the different changes can be considerable work for that central editor. With document workspaces, the file has only one copy, and access is restricted to only approved individuals.

> NOTE
>
> *Simply circulating the document from one person to another doesn't tell your colleagues who's edited it and it doesn't indicate what changes have been made. You can track changes and comments made to the file by multiple individuals. Do this by activating the Reviewing toolbar tracking changes in Word (or another Microsoft Office application you want to use). You also need to assign the appropriate permissions to users who must be able to upload new documents to the workspace. Otherwise, you'll be confused by multiple copies of the file circulating around your office.*

Customizing the Workspaces

When you are configuring workspaces, Office Live gives you a set of Web Parts with which you can work. These are the utilities you're most likely to need. The default options, called *Web Parts*, enable you and your coworkers to perform common tasks, such as scheduling events or adding agenda items. But, the exact Dashboard components differ, depending on the workspaces you're using:

- **Basic Meeting workspaces**   You see four basic options that can help you set up meetings: Attendees, Document Library, Objectives, and Agenda.

- **Customer workspace**   You see a Calendar for announcing meetings and a Links section for making links to important documents or web pages.

- **Team workspace**   You see announcements, Calendar, and Links.

- **Wiki workspace**   You see a simple page divided into the columns Type (for file type), Name (name of the document), and Modified By (to tell you who changed the wiki most recently).

But these are by no means the only Web Parts you and your colleagues can use. You can customize any workspace to provide specialized utilities.

Adding Web Parts

The first step in customizing the Dashboard is to open the type of workspace you want to edit and click the Dashboard tab, if necessary, so you are viewing the Dashboard. The next step is the same for all four types of workspaces: click Common Tasks, and then choose Customize Dashboard from the drop-down list.

The Dashboard refreshes, and you see it is now divided into several columns called *Web Zones*. In the case of the Basic Meeting Workspace, the columns are labeled Left, Center, and Right. Each of the columns has a link above it: Add a Web Part. Click this link in the column where you want a new Web Part to appear, and the Add Web Parts dialog box, shown in Figure 5-11, appears.

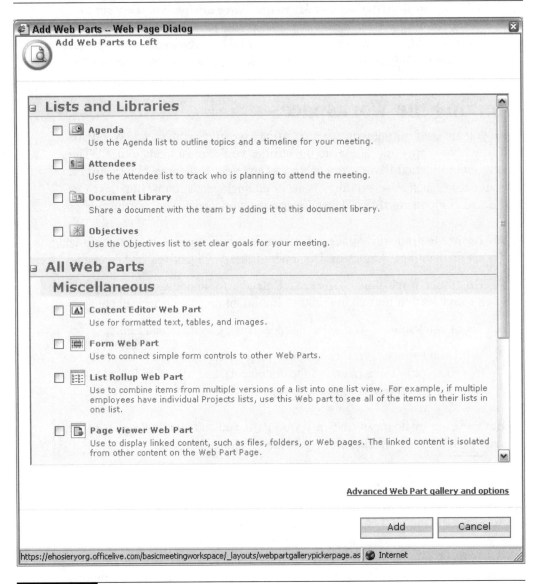

FIGURE 5-11   Add new utilities, called Web Parts, to the Dashboard using this dialog box.

The Lists and Libraries section at the top of Add Web Parts lists the current Web Parts you see in the Dashboard. The ones in the section labeled All Web Parts are new ones you can add. One sort of customization is graphical. By opening your site in the Content Editor Web Part, for instance, you can make a change as simple as adding a logo or adding your company name. You can also change the color scheme or hyperlink colors to get away from the standard look and feel you are initially given by Microsoft.

Another kind of customization is performed by adding Web Parts to your workspaces. At the very least, you should do some "shopping around" for available Web Parts when you establish workspaces, to see if any are available that can make the site more functional. Do this by clicking Common Tasks and choosing Modify This Application or Workspace. When the Site Settings page appears, click Web Part page under the heading Create.

Click Web Part page, and the page shown in Figure 5-12 appears. Choose an arrangement of Web Zones, give the page a name, and then click Create.

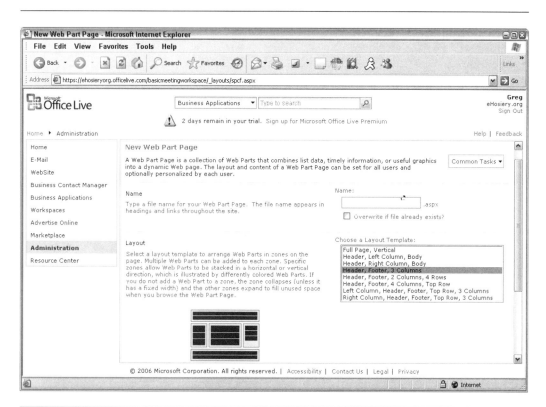

FIGURE 5-12 You can customize your workspaces by adding Web Parts.

The page is saved by default in the Document Library and it opens in its own browser window. The Add Web Parts dialog box appears. You can either choose a Web Part from this dialog box or click the link Advanced Web Parts and Options at the bottom of the dialog box.

If it doesn't appear initially, you may have to initially authorize Internet Explorer (IE) to enable this active content to appear.

When you choose Advanced Web Parts and Options, the browser window refreshes, and a new Web Parts pane (see Figure 5-13) opens in the workspace window you are working with. The first Web Parts on the list (Attendees, Agenda, and so forth) are already included in your workspace. You might want to add some of the other items, though, such as Things to Bring or General Discussion.

The items initially displayed in the Web Parts pane are ones that apply to the current workspace you have open (in this example, a workspace). Many more

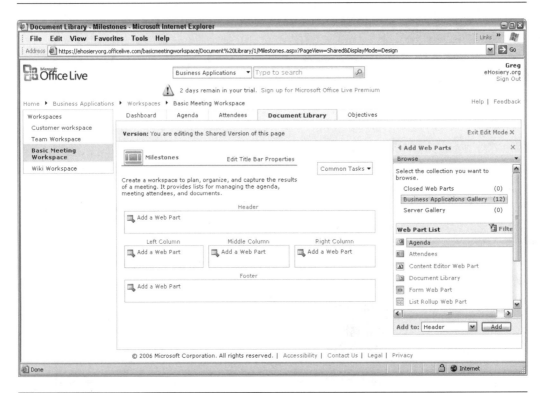

FIGURE 5-13   Choose additional collaborative tools from the Web Parts pane.

are available, however. If you click Search or Import by clicking the down arrow
next to Browse at the top of the Web Parts pane, you can locate sets of Web parts
applicable to other types of shared spaces.

You can add a Web Part to a workspace by dragging it into the body of the web
page in which the site is displayed. In the column (otherwise known as a "zone"
or "Web Zone") immediately to the left of the Web Parts pane, you see a message
instructing you to Add a Web Part to this zone by dropping it here. In fact, you can
add a Web Part to any part of the workspace page, not only this zone. And, if you
don't want to drag-and-drop, you can choose a zone from the drop-down list at the
bottom of the Web Parts pane, and then click Add.

Working with Web Parts

A workspace layout, then, is constructed of a variety of Web Parts. The layout of
those parts is not fixed. You can move or remove a Web Part by clicking the down
arrow in its blue title bar and choosing one of the available options:

- ■ **Minimize**   Choose this option to display only the title bar on the page and
  not the contents, to conserve space.

- ■ **Delete**   Choose this to delete the Web Part from the workspace. (This
  option only appears when you are working in the Modify Shared Web Part
  tool.)

- ■ **Close**   Choose this to remove the Web Part from the workspace (instead of
  the previous option).

- ■ **Modify Shared Web Part**   This option has its own set of options. They
  appear in the List Views pane on the right side of the workspace (see
  Figure 5-14). They let you change the alignment or positioning of the Web
  Part or work with the contents. To apply your selections, either click OK or
  Apply in the blue bar at the bottom of the List Views pane.

- ■ **Connections**   Use this option to establish a connection between one Web
  Part and another one. You can filter the information in the Objectives pane
  by connecting to items in your Document Library, for instance. You can
  also display a row in one Web Part that displays information from another
  part. The *Connections option* has its own submenu, which lets you build
  connections between Web Parts. (This option only appears when you are
  working in the Modify Shared Web Part tool.)

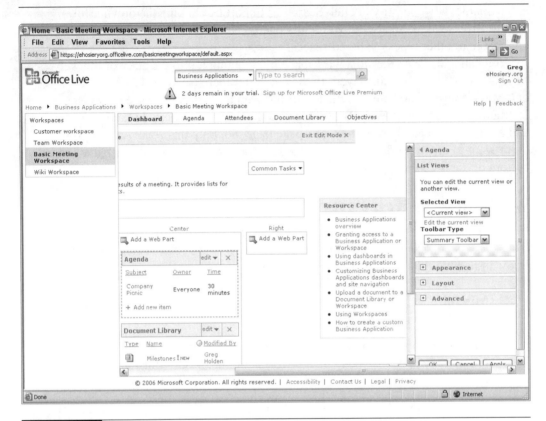

FIGURE 5-14 Use the List Views pane to change display options for Web Parts.

■ **Help** This option displays a special Help window. It's not the usual Office Live Help window but, rather, a Windows SharePoint Services Help window with information about working with Web Parts. (Remember, Web Parts and workspaces are based on SharePoint technology.)

 *If you have a pop-up blocker open in your web browser, you might not see the Connections dialog box, which helps you establish a connection between Web Parts. You might be unable to add new Web Parts at all. If you have problems seeing Web Parts, turn off your pop-up blocker or adjust it to temporarily allow pop-ups from this site.*

Best Practices for Working with Workspaces

Workspaces improve collaboration for a workgroup, but they also open some potential security problems.

Uploading Your Files

One potential problem was mentioned earlier in this chapter. When you want to upload multiple files to a Document Library on your Office Live site, Office Live opens a connection to your computer and displays, on your web page, the contents of your local file system. Is this secure? Microsoft would undoubtedly say yes: they protect such connections with user passwords. But passwords are notoriously insecure. They can be "hacked" by clever computing experts or stolen by people looking over your shoulder as you type. What would be better is if Microsoft would encrypt such a connection by presenting the site on a secure server. But, when I set up a "multiple files" connection using the Document Library, I didn't see the "closed lock" icon in the IE status bar that normally tells me the connection is protected by encryption.

To reduce the chances that a connection could cause problems, you need to protect yourself. You have several options:

- ■ Conceal part of your file system. When you connect to Office Live, do so from a computer that isn't connected to your entire file system, such as an Office server.

- ■ Password-protect sensitive directories.

If your office works with customer information, for instance, a good practice is always to isolate the names, addresses, credit card numbers, and other sensitive customer data from the Internet, so no one can gain access to it.

Protecting Your Information

The best defense is to observe good password management. Pick a long password (six to nine characters) that uses a mixture of characters and numerals, and capital and small letters, which isn't a recognizable word in the dictionary. And don't share your password with anyone. Protect your computer with firewall and antivirus software, so hackers can't install programs that track your keyboard entries or other harmful software.

 *Remember, when you have Office Live open on your computer and you are logged in to your account, anyone who works with you in the same space can make changes to your workspaces or other content—or possibly even delete the workspaces altogether. Be sure to log out every time you leave your computer or finish working with Office Live, so no one can gain unauthorized access.*

Where to Find It

■ **Additional Services**

http://membercenter.office.microsoft.com/Settings/Pages/Upsell .aspx?Source=Shop

Click Member Center, and then click Additional Services to add storage space or more users for your workspaces.

■ **Windows SharePoint Services Help**

https://[your_domain_name].officelive.com/[shared_site_name]/_vti_ bin/help/1033/sts/html/wstoc.htm

You know how to find Office Live Help, but to find SharePoint Services Help for workspaces, choose Help from a Web Part's menu or try the previous URL.

Chapter 6

Giving Your Employees Access to Your Workspaces

How to...

- Navigate through business applications with the Dashboard
- Manage employee hiring with human resources applications
- Track sales leads and follow-ups with the Business Contact Manager
- Share plans and upcoming events with a shared calendar
- Manage estimates and expenses with financial applications

Perhaps the most common reason to create workspaces for your employees is to give them the ability to access their e-mail from any computer connected to the Internet. But, many other business functions can be performed with Office Live workspaces. This chapter gives you some ideas for the kinds of workspaces you can set up for your employees, and how you can use them to increase efficiency and productivity.

In a small office, you probably lack IT support; you might not have a full-time IT person on call. Using Office Live helps reduce the burden on the technical staff you do have. You do that through creating workspaces. What do you do in those workspaces? You use a shared business application.

Working with Office Live Business Applications

Office Live may not be a miniature version of the business application suite called Microsoft Office, but it does provide some valuable software programs of the sort that companies pay big bucks to install on their workstations or access from a shared server. These applications help members of a workgroup get on the same page: if you have customer contact information and project milestone dates available to everyone in your group, you dramatically reduce the risk of something "falling through the cracks" and being overlooked. The following sections describe how to get started with the many business applications that come with Office Live.

NOTE   *The difference between the business applications provided with an Essentials or Premium subscription is not in the number of applications, but in the amount of space for storing data accumulated by their users. Essentials customers get 500MB of storage space, while Premium users get 1GB. In addition, an Essentials subscription enables 10 users to take advantage of business applications, while Premium subscribers can give access to a maximum of 20 users.*

Getting Started with Business Applications

A *business application* is a tool you use to view and work with data more efficiently. One of the most obvious business applications is a shared calendar, such as the one shown in Figure 6-1. But all the applications share the same goal of giving a group of people the same information to work with, so they can all be on the same page. These days, members of a workgroup may or may not be in the same location. Contractors may be working at home. A company may conceivably have branch offices in different parts of the country or overseas. Having a centralized repository of business information on the Web is essential because it enables staff to access the same information, despite time differences.

6

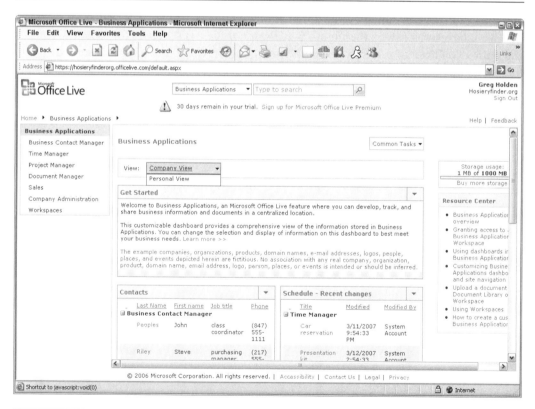

FIGURE 6-1   The Dashboard tracks events and points you to other applications.

Office Live offers more than 20 different business applications to Essentials and Premium subscribers. You access them by clicking Business Applications, and then choosing them from the navigation bar. The Business Applications page appears, but no applications are listed. To access the programs available to you, click the name of the first shared application you are likely to use: the Dashboard.

Steering Through Shared Applications with the Dashboard

In any work environment, a Things to Do list or Daily Planner is essential, so you can keep track of everything you have to do in a given period. The Dashboard, a standard feature with Office Live's business applications, performs the same function. The *Dashboard* is, essentially, a planning tool that lists upcoming contacts, tasks, and events for you and your coworkers. The exact contents of the Dashboard differ, depending on the application you are viewing. The Dashboard has two tabs, as you saw in the Figure 6-1. *Personal View* is set aside for meetings and duties you need to perform in the upcoming future. *Company View* is reserved for events the whole office or workgroup need to perform or at least be aware of.

As you might expect, the individual sections of the main Business Application Dashboard reflect the contents of individual applications you can work with:

- **Schedule**   These are events that describe what's going to happen on a specific day: a meeting, a phone call, a completion date, and so on.

- **Opportunities**   These are sales opportunities you need to be aware of to keep up good relations with your business contacts.

- **Project Issues**   These are issues you record using the Project Manager application.

- **Projects**   These are projects your company needs to address, as described in the Project Manager application.

 *Before you create a new event or resource, you first need to decide whether it should appear on Personal View or Company View. Click the view on which you think the item should appear before you add it.*

Scheduling is one of the most important functions you can perform with the business applications. You can specify them in the Dashboard that appears when you click the Time Manager application; a visual calendar appears in the

Scheduling & reservations section of the Dashboard. Before you start recording upcoming events and items, a good idea is to identify the types of events you expect to record, as well as the kinds of resources you plan to use. If you do this in advance, the options you specify appear conveniently on drop-down lists, which are part of the forms you need to fill out to record items on the calendar. To create a calendar item, or to record events and resources you might want to list, follow these steps:

1. Click Time Manager and scroll down to the Scheduling & Reservations section to view the online calendar.

2. Click the date of the event you want to record (see Figure 6-2). An hour-by-hour schedule for the selected day appears.

3. Click the hour when the event is scheduled to occur. The Schedule and Reservations: New Appointment screen appears.

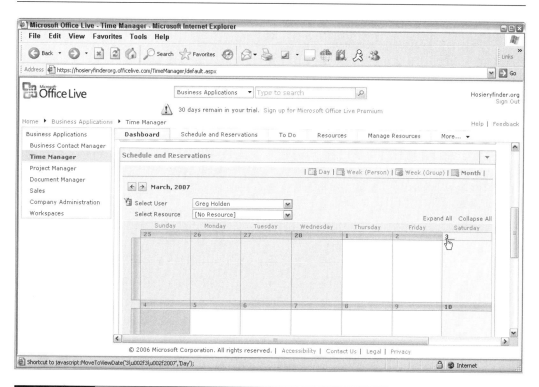

FIGURE 6-2   Record upcoming events using this visual calendar.

4. If you need office resources to conduct your event, click the Manage Resources tab (see Figure 6-3) and fill out the form that appears to identify the resource. Until you do this, the Add Resource drop-down list in Schedule and Reservations is blank.

5. Enter a name for the event in the Title box.

6. Complete the rest of the form to specify any resources you need, and then add a description, so your coworkers can find out about what's going to happen.

7. Click the calendar icon next to the Begin or End fields, or type a specific date for the item.

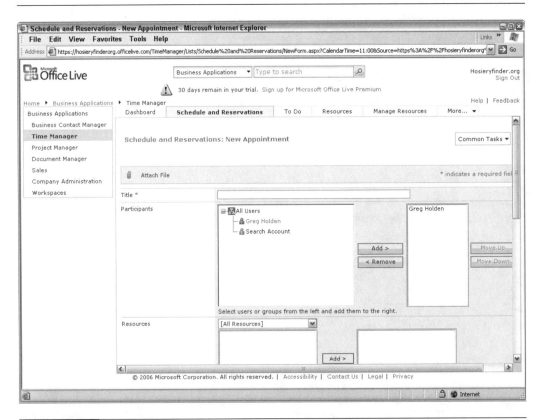

FIGURE 6-3 Fill out this form to place an item in your Dashboard's scheduling section.

8. Optionally, you can choose a color from the toolbar above the Description box to designate, for instance, an in-house meeting, a reminder, or a client meeting.

9. When you finish completing the form, click OK. The screen refreshes and you return to the hour-by-hour version of the scheduling and reservations utility, where your meeting is now displayed (see Figure 6-4).

Other scheduling applications let you specify different types of options. For instance, with Time Manager open, you can click the To Do tab. When the To Do list appears, click New, and then choose New Item. The New Item list appears; this is a list commonly used not only in Time Manager, but many other business applications.

In the New Item form, you are required to assign a level of urgency to the task from the Priority drop-down list. The list is populated with default options: High, Normal, and Low. You can also describe the status of the event (Not Started, In Progress, Completed, Deferred, Waiting, or something else). When you click OK, your new item is added to the To Do list. You probably want to eliminate any default information already included as sample data by Microsoft, so you can see

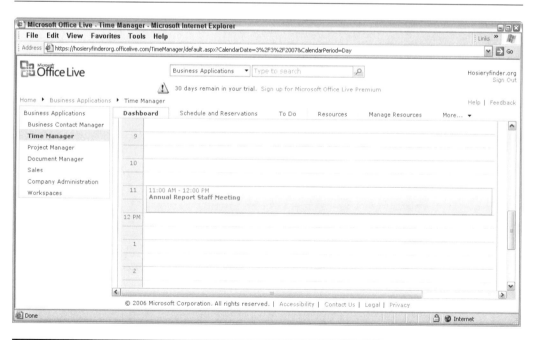

FIGURE 6-4   Your meeting appears in this shared area where your coworkers can see it.

your new information more clearly. Click the down arrow in the upper right-hand corner of any list and press DEL to clear the default information.

If you click the Manage Resources tab in Time Manager, you click New and then choose New Group to specify typical company resources: Company Car, Conference Room, or Computer Resources, for instance. To add individual resources, click the Resources tab, then click New, and then click New Resource. When the New Resource form appears, type its name and description, and then click OK. You should take the time to include your own company resources (see Figure 6-5). These might include:

- Cameras or photo equipment

- Your reception area

- Your archives of past publications (examples of your work)

- An office laptop

- Office cell phones, tape recorders, or other electronic devices

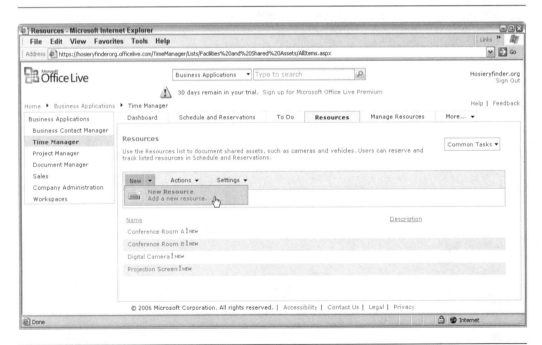

FIGURE 6-5   You can customize your calendar by specifying your own events or resources.

Editing Projects and Contacts

Scheduling details are only one type of information you view with the Dashboard that appears in the main Business Applications. The others, Opportunities, Projects, Project Issues, and Contacts, also come with pre-entered default information. To delete the default information, click and click Remove Sample Data from the drop-down list that appears.

 *See the section "Managing Contacts" for more on Business Contact Manager. See Chapter 7 for more on that application.*

Managing Contacts

6

Salespeople are naturally protective of their accounts. But their need to protect their livelihood needs to be balanced with the organization's need to track clients. Not only that, but it's often essential to maintain a record of which clients have been contacted in the recent past and which need to be called or e-mailed on a periodic basis.

The Business Contact Manager business application enables workgroups to maintain a list of individual clients, as well as business accounts. As you can see in Figure 6-6, the application is divided into five tabs:

- **Accounts**   This tab is for companies you work with. You can assign a "business rating" to indicate what sort of client they are.

- **Contacts**   This tab's information is essential for any office and includes contact information for individuals you work with. Listing their correct job title is often important, so new salespeople don't make a mistake. The Business Contacts tab includes a tab for this bit of information, as well as a Follow Up Flag to let everyone know if the person should be contacted soon.

- **Opportunities**   This tab is for recording people or businesses that are possible, rather than upcoming, clients. You can record not only the name of the account, but the probability that they'll sign a contract with you and even the amount of revenue you project to gain.

- **Products**   This tab is to associate each of your business contacts with a product you produce. You specify the products in this list.

- **Business Documents**   This tab stores résumés, CVs, or other documents associated with your contents in this area.

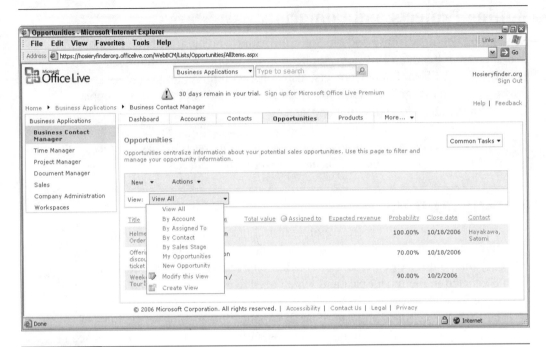

FIGURE 6-6   Business Contact Manager helps you manage clients through its lists and views.

If you have Microsoft Office 2003 or 2007 installed, and you are more comfortable with databases, you can click the Edit in Datasheet button to open a database application.

Contact Manager not only has five tabs (each of which presents a list), but also a variety of Views. The number of views depends on the list you are in. For example, in the Opportunities list, you have a long list of views, including: All Opportunities, My Opportunities, Active Opportunities, and By Contact. Use these Views to sort your data and view it selectively. By filtering and sorting it into these categories, you can make sense of it more easily.

You can export your Business Contact Manager data to common Office applications you work with. Office 2007 also uses XML as the file format for Word, Excel, and PowerPoint, so it should be even easier to make use of this exported data.

Using Applications to Manage Your Staff

Managing staff is enough of a challenge when everyone works standard 9-to-5 hours in the same physical space. When some workers telecommute from home, some work in branch offices, and everyone works flex hours, management becomes even more difficult. Shared business applications can help your staff find one another, track projects they are working on together, and keep everyone in the loop, no matter what time zone they are in. The following sections describe some of the applications that can give employees access to shared documents, notes, dates—and each other.

Working with the Jobs and Hiring Application

The Jobs and Hiring Workspace is one of the business applications included with Office Premium. Setting aside workspaces and giving individuals access to them isn't difficult. But, once you create workspaces, what do you do with them? Keeping employees in the loop about job openings, and communicating news and notes about job candidates to the appropriate personnel (the ones who need to approve and/or interview the new hire) is essential for virtually any office. Once you open the Jobs and Hiring application, you can use one of the built-in lists to make it work for your office.

TIP   *To find the Jobs and Hiring application, first, log in to Office Live Premium, and then click Business Applications. Next, click Company Administration. Finally, click Jobs and Hiring.*

Listing Jobs and Hiring Status

Suppose a job position opens in your office. You advertise for the position, both in-house and in public venues, such as trade publications or classifieds sections. How do you keep track of who has already been interviewed, who remains to be interviewed, whether résumés were received, and each candidate's status? You open Jobs and Hiring, and then list the openings in the shared space provided for you.

When you first open Jobs and Hiring (shown in Figure 6-7), you see a set of sample data in Requisitions, one of three lists with which you are presented. Scan the data to get an idea of the kinds of information the application requires. Besides the basics (name, address, phone, email), you have the opportunity to add some notes, as well as to attach one or more files such as a résumé or a sample of the candidate's work.

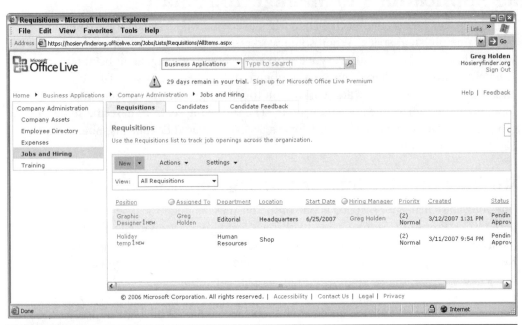

FIGURE 6-7 You can attach résumés to candidate listings.

To add your own data to the application, remove the sample data (click Common Tasks, and choose Remove Sample Data), and then click New. Choose New Item and fill out the New Item candidate form that appears (see Figure 6-8). Be sure to scroll down the list and complete all required fields (each field is marked with an asterisk [*]). The tricky ones are the Assigned To and Hiring Manager fields: you have to enter the name exactly as it appears in Office Live's database (for instance, I had to enter Greg Holden, rather than simply Greg). Click the checkbox to the right of each field to open a Find box. Enter the name you want to find, and then Click Find. The correct name is then displayed.

Once you receive some responses to your job listings, you can record each candidate's name in the Candidates list. If you're really organized and want to provide comments about your company that others in your organization can view, click Candidate Feedback and enter it.

NOTE *The sample data is common to all business applications and appears the first time you open one of them. Click Remove sample data from the Common Tasks lists, and then type your own information to customize the form for your needs.*

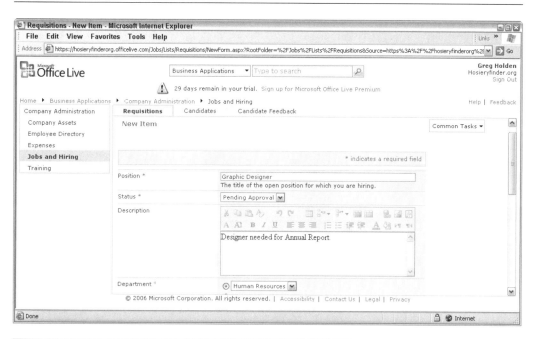

FIGURE 6-8   Enter information about job openings in the New Item form.

Training Your Workforce

The Training business application gives you the opportunity to track training courses you set up for your employees, as well as your customers. If you conducted training, you know that only half the battle is creating and scheduling the courses; the other half is getting employees to be present for the courses and to ensure they don't forget when those courses are. By recording events in a calendar that you distribute to employees, you give your employees a way to easily access and track the available courses. You also deprive them of the excuse that they weren't made aware of the courses. You only have to send them a reminder that the courses were all listed online.

The Training application, shown in Figure 6-9, is divided into two tabs: Training Courses and Training Enrollments. The Enrollments tab is used to give employees or customers a place to be enrolled. If you give all your employees access to the Human Resources Workspace, you can encourage them to enroll themselves. Otherwise, you have to do the recording of who is going to attend. The Training Courses tab enables you to record the name, location, time, instructor, and other information about each course.

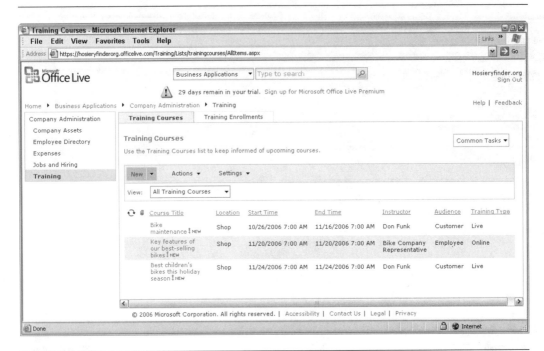

FIGURE 6-9   When you use this application, your employees won't have any excuse for not enrolling in courses.

At the bottom of the Training Courses form, you can find a useful, but easily overlooked, item called Workspace. Check the box to create a Meeting Workspace for the event. This gives your employees a place to organize notes and set agenda items for the course. See Chapter 5 for more on meeting workspaces.

Creating an Employee Directory

The larger the organization, the more critical it becomes to give all interested parties access to your employee contact information. Employees themselves need to get in touch with one another, of course, as do customers and business partners who need to call them quickly. Printed directories are good for use in an office. But, do you really want to carry one on the plane or in the car when you're traveling? When you're on the road, or when it's after hours and you can't call the receptionist, the capability to access the employee directory at any time—from a laptop or other Internet-connected computer—can help you get a question answered or a problem solved at a critical time.

To create an online employee is a simple matter. Click Company Administration, and then click Employee Directory. At this point, you have two options:

- Type each employee's information from scratch

- Import the employee information from Microsoft Outlook

If you have multiple employee listings to add, choose Edit in Datasheet view from the Actions drop-down list. A *datasheet* is a view divided into rows and columns, much like a spreadsheet, which makes it easy to import information.

If you have an address book compatible with SharePoint Services installed on the computer that holds the employee information, you don't necessarily have to import the contact information to Office Live. You can link your Employee Directory to your Outlook file. Click Link to Outlook at the top of the Employees tab, and then follow the instructions on the page that appears.

In either case, it's a matter of setting up an employee database. You type the last name, first name, job title, e-mail address, and phone number of each person you want to add. The Employee Directory looks rather simple. However, when you click New employee to add an individual to your list, you access a form with many more possible fields than displayed in the Employee Directory. For instance, if you have a photo of the employee available, you can post it on your Office Live web site, and then enter the URL for the image in the Image field. That way, a photo appears, along with the employee's other information (see Figure 6-10).

CAUTION   *As you can see from Figure 6-10, depending on the size of the photo, it can make the layout of the employee profile difficult to read. Make sure your photo is saved in a small thumbnail size—about one-inch square—before you post it online.*

Managing Time

Even for those of us who extend their work hours into the evenings and weekends, you can devote only so many hours in the day or week to work. If you lose valuable time by missing meetings, having to reschedule meetings, or having to sit through meetings that go on twice as long as they should due

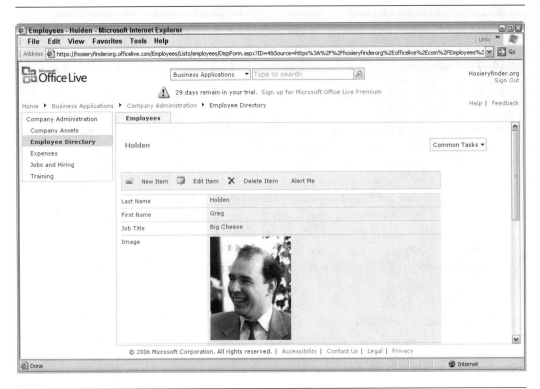

FIGURE 6-10   You can add a photo to an employee listing, but keep it small.

to lack of organization and preparation, your jobs fall behind, and the whole organization suffers.

Many of Office Live's business applications are designed to help busy workers with time management. In the following sections, you get an introduction to applications that help you track office activity of all sorts, as well as hours spent on various projects.

Creating a Shared Calendar

As anyone who has worked in an office knows, missing or being late for meetings is a serious black mark on an employee's record. Setting up a shared calendar for office use relieves people of the excuse that they weren't told about the time or location of a meeting.

But, more than that, a shared calendar also helps people track the progress of jobs on which they are working together. Deadlines and milestones toward a project's completion are essential things to track, because they reassure everyone that the job is on time. If it is not, you get early warning that it's going to be late, so you can adjust the end date as needed.

When you click the Time Manager application and choose the Schedule and Reservations tab described earlier in this chapter, a shared calendar application appears. It enables you to schedule events and reserve resources you need for them. Along with the traditional calendar, which is the same as the one that appears in a small "snapshot" size on the Time Manager application's Dashboard, you are presented with several other options for viewing upcoming events:

- **All Schedules**   This is a list of all events you or others in your workgroup have scheduled.

- **Calendar**   This option is pretty misleading, frankly, because all the views are presented in the form of calendars. This is literally a catch-all, a place to turn when you want to review company events, training sessions, and resources—all in one place.

- **Current Schedule**   These are the events scheduled by the user who is currently logged on to the Office Live site.

Managing Money

Every office needs to track budgets, available funds, and expenses. But not every office has financial staff who are dedicated solely to bookkeeping or accounting functions. Several Office Live business applications can help small businesses at least keep track of their expenses, so nothing slips through the cracks.

Tracking Expenses

When you click Company Administration | Employees | Expenses, the Expenses application appears. This program asks for the basics, including:

- Title (a brief description of the expense)

- Expense Type (a designation to help with accounting: travel, supplies, training, and so on)

- Expense Amount (the amount spent)

- ■ Date Incurred

- ■ Date Paid (the date the expense was paid for out of your accounts may be different from the date the expense occurred. You can sign a purchase order and receive equipment, and then pay for it later on, for instance)

Some repetition is in the default form: the Expense Type item occurs twice, for instance, and Title and Expense Description are pretty much the same thing—although you can add more details about why the expense occurred in the Expense Description box. Click Customize List to change the columns. You can change the name of a column by clicking it, and then changing the name in the form that appears. You can also move columns by clicking Changing the order of the fields in the Column section of the Customize form. But you can't delete a column—not at press time, at least. By leaving the name of the column blank and moving it to the far end of the form, however, you can ensure it will be ignored.

One of the most useful applications related to Office Live is called Office Accounting 2007. This isn't one of the business applications described in this chapter, but it can help you process the data you capture in the Expenses and Estimates applications. See Chapter 15 for more information.

Estimates and Budgets

The *Estimates business application*, which appears under the Sales category, is intended to give your staff a place to record the estimates you give to prospective clients for your products or services. You don't want to duplicate estimates someone else on your staff has already issued, and you certainly don't want to provide different quotes than the ones already released. You record Requests for Proposals (RFPs) on the Quotations tab, one of two included with the Estimates application.

The other tab, Order Information, gets specific about the quotations. The *Quotations tab,* by default, only lets you record that an estimate was made, as well as who made it, and when it was made. The *Order Information tab* provides fields for the specific amount of the estimate itself.

The other essential aspect of tracking office finances—budgets—doesn't exist in Office Live's business applications. You can use Microsoft Office Accounting 2007 quite nicely for that purpose. But, if you only want a quick statement of available funds, consider "adapting" the Estimates application for your purposes.

Default column headings	Quote Title	Effective from	Status	Sales Person	Account
New column headings	Account #	Account Name	Budget	Description	Department

TABLE 6-1	Customizing the Estimates Application

You can't change the name—Estimates—but you can change the names of the column headings, as Table 6-1 indicates.

To be sure, it's only a workaround. But, for a small office with a fairly simple budget, it might be adequate. You find out more about customizing applications in Chapter 10.

Where to Find It

- The Dashboard: A planner that links you to Office Live business applications

    Log in, click Business Applications, and click Dashboard

- An Employee Directory

    Click Employees and choose Employee Directory

- A shared calendar with all upcoming office events

    Click Company, choose Calendars, and then select Calendar View

- Information on orders you received

    Click Sales, choose Estimates, and then click the Order Information tab

Chapter 7

Opening Your Business to Vendors and Customers

How to...

- Provide workspaces where your customers can track orders
- Custome workspaces to refer to specific clients and projects
- Create a library of shared documents you can view and edit
- Keep track of changes to documents with file versioning and check-in/check-out
- Configure a discussion board or survey, so your colleagues can "talk back"
- Open shared workspaces for your vendors

The way your employees communicate with your customers is of paramount importance to your overall business operations. Yet, you can't monitor exactly what individual staff are going to communicate and how they are going to do it. Customer workspace can help you establish uniform procedures for how staff maintain ongoing relationships. It can also give you a space for lists that can keep your vendors on their toes regarding orders and deadlines they must meet, so you can achieve your sales quotas. By creating shared workspaces, you strengthen connections with customers and vendors alike. You build customer loyalty, and you also give vendors a place to monitor important milestones and issues.

In this chapter, you discover ways to open your Office Live site to "outsiders" who are critical to your operations and who can benefit from improved sharing of information—an improvement that can carry forward to your business's profit margin.

Creating a Customer Workspace

A few years ago, I visited a factory in Chicago that manufactures what might seem the most boring product imaginable: corrugated paper. This place didn't create just any kind of paper. Rather, Corrugated Supplies Corporation (CSC) makes specialty papers in different colors and surfaces, so it can be folded and printed with the brands and logos of well-known retailers. I wasn't visiting the place to check out the paper itself. Instead, I was assigned to write the news that the company had opened its entire supply chain to customers and suppliers, who could place their orders directly into the system without even having to place a phone call.

CSC is a small operation. It has to compete with much larger corporations that can turn around a greater quantity of paper with lower cost. How can CSC compete? Besides using unusual colors and papers, it succeeds by offering rapid turnaround times and a level of customer service the bigger paper producers can't match. Those last two qualities are achieved by letting outsiders have direct access to the CSC computer network. They can track orders, place orders, and make adjustments directly. This provides customers with greater control and faster delivery than they could get otherwise. You, too, can use Office Live's Customer-centric business applications to make stronger connections than ever before with your valued clients. The tools and strategies for doing so are described in the following sections.

Customizing Workspaces

When you set up workspaces for your customers, you want them to feel special. Instead of using the generic Customer Workspace name, a good idea is to refer to their own company name. Doing this is easy enough by customizing the Customer Workspace in Office Live:

1. Log in to Office Live and click Workspaces.

2. When the Shared Sites page appears, click Customer Workspace.

3. When the Customer Workspace opens, click Common Tasks, and then choose Modify this application or Workspace.

4. When the Site Settings window appears, click Change left menu options.

5. When the list of items that normally appear in Office Live's left-hand menu appears, click Customer Workspace to display the categories beneath it.

6. Click the Edit button to display a Title box shown in Figure 7-1. Type a name unique to your customer.

7. Click OK to refresh the Site Settings screen, where your customized workspace name is listed.

Another good idea is to review the columns in the Customer Workspace to make sure they're specific to your project. Open the Customer Workspace, click Common Tasks, and then click Manage this Application or Workspace. Scroll down to the Develop and Customize section of the Customer Workspace Site Settings window. Click Change columns, and then review the names of the default column headings. Many of those names are generic, such as Address, Assistant's

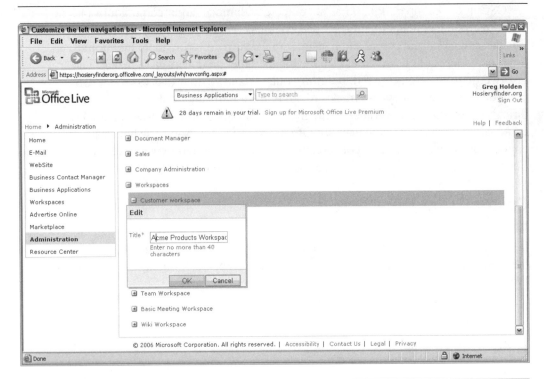

FIGURE 7-1 Customize your workspace to make it unique to your customer.

Name, and so on. Consider changing those names to something more specific, such as Acme Products Manager.

 *Click Basic page under the Create heading in Site Settings to create a new page for your shared site if you don't see one in the default list that meets your needs. You might want to create a page that's specific to your client, such as Layouts for General Information Brochure or Paper Orders for 2007, for instance.*

Exploring the Project Manager

Once you customize the workspace, click Business Applications, and then click the custom name you just gave it. Once there, you can click the Project Manager menu option. When the Project Manager opens, click Projects, then click New, and, finally, click New Item from the drop-down list. When you create a new project from scratch, you get a lot of flexibility. You can refer to a specific project or use it as a `sort of catchall for any of your shared needs—orders, inventory, publicity, or sales. When the New Item form for Project Manager shown in Figure 7-2 appears, enter the name, status, start and end dates, and other information.

When you finish, click OK. The New Item form closes and you return to Project Manager, where your new project appears at the top of the list of Open jobs. You can move on to the other tabs in Project Manager—Milestones, Tasks, and Issues—and add more data related to the new project or to other projects you have underway. The *Project Issues tab* is especially important for customers who want you to pay attention to particular concerns, and you should encourage them to use it (see Figure 7-3). Giving customers a place to speak their minds and make sure you are aware of priorities is critical to maintaining customer satisfaction.

7

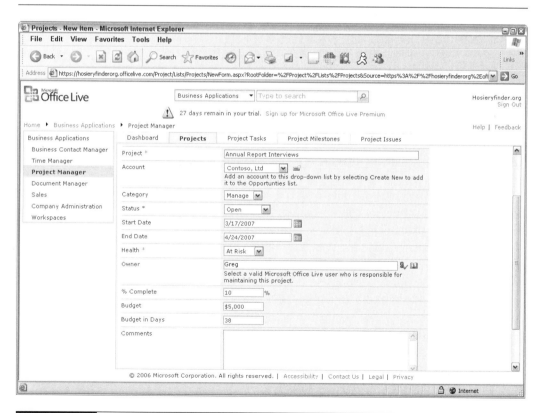

FIGURE 7-2   Project Manager gives you and your customers the chance to collaborate on specific jobs.

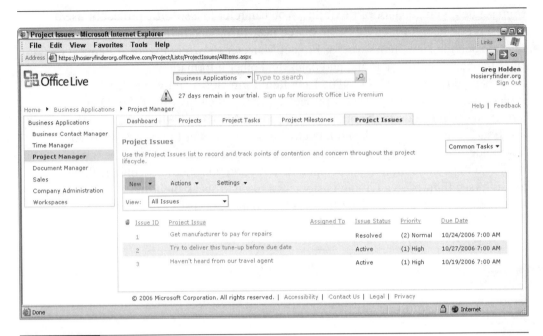

Just be sure you and your coworkers keep checking the Project Manager on a regular basis, so you can keep on track with the issues your customers are pointing out.

Of course, to grant customers access to their customized workspaces or to the Project Manager, they need to be issued user accounts. Click Home, then click Administration, and then click Users & Permissions. When the User Permissions window appears, click Add User. You are prompted to create an Office Live e-mail account first, if one doesn't exist yet. Once the customer has an e-mail address, you create a user account: open Users & Permissions, click Add user, and then enter the e-mail address and user name. Click Next, and the Add User—Web Page Dialog window appears, where you assign the individual Reader, Editor, or Administrator permissions to the custom workspace or Project Manager. Depending on the permissions level, the person's view of the workspace or application might be slightly different from that of the Administrator. He/she might not be able to add new items or change the contents, for instance.

If you ever want to customize Project Manager (or any Office Live application), click the Customize this page link in the application itself.

Working with the Document Library

A *document library* is a collection of files exchanged by your company and your customer's organization. You don't have to think long and hard about the kinds of files you can place there. Examples include:

- Copies of e-mail messages with critical information about projects

- Orders for work

- Samples of layouts or drafts of documents you're preparing for the client

- Logos or other images the client sends you

- Financial data or background information you need to prepare web sites or articles

When you're in your customer workspace, click the Documents button, and then click Document Library to enter the space. To add a file to the Document Library, you have two options:

- Upload a file from your computer to the library. (See the following instructions.)

- Create a new file on the Office Live site. Click New Document on the Documents page. If you have Office 2003 or later installed, Microsoft Word opens, so you can create a new file. Save the file on your file system, and then upload it to the Document Library.

The term *upload* is used to describe the process of transferring data from a local computer to a network server. (You *download* a file when you move it from the server to your computer. Every time you view a web page, you are downloading text and image files.) Follow these steps to add a file to the library:

1. Click Upload, and then choose Upload Document. When the upload form shown in Figure 7-4 appears, click Browse.

2. When the Choose file dialog box appears, highlight the file on your file system, and then click Open.

3. The path leading to the file is added to the form. Click OK to add the file to the list (see Figure 7-5).

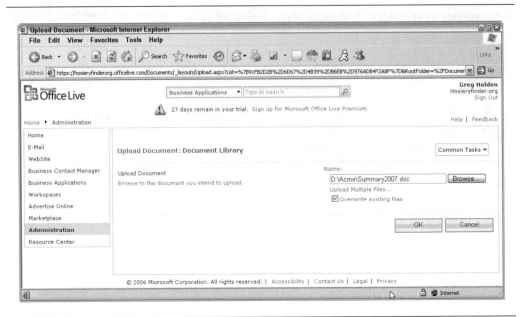

FIGURE 7-4   Uploading a file to the Document Library only takes a matter of seconds for you or your customers.

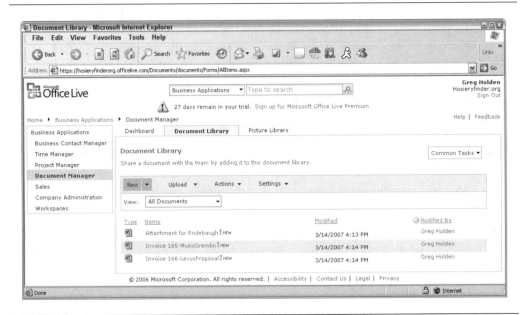

FIGURE 7-5   A Document Library can hold files that coworkers can view and create.

 *When you create or edit a new file on Office Live, you won't have a backup on your local system. If the file is important, be sure to save a copy. When you finish working on a Word file, for example, and you click Save, you are prompted to log in, so you can save the file using your .NET Passport account.*

When you have documents stored in a library, you view any one of them by clicking its filename. A .NET Passport dialog box appears. Obviously, this assumes you have a .NET Passport account with Microsoft, because the dialog box doesn't give you the opportunity to enter the Windows Live ID you use to log in to Office Live. If you need one, click the Get a .NET Passport link in the bottom left-hand corner of the dialog box. Enter your .NET Passport e-mail address and password, and then click OK. The file you want to view opens in Microsoft Word (you don't need Word 2003 for this feature).

When you start to organize and edit your shared documents, you want to know Document Libraries support the features described in the following sections.

 *Not everything can be transmitted from your client to you by uploading it to Office Live. One thing that won't work is a contract, which requires actual physical signatures. You have to send those by mail or delivery service, or sign them in person.*

Keeping Track of Document Revisions

If you have worked on a complex or lengthy project, you know files go through multiple versions before they are approved. As they are circulated for approval, files are usually designated Version 1.1, Version 1.2, or something similar. Circulating such documents by interoffice mail as physical printouts can be time-consuming. Even by e-mail, sending a document in a "chain" from one person to another can be awkward, especially if someone in the chain is out of the office for a few days. Sending mass e-mails to everyone in the group at once is more efficient, but then you have the burden of collating all edits and comments into a single document—and this file, too, may need to be circulated for final approval.

By posting one document in your Office Live Document Library, you save yourself some work and trouble. Everyone can access the same file. Duplication is prevented by using the Check in/Check out feature described in the next section. And, you can keep track of how many versions the file has gone through by simply viewing who edited it last. You can take an extra step and save a copy with a new

version number, if you choose. To view edits and assign a version number to a
document, follow these steps:

1. Click Workspaces.

2. Click the name of your customer or vendor workspace (or the workspace
   with the documents you want to circulate).

3. When the workspace opens, click the Shared Documents tab. (If you're
   working in Document Manager, click Document Library.)

4. Locate the document to which you want to assign a version number. Slide
   your mouse pointer to the right of the filename. A blue box with a down
   arrow appears (see Figure 7-6).

*The gray box and the down arrow only appear when your mouse arrow
passes over the apparently blank area to the right of the filename.
Otherwise, the Name column appears blank.*

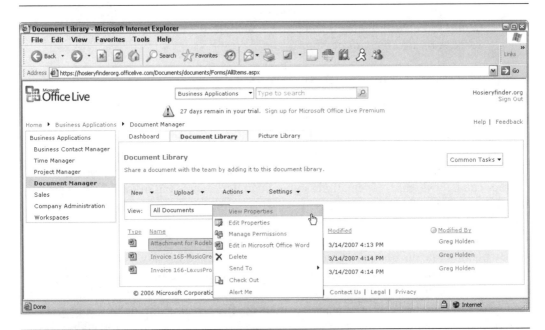

FIGURE 7-6   You can perform functions on each document in the library with these menu
options.

5. Click the blue box/down arrow and choose View Properties from the drop-down list that appears. The detailed information that appears includes a statement about who last edited the file and when it was revised.

6. If you want to take an extra step and create a copy of the file with a new version number, so you can make changes while preserving the previous version, click Manage Copies.

7. When the Manage Copies screen appears, click New Copy.

8. In the Edit Copy screen, you can change the filename. In Figure 7-7, I added v.2 to the name in the box labeled Filename for the copy.

9. Click OK to save the copy with the new version number.

Now that you have created a new version of the file, two copies should appear in the Document Library or Shared Documents list, each with different version numbers.

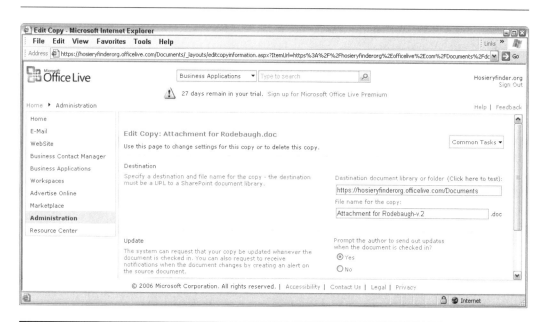

FIGURE 7-7   You can create a copy of a file with a new version number if you choose.

Using Check-In/Check-Out

If you work in a group with other staff who need access to the same files, keeping track of documents and who has them open is hard enough. When it's possible your staff or your customer's staff might be working on the same files, things get even more complicated. To make sure two people don't try to open and change the document simultaneously, you can take advantage of check-in/check-out for Document Library files. You don't want to duplicate one another's work. You check out a file, make the changes, and then check it back in.

Checking out a file is a snap. You follow Steps 1 through 5 in the preceding section, but you choose Check Out from the drop-down list. Your name then appears in the Checked Out column. Anyone who connects to the same document library can see the file is checked out, and then they know they should either wait until you check the file in again or e-mail you to let you know they're waiting for it. When you finish and save your changes, be sure to select Check In from the drop-down list to let others know the file is "available" once again.

Click Alert Me from the drop-down list next to a document's name if you want to receive an e-mail alert when the file has been changed. The e-mail message is sent to you automatically by the Office Live server.

Creating a Discussion Board

Giving your customers and vendors a place to conduct online discussions with each other and with your own staff can bring obvious benefits in terms of customer satisfaction. Customers who feel they are "in the loop" and who have an open communication channel with your company, naturally feel more invested in you and connected to your organization. They are less likely to jump ship and sign up with a competitor. But, more than that—ultimately, your customer profitability depends on how loyal your customers are. Customers develop a sense of loyalty when they have a reason to visit your site regularly and remain on the site for longer periods of time.

One of the best ways to encourage visitors to remain on your Office Live site (or on any web site, for that matter) is by creating a discussion forum. What, you ask, is an online discussion forum? You might liken it to clubs of members who meet in coffee shops or church basements who share their enthusiasm for a hobby, such as collecting dolls, or an interest, such as old-time radio. But, rather than meeting at a specific place at a fixed time, an online discussion group can meet any time of the day or night. They hold conversations by typing notes to one another.

The benefits of a discussion group might not seem obvious if your immediate goal is selling products online. But, experience shows that, by creating a place for vendors or customers to gather, you can realize a big return on your investment. I own a Volkswagen car, and owners like me flock to a lively community discussion area called VW Vortex (www.vwvortex.com, shown in Figure 7-8). This is a place where owners can ask questions about parts and inventory, features, and experiences with this line of cars.

Creating a Workspace Discussion Board

You have two options when it comes to permitting discussions in a shared site. You can use the Team Workspace, which has a ready-made discussion area within it. Choose More and Team Discussion to open the discussion area immediately.

7

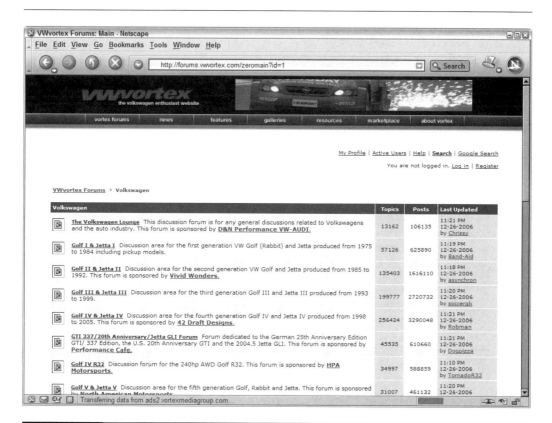

FIGURE 7-8   A discussion area can build loyalty, which leads to sales.

Otherwise, you have to add a discussion area to the workspace itself. To configure a discussion area for a customer or other workspace, first open the workspace you want, then follow these steps:

1. Click Common Tasks and choose Manage this application or workspace. The Site Settings page appears.

2. Under the heading Create, click Lists and Libraries.

3. In the Site Libraries and Lists window, click Create new content.

4. In the Create window shown in Figure 7-9, click the Discussion Boards option in the Select a View list on the left-hand side. When you hover your pointer over Discussion Board, more information appears above the list.

5. Type the name and other settings for your discussion area in the New form. If you want the discussion area to appear in the navigation bar, leave Yes selected. When you finish, click OK, and then click Create. In a few seconds, your discussion area appears (see Figure 7-10).

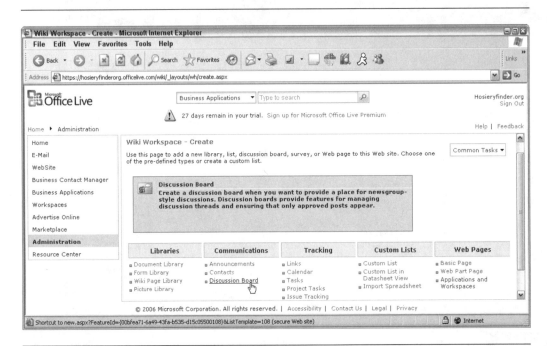

FIGURE 7-9   Create a new Discussion Board page within the shared site or workspace.

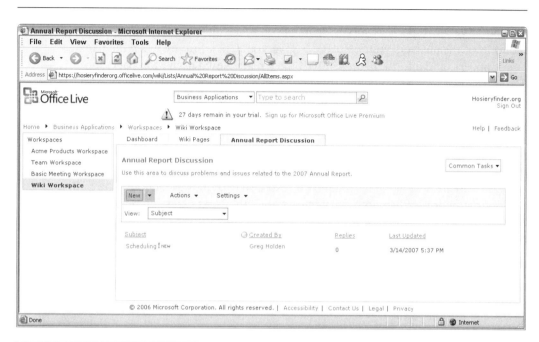

FIGURE 7-10   Once you create a discussion area, you should start the discussion by posting the first message.

6. A good idea is to start the discussion yourself, once you create the site by clicking New, and then choosing New Discussion.
7. When the New Item form appears, click the subject for your post (Welcome to the Discussion, for instance), type your text, and then click Save and Close.

If you are anxious to know when someone has posted a message to the board, click Alert me in the list of Actions on the left-hand side of the discussion board.

Creating a Survey

You always want to know what your clients think of your work, whether or not you explicitly ask them for their opinions. But, you can ask them for their opinions in a formal and systematic way once you create a collaborative workspace with Office Live: you can follow the steps for creating a site-wide discussion area and click Surveys. A *survey* is a poll of all the people who have been admitted to your collaborative workspace. A survey enables you to ask questions and even control the form of the answers your colleagues give you. Click Survey when the Create Page appears, and a form that resembles the Create New Discussion page appears. The difference is, after you enter the name and description of your survey, you click Next, and then go the page shown in Figure 7-11.

As you can see from the options on the Add Question page, you can check one of the buttons to specify the type of answer the user must supply. This can be in the form of a number, currency, text, a date and time, or a Yes/No check box, among other possibilities. You can also provide multiple choices from which the user can choose. If you want to require a response to a question, choose the button next to that option. When you finish, either click the Next Question button to add another question, or click Finish to save and post your survey online. You display the List Information page, where you can add a question in the Questions section.

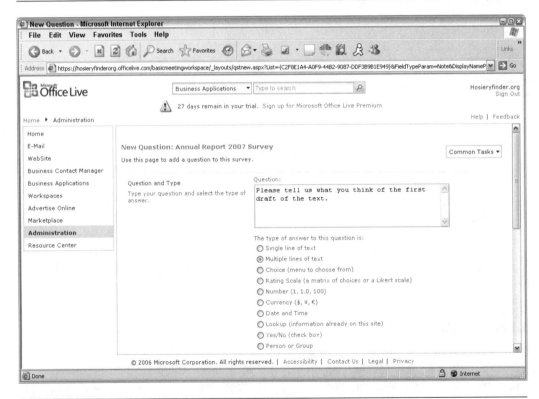

FIGURE 7-11   You can pose questions and require they be answered in a certain way.

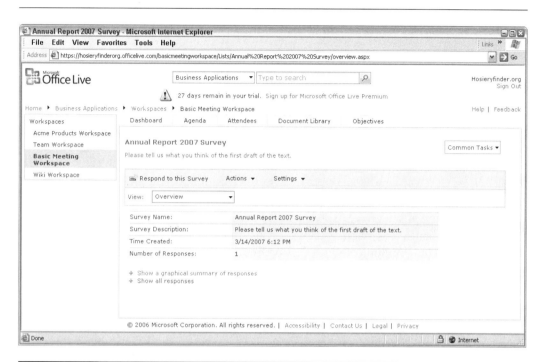

FIGURE 7-12   You and your coworkers can view survey questions and view responses to them.

At the top of the List Information page, you see the URL for the survey you created (for instance, https://[mydomain].officelive.com/basicmeetingworkspace/Lists/Annual Report 2007 Survey/overview.aspx). You can view the survey either by copying and pasting this URL into your browser's Address bar and pressing ENTER, or you can navigate using the links on the left.

When the Survey page shown in Figure 7-12 appears, review the survey, and test it by adding a response if you want. You or your coworkers can respond by clicking Add a response just above the question. The New Item form appears, where you type a response, and then click Finish. Clicking Finish returns you to the survey page. You or your coworkers can then click View all responses to see what others have said.

Collaborating with Vendors

Why would you want your suppliers and vendors to have a workspace within your Office Live web site? One answer is control; another is speed. When you are providing materials or services to business suppliers, they need to get those goods quickly. Rather than having to double-key the order data by faxing or even e-mailing an order. they type it right in your workspace. This makes for more efficient workflow.

Project Manager

The options available to designers in the Vendor workspace are much the same as those in the Customer Workspace. The Project Manager application is one of the primary tools you can use. The structure is basically the same as that of the Project Manager in the Customer Workspace. But, the way the application is used is different. Your main concern here is the set of supplies you procure from a particular vendor. You need to keep track of what you ordered, when it was shipped, and when it will arrive. You also need to discuss any issues pertaining to the products themselves, such as their composition, color, and size. In other words, you need to communicate information to the outside collaborator as much as that collaborator needs to transmit data to you. The discussion groups and other features discussed in the Customer Workspace section certainly apply. But, in the case of vendors, you might want to refer to the lists you can add to the workspace. You find these by following these steps:

1. Open Site Manager (click Common Tasks, and then click Manage this application or workspace).

2. Click Settings next to Vendor Workspace.

3. Click the Lists and Libraries option under the heading Create.

4. Click Create new content.

5. Scroll down to the Customize List section of the Create page.

Most of the options on the Create page were already discussed. But, the items under Tracking give you the capability to add useful content in an easily digestible format. Links, for example, is a set of links to web pages on the Internet, on your own web site, or within your workspace. The last three items are more directly relevant to the Vendor Workspace and are described in the following sections.

Adding Lists

A *list* is a simple collection of data that can be read and used by multiple individuals who connect to your Office Live site. You get a good idea of what a list looks like when you open Project Manager, and then click Milestones, Issues, or Tasks. A task list is shown in Figure 7-13.

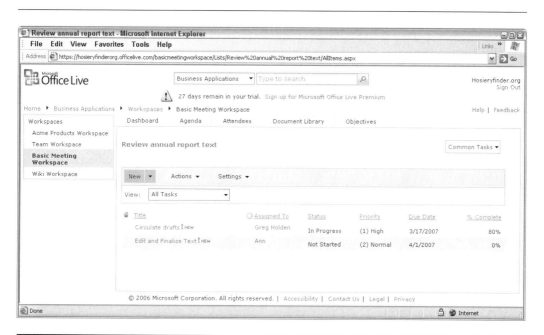

FIGURE 7-13   Lists can make critical supply-chain information easy to absorb for vendors.

The kinds of lists that can apply to vendors may not fit into categories, such as Events or Issues. Remember, you can always customize the names of lists by clicking Customize List | Change general settings, and then typing a new name and description for the list.

Vendor "Events"

When you are populating your vendor workspace with data, you might think of *Events* as representing your own deadlines—the deadlines you impose on yourself to put items up for sale, and the deadlines you agree on with your vendors for when your supplies need to arrive. Consider listing meetings between you and your vendor or sales deadlines you need to meet for your customers.

Vendor Milestones

Giving a supplier access to a shared workspace should improve communication, but only if you clearly instruct the vendor on what your expectations are. If you expect 10,000 widgets by November 10, you should spell that out in an e-mail or phone call, and then also record it on the milestones list. Also communicate to the vendor that you want him/her to use the milestones list to tell you when shipments will go out. Set up the list so you receive an alert e-mail when a new bit of data is added to the workspace.

Vendor Issues

If you have problems or concerns with the quality of your supplier's work, you should probably discuss them in person. Leave the Issues list for noncontroversial concerns that need to be addressed in the near future, such as obtaining new lumber for a building project or new paint supplies for a signage project. Shared workspaces are good resources, but they're no substitute for face-to-face (or voice-to-voice) conversations about urgent matters.

How to Do It

Change a Shared Site's Title and Description	Click Shared Sites, Site Manager, Site Settings (next to the site you want to rename), and click Change site title and description
Upload a file to a Document Library	Open your Shared Site, click Documents, choose Document Library, click Upload document
Edit a file stored in a Document Library`	Open the Document Library, click the file's name, log on with your .NET Passport e-mail address and password if prompted, make changes in Microsoft Word
Create a Web Discussion forum	Click Site Manager, open Workspace, click Modify this Workspace, choose Site Settings, click Modify Site Content, Click Create New Content, Click Discussion Boards
Opening a discussion pane within a document	Open Document Library, click down arrow to the right of the filename, choose Discuss from the drop-down list

Part III

Working with Business Applications

Chapter 8

Managing Business Projects

How to...

- Configure Project Manager's default lists to track your work
- Schedule your projects by establishing milestones and alerts
- Delegate tasks to workgroup members and create To Do lists
- Tracking issues and problems you need to resolve
- Filtering items in one of Project Manager's list views
- Customizing category designations for better organization

Obtaining a free web site, domain name, and e-mail is a good thing, no doubt about it. But you can get two of those services elsewhere, and you can register a domain name for less than $10 a year. Office Live becomes valuable when you use it to bring workgroups together, so they can collaborate on a project.

The core of Office Live's shared business applications is Project Manager. Once you learn how to manage workflow and users with this application, you can do so with all applications. In this chapter, you follow the creation and online management of a project, so you can learn all aspects of this individual application. When you need to set up your own project, you'll be able to follow the instructions in the following sections.

Getting Started with Project Manager

The next sections are based on the following scenario: You work for a small public relations firm that produces brochures, posters, and other promotional materials for institutions of higher learning, as well as commercial operations. You are assigned to assemble an annual report for a local community college. Your four staff need to subcontract aspects of the job to ensure its timely completion. On staff, you have a project manager, a writer, an editor, and a graphic designer. You need to hire a photographer and you need to solicit bids to find the best printer for the job. You are given a budget of $15,000 to do the job, and you are told it needs to be done in three months. Where do you start? You use your existing Office Live account and create a new shared project with the Project Manager business application.

The Project Manager environment, shown in Figure 8-1, was designed to resemble the Microsoft Office working environment you already know. But some of the tools you work with are different. Before you get started, you need to get used to working with forms, lists, and data:

■ **Forms**   These are familiar web pages that contain text boxes, check boxes, and buttons used to submit information.

■ **Lists**   In the world of Office Live, a *list* is any collection of information. It can be a series of names, a set of dates, a series of financial data, or anything that can be part of a business application.

■ **Data**   These are the dates, figures, deadlines, names, and other information you enter in Project Manager or another business application.

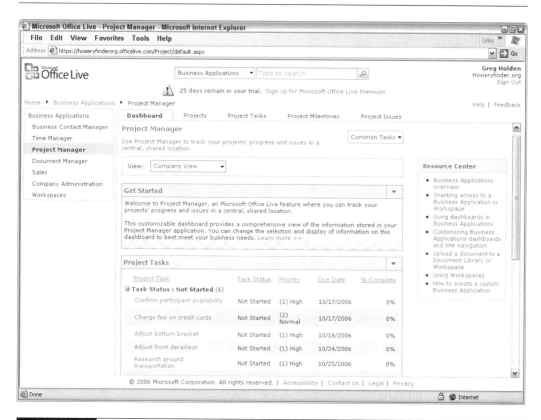

FIGURE 8-1   Project Manager should be at least somewhat familiar to Microsoft Office users.

Component Lists

Project Manager comes with various sets of lists built into it. You can customize the application to create your own lists, but when you're just starting out, you should familiarize yourself with the lists that are already present. They represent the most common collections of information you're likely to work with, and are described in the following sections.

Projects

This list gives you an overview of the project's progress and lets you track it visually. Use this list to describe the overall goals for your project. If any changes are made to the scope of the project, you would record them here.

Project Milestones

Every project has milestones: important phases in its development, which are usually associated with dates. In the construction of a skyscraper, one milestone would be laying the foundation, another would be completing the framework for the building, and so on. This list gives you a place to record important milestones and deliverables.

Project Tasks

This list lets you divide work, assign duties and responsibilities, and have a way to keep tabs on the coworkers who are contributing to the project.

Project Issues

Issues aren't the same as tasks. They come up when you're trying to perform tasks and run into trouble, or when you're trying to create a list of tasks. *Issues* are problems or questions your team members need to discuss. The Project Issues list lets you assign a high priority to an issue that hasn't been resolved as yet.

Custom Lists You Might Configure

Look on Project Manager's built-in lists as a starting point. You can customize the list by clicking Common Tasks, which appears on virtually any page that works with data. Click Manage applications and workspaces. When Site Manager opens, click Settings next to Project Manager, and then click List and Libraries. When the Site Libraries and Lists page appears, you can either click Create new content to add a new list to Project Manager or click Customize next to one of the existing lists (Projects, Project Tasks, and so on).

■ **Project Risks**   Describe any situations or problems you need to watch for and that represent risks to the project's successful outcome.

■ **Project Roles**   Consider setting up a list that clarifies which of your team members is responsible for budgeting, who will handle editorial, who will do design, and so forth. You can never state this too many times. The clearer you are, the less your chances of confusion.

■ **Project Teams**   If your project is large enough that multiple teams will handle different aspects of it, you can identify the teams and clarify the team members who are using this list.

Creating a New Project

Once you have an introduction on Project Manager's vocabulary and component parts, you can start configuring the program for your project's characteristics. When you start filling out the New project form, however, you are asked for some preliminary information: the account name and the project "owner."

Identify Your Project

To get started, log into Office Live, and click Business Contact Manager. When the Business Contact Manager application appears, follow these steps:

1. Click Contacts to bring it to the front.

2. Click New, choose New Item, and fill out the form with the contact information for the person you'll be working with at your client company. Leave the Account Name field empty for now.

3. Click OK to close the form and save your changes.

4. Click the Accounts tab to bring it to the front.

5. Click New and choose New Item. The New account form appears.

6. Enter an account name in the Account Name box.

7. Scroll down the page and click the Contacts tab.

8. You are prompted to save the form. Click the option to save the form. The new form, shown in Figure 8-2, appears.

9. Fill out the Contacts—New Item form with a contact name. Notice the Account name you entered earlier appears in the Account drop-down list.

8

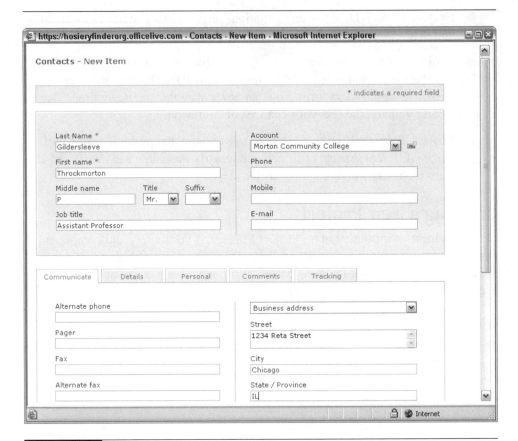

FIGURE 8-2 Begin by identifying your account, so you can create a new project.

When you're done, click OK to close Contacts—New Item. You return to the Accounts tab, where your business contact was added. Click Project Manager to switch to that business application. Then, click Projects to open the Project list.

Creating a New Project

Now that you have assigned your project a name and a primary contact person, you can move to setting up the project itself:

1. Click New and choose New Item.

2. In the New Item form, enter the project name, and choose the account name you created in the preceding section from the Account drop-down list (see Figure 8-3).

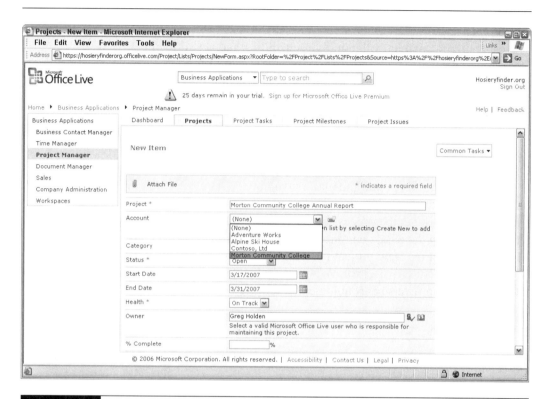

FIGURE 8-3   The account name you created earlier appears in the New Project form.

3. Be sure you enter the name of a valid Office Live user in the Owner list. Your project must be assigned to someone in your workgroup—someone with a valid Office Live account. And the name of the user must be in the correct form. If you don't know the form, enter part of the name in the Owner box. Then, click the Check Names next to the Owner box. The name is now changed to the correct format.

4. Finish completing the form, and click OK when you are done.

When you click Save and Close, your browser refreshes and you return to Project Manager, where your project is now included in the list.

CAUTION   *When you fill out the Project name box at the top of the New project form, make sure you don't use blank spaces. The name you enter here will be part of the URL for the project, and blank spaces will appear as %20 in the site URL, which will make it harder to read.*

Setting Up a Schedule

The capability to conduct collaborative scheduling and get all members of a workgroup on the same page regarding dates is one of Office Live's great benefits. In Project Manager, the primary tool for setting schedules is the Milestones tab. After you create your project, click the *Milestones tab* to set deadlines for your project.

Milestones aren't necessarily deadlines: instead of dates, by which a portion of a project needs to be completed, they may also represent stages of completion. One date can represent the desired starting point for the job, another can be the 50 percent completion point, and another can be the date by which the printer or other vendor needs to be chosen.

Here, as elsewhere, the process of creating content is a matter of completing a form and saving the data, one milestone at a time. You click New Project Milestone, fill out the New project milestone form (which, thankfully, is less detailed than the New project form), and then click OK. The items you create are added to the list in reverse chronological order (see Figure 8-4).

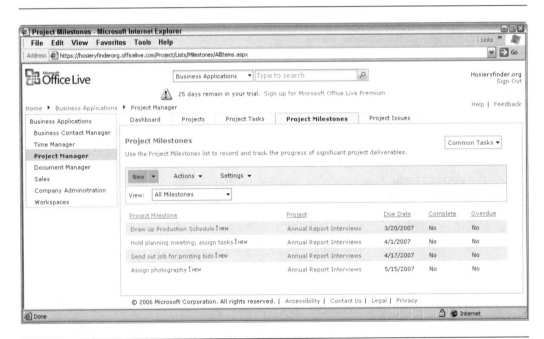

FIGURE 8-4   Milestones are automatically arranged in reverse chronological order.

NOTE *To edit a milestone, pass your mouse over its name, so the drop-down arrow appears. Click the arrow, and then choose Edit Item from the context list. At any time, you can attach a file to a milestone by choosing Edit Item, and clicking Attach File (which has a paper-clip icon next to it).*

Notice no field in the New project milestone form allows you to associate a milestone with a particular individual. You can do that by clicking Common Tasks, choosing Customize this application or workspace, and then clicking Site columns. Click Customize list while the All Milestones tab is displayed. Click Add a new column under the Columns section. When the Add Column form, shown in Figure 8-5, appears, click Create. In the New Site Column form, type a name for your column (such as Personnel), and then click the button next to the type of content you want the column to contain (text, dates, and so on). Next, click OK.

NOTE *Milestones appear on the Dashboard when you create them. They don't appear on Calendar Events, but they are listed next to the calendar in the Projects section. This gives everyone in the workgroup a chance to track deadlines they need to meet in a given period.*

8

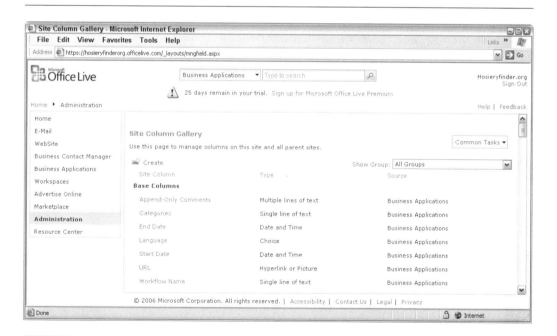

FIGURE 8-5   You can customize the Milestones list, as well as any others in Project Manager.

Setting Up an Alert

When it comes to meeting deadlines or milestones, you can never remind people too often. But, simply having to remember to remind people is another burden on the project manager. You can configure Office Live to send out alerts to remind people when a deadline or milestone has arrived. Alerts can also be used to tell you or others when an item has been changed or a new piece of information has been added to a project list. Follow these steps:

1. Click Business Applications and choose Project Manager to open this application if it isn't open already.

2. Click Projects.

3. Click the view you want. Chances are this will be All Current Projects, but you can choose My Projects, Completed Projects, or Overdue Projects if you want a more focused set of data.

4. Click the down arrow next to the name of the item for which you want to create an alert.

 If you click the arrow next to the name of the entire project, you cause an alert to be sent every time new information is added to any aspect of the project. This may quickly get to be more alerts than you want to receive. If you don't want to receive this many alerts, set up an alert for a specific task, milestone, or issue. When the context menu appears, click Alert Me.

5. When the New Alert page, shown in Figure 8-6, appears, follow the instructions.

6. When you finish, click OK.

Viewing Alerts

As you can see from Figure 8-6, the options for sending and receiving alerts are somewhat limited. By default, the form only gives you the option of sending an alert to your own e-mail address, and only when an item changes. Presumably, once you receive the alert, you can pass it on to others in your workgroup as needed. You can also change alert settings for the shared site in which you are working, as described in the next section.

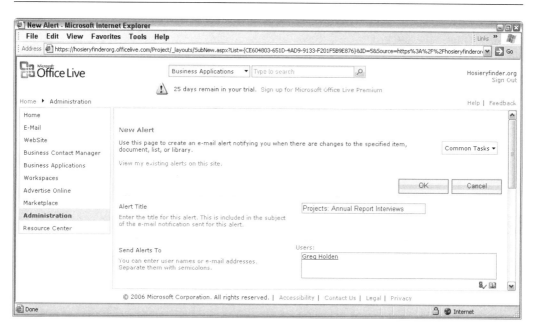

FIGURE 8-6   You can be alerted when information changes on one of your projects, milestones, tasks, or issues.

You can create alerts for document libraries as well as lists. You can even create alerts for individual files held in document libraries, so you are notified when someone checks them in or out.

Changing Alert Options

To reconfigure alert options to automatically send messages to other employees, or for different "trigger" events, click Common Tasks, and then choose Modify this Application or Workspace. The Project Manager Site Settings window opens.

When you click Site Settings, the Site Administration options appear. Under the View heading, click User Alerts, and the Manage User Alerts window appears. For any options to appear in this window, you first need to set up some alerts for individual aspects of your project. If you have some alerts created, choose the passport code of the person receiving those alerts from the Display alerts for drop-down list in the Manage User Alerts window. Click Update, and the alert appears (see Figure 8-7).

Check the box next to the name of the alert you want to customize, and then click Update. The options you see vary, depending on the kind of item for which

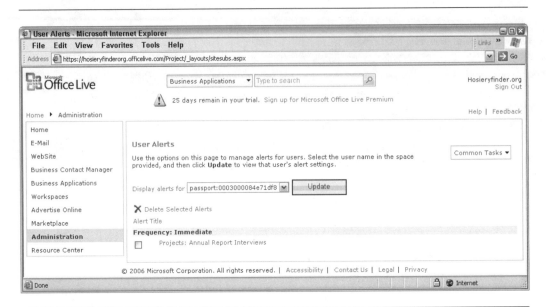

FIGURE 8-7   This screen lets you change alert settings for your projects.

you are creating an alert. Some items can only have alerts sent when they are changed, and no other options are available. But, if other options exist, you change them here, You can also select an alert and delete it using this screen.

When you finish configuring alerts or other site administrative tasks, to return to the Project Manager, click Business Applications, and then Project Manager on the left side of the Office Live window.

Delegating Tasks to Employees

Once you configure a project and establish the stages through which it must proceed, the next step is to make sure the right staff have access to the shared site and that they receive tasks to perform. The delegation of who is going to work on a job and which individuals are going to be responsible for different stages is something you may want to discuss at an in-person staff meet or phone conference.

You can also use another Microsoft "Live" Product, Live Meeting, to get all the members of a workgroup together, so they can discuss a project at the same time. Find out more in Chapter 16.

Checking Access Privileges

In Chapter 6, you learned about how to give employees access to workspaces. But access needs may change, depending on projects that come up. For a particular project you are initiating, you may want to add more people; you may want to restrict others from participating. When you are in the early stages of configuring your project, a good idea is to review users and accounts to make sure the right people have access. The Site Manager window gives you a fine-grained level of access control: you can allow some users access to one application, others to a workspace, and so on. Follow these steps:

1. Click Common Tasks, a button present in virtually all windows on Office Live, including business applications and workspaces.

2. Choose Manage Applications and Workspaces.

> **NOTE** *Because you are working with Project Manager for this example, these steps examine how to control access to this particular business application. Other business applications, such as Business Contact Manager, can be controlled by following the same steps, however.*

3. When the Site Manager window appears, click Settings to the right of Project Manager.

4. Under the heading Modify, click Settings. The Permissions page appears with a list of all the users who have access to this current application or workspace.

5. Review the list and click Add User to add another user if you want to expand the list of those who have access.

6. Click Edit next to any existing users you want to adjust. When the Site permissions list appears, check the permissions level for this application and adjust, if necessary.

You can adjust the same users' permission levels for other workspaces you have created by choosing the name or workspace from the View drop-down list in the Permissions window. Then, click Add User or Edit as needed for the new application or workspace.

Working with the To Do List

As mentioned in the preceding section, when you work with the Project Tasks list, you fill out a form that enables you to assign a task to an individual in your workgroup. You can further customize the list and add a column called Staff, which identifies each person who is going to work on each task and spells out what each individual is to perform in more detail.

Or, you can use another business application list, the To Do list, which is found under the Time Manager. This list also lets you identify a set of tasks, but it's much shorter and simpler than Project Tasks. Why? The To Do tasks aren't necessarily associated with a particular project. However, you can add a note in the Description field in the To Do list's New Item form that lets you identify a task as being part of a project you're working on (see Figure 8-8).

By default, the Description field doesn't appear in All Tasks view. Make sure you check the box next to the Description field to make certain it's visible. You need to click Common Tasks and choose Manage this application or workspace, then click Site Libraries and Lists, and then click Customize To Do. Click Column Ordering and move this column up in the list to require that it be displayed.

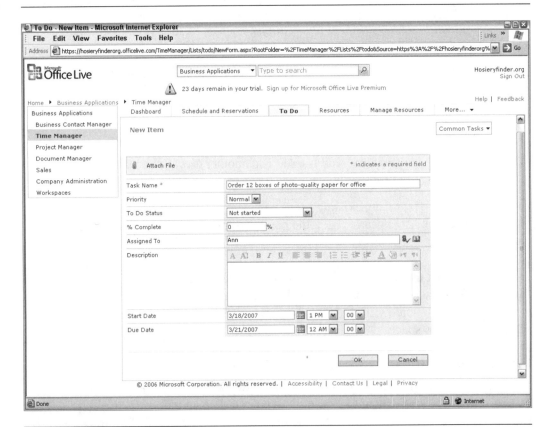

FIGURE 8-8   The To Do application is intended to create a series of tasks.

Adding a New View

Suppose you have lots of different tasks to track and you want to group them all into different projects. You can do this by customizing the To Do list. Follow these steps:

1. Click Common Tasks and choose Manage this application or workspace.

2. Click Site Libraries and Lists, and then click Customize To Do.

3. Click Create view under the Views heading.

4. Click Standard View or another type of view.

5. Enter the name for your view, such as By Project.

6. Click OK.

7. Return to the To Do window, where By Project appears, along with the default views My Tasks, Due Today, and so on.

Click the new By Project tab to bring it to the front. Your projects are sorted by project order—if you placed the Description field first in the list, this is especially easy to see because all your project descriptions appear on the left.

Tracking Project Issues and Problems

Projects rarely go completely smoothly. In fact, the more people you have working on the project and the more milestones you go through, the chances that you'll run into what Office Live calls "issues" goes up proportionately. Issues are presumably different from tasks. Issues are situations that need to be resolved at some point for the project to go forward. In a group environment, keeping issues to yourself isn't good. Your colleagues might be able to help or come up with solutions. The Project Issues tab in Project Manager is designed especially for tracking problems, complications, dilemmas, or other concerns that need to be addressed. The Issues list, like others in Project Manager, is divided into multiple views:

- **All Issues**   These include issues that are current, as well as those already resolved.

- **My Issues**   These are issues assigned to you to be resolved.

- **Active Issues**   These are only issues that remain to be addressed and have not been resolved as yet.

- **Overdue Issues**   These are issues that have fallen behind schedule.

- **Unassigned Issues**   These issues might be active or overdue, but they need to be assigned to an individual, so they can be completed.

 Including resolved issues along with issues that are still outstanding can be useful because it keeps all workgroup members informed about the status of the job as a whole.

Recording Issues

Adding an issue to the list is similar to the process of adding projects, milestones, or tasks. But, with the Issues list, you have more columns to add. Some of the columns contain information that needs to be changed as issues change their status. They include:

- **Project Issue**   Assign a short name for the issue.

- **Project**   Identify the project affected by the issue. You can record issues that have to be resolved for all your projects, not only the current one.

- **Owner**   This is the person responsible for resolving the issue—not necessarily the one who is working on it.

- **Assigned To**   This individual is tasked with resolving the issue and reporting the status to the owner.

- **Issue Status**   The options are Active and Resolved.

- **Priority**   Choose one of the three options: High, Normal, or Low.

- **Description**   Type some details about the issue, so people understand what you're talking about.

- **Category**   Choose an option that describes the type of issue you are experiencing.

- **Due Date**   If the issue needs to be resolved by a specific date, enter that date here.

- **Related Issues**   If the current issue is tied to others your workgroup is facing, enter them here. Current issues are listed on the left box (see Figure 8-9). Click Add to move one to the right box to show it's related to the current issue you're describing.

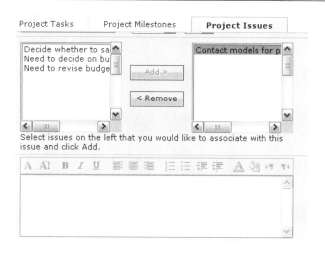

FIGURE 8-9   Issues you have already identified can be related to a new issue.

8

Once you finish, the issues you entered appear in the list in the order in which you created them, as described in Figure 8-10. You can order them by setting up filters, as the next section describes.

Setting Up Filters

When you pass your mouse pointer over the name of one of the columns at the top of the Issues list (or any list in the business applications), a drop-down list appears. (One is at the top of each column in the list.) Choose options from one of the lists to filter the issues in Ascending or Descending order, or by user.

The options that appear in each of the drop-down lists are the same as the ones you entered for the individual items in the column beneath them (see Figure 8-11). Choose one of the items, and the list is reconfigured. To undo the filtering, choose Clear Filter, and then select another option from the drop-down list.

Getting Specific About Categories

When you complete any one of the forms in Project Manager, and you choose the options in the Category drop-down menu, you see the generic options Category 1, Category 2, and Category 3. These designations aren't useful unless you customize this field and create categories that apply to your project. The following steps

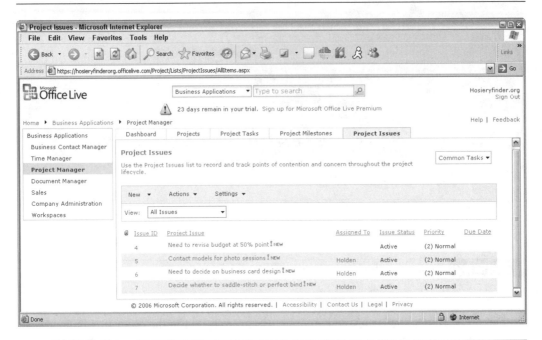

FIGURE 8-10   Issues appear in the order in which you enter them and can refer to multiple projects.

apply not only to the Issues list but also to any list in Project Manager (or in other business applications, for that matter):

1. With the Issues list visible in Project Manager, click Common Tasks, and then choose Manage this application or workspace.

2. Click Site Libraries and Lists.

3. Click Customize Project Issues.

FIGURE 8-11   Choose an option to filter your list items.

4. Click Category.

5. In the Change Column screen, in the Optional Settings for Column section, provide some details in the Description box to help your colleagues decide when to use this drop-down list.

6. Optionally, you can click Yes to require that the user choose an option from this list.

7. In the box labeled Type each choice on a separate line, replace the generic Category 1 and other designations with some more specific options that apply to your job. In Figure 8-12, I typed (1) Money, (2) Textual Content, (3) Photos, and (4) Graphic Design.

8. You can select an item under Display choices using to change Category from a drop-down menu list to a series of buttons or checkboxes.

9. When you finish, click OK.

8

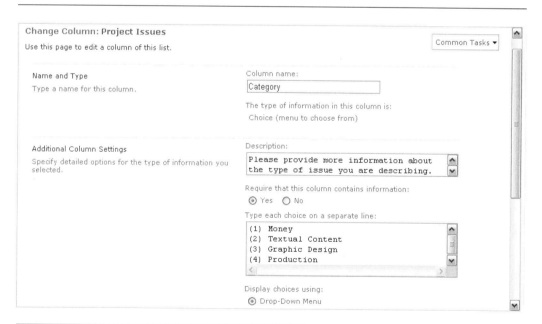

FIGURE 8-12 Create specific categories for your project issues.

Click New project issue to open the New project form, where you can test your customization by choosing the Category drop-down menu and verifying your desired options are present.

How to Do It

Create a new project you can track using Office Live	Click Business Applications, click Dashboard, click Projects, choose Project Manager, click New project, and then fill out the form
Identify the client contacts for your project	From the Dashboard, click Customers, choose Contact Manager, click Business Contacts, and then choose New contact
Establish a series of deadlines for a project	Open Project Manager, click Milestones, click New project milestone, and fill out the form
Attach a file to a project, milestone or other type of list item	Click the down arrow next to the name of the project or item, choose Edit Item, click Attach file, click Browse, locate the file, click OK, click Save, and then close
Create an alert for a task or milestone	Click the down arrow next to the name of the project or item, click Alert me, and follow instructions on the New Alert page
Make sure the right workgroup members can access your project	Click Shared Sites, click Site Manager, click Business Applications, click Site Settings, click Manage Users, and add users if needed
Create a New View for your project	Click Customize List, click Add a new view, enter the name, click Save, and then close

Chapter 9

Tracking Assets and Inventory

How to...

- Configure the Products list to manage inventory

- Record equipment and other company assets

- View inventory and assets in datasheet form

- Export inventory and asset data to a database

- Track an inventory list in Microsoft Access

- Query your list with Microsoft Excel

- Chart your list with Microsoft Excel

When you work with only a limited number of staff, you probably don't have employees dedicated to managing the "stock room." And, when you run a small web-based business, your stock room may be no more than a set of shelves along one wall of your office. Nevertheless, you need to perform the same basic tasks large corporations that have warehouses full of inventory at their disposal must do. You need to keep track of what you have in stock, know what you paid for it, and reorder when stock runs low.

This sounds like a straightforward list of functions, but when you have many other business tasks to perform to run your company, keeping track of your inventory can be cumbersome and awkward. Yet, if you run out of stock, your customers have to wait to receive what they ordered, which can directly affect your bottom line. Keeping track of your assets—your business equipment and other tangible property—is also important both for accounting and generally keeping your company operating at peak efficiency. This chapter explores how Office Live can help you manage your inventory and assets to keep your supply chain flowing smoothly and maintain customer satisfaction.

Working with the Products List

Inventory management seems simple enough: you count what you have to sell, and you order new stock before you run out. But any business owner, from the lone entrepreneur to the corporate president, can tell you managing products is much more than that. Electronic sales catalog and computer software have transformed inventory tracking. Inventory items used to simply be assigned numeric codes: part numbers, or item numbers. Now, using computer programs to track inventory is the rule, rather than the exception. With Office Live, you have two options for tracking inventory:

- Use the default list best suited to tracking stock, so you don't have to create your own application from scratch. This is Products, which is part of the Business Contact Manager application, available with either Office Live Essentials or Premium.

- Create your own business application. You can create an application called Inventory Manager from scratch, and populate it with the data you need. You need a special software tool called SharePoint Designer to do this. See Chapters 10 and 11 for more information.

Creating your own application is a bit of extra work, but the advantage of creating your own Inventory Manager is you don't have to customize the default columns you're given in the Products list. You can keep it simple, and only create the items you need. On the other hand, if you're pressed for time and don't want to do much customization, you may find Products serves your needs well. The Products list option is examined in the section "Adding New Inventory Items."

9

Inventory Vocabulary

Knowing something about the vocabulary of tracking and managing inventory can help you do a better job. The following is a "short list" of commonly used inventory management terms you might encounter in the process of ordering, storing, and replenishing your own stock:

- **Allocation**   The amount of merchandise you need to meet a specific demand.

- **Available**   The amount you have available to sell. This is different from your total inventory because it subtracts the quantity on hold.

- **Carrying cost**   The cost of holding the current inventory on hand. Auto dealers, for instance, have to pay a monthly carrying cost to hold autos for sale on their lots.

- **Container**   Commonly used to describe a standard ocean-going container used for storage and transport. A common container is 8 feet wide, 8.5 or 9.5 feet tall, and 20 or more feet long.

Continued

Inventory Vocabulary

- **Drop-ship (also called direct-ship)**   A process in which the buyer initiates a purchase with the seller, who then arranges with the supplier to ship the product to the buyer. The buyer does not store inventory of the product.

- **Electronic Product Code (EPC)**   A version of the UPC bar code that both identifies the product with its SKU and can include information about its origin and history.

- **Enterprise Resource Planning (ERP)**   Software systems used to handle many or all of a distribution process. The Office Live Product & Service Items application performs ERP, for instance.

- **Fill rate**   The rate at which inventory must be replenished to avoid shortages.

- **Fulfillment**   The process of satisfying customer orders.

- **Lead time**   The amount of time needed for an item to be available from the time it is ordered.

- **Stock-keeping Units (SKUs)**   This is a fancy way of describing the number of items you have in inventory.

- **UPC**   Universal Product Code, the bar code placed on a product, so a scanner can electronically record its product number, name, and price, as well as other information. If you use UPC tags to record the price and other information for your merchandise, this field can help you keep track of what's on hand.

Inventory tracking is more important than ever because online ordering is an uncertain business. Customers who order remotely want to receive their merchandise as quickly as possible. Netflix, the video rental service, has succeeded because it has inventory distributed around the country, which means it is less likely to run out, and more able to ship and deliver as quickly as possible. You might be unable to have your sales stock all over the country, but even if your stock is contained in a single room, simply knowing what you have and replenishing it in a timely way can help you work efficiently.

Adding New Inventory Items

The first step in managing inventory is adding stock when you obtain it. When you obtain an item, you need to add to your inventory, open Products, Click New, and then click New item. The New product item form, shown in Figure 9-1, opens.

Consider using a datasheet to quickly enter new inventory items without having to open a separate form as described in the section "Tracking Inventory with a Datasheet."

By default, the Products list's New item form includes the following fields:

■ **Item Name**   Give your item a short and descriptive name.

■ **Description**   Describe the item as you would in your product catalog.

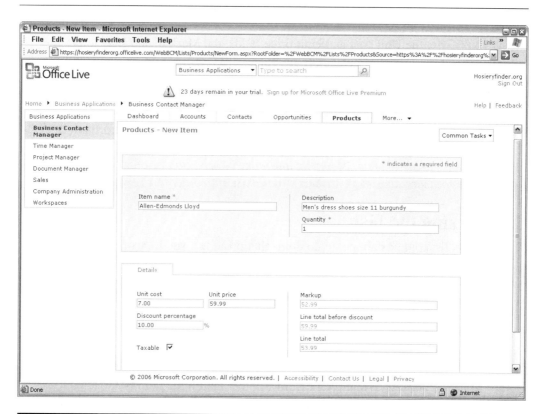

FIGURE 9-1   To manage your inventory, you need to enter stock items in a list.

■ **Quantity** Is the item currently for sale or being held for a future promotion? Enter its status here.

■ **Unit cost** Type the cost you paid for the item.

■ **Unit price** Type the sales price here.

■ **Discount percentage** If the item is offered at a discount, record how much here.

■ **Markup** This is the difference between what you paid for the item and what you are charging for it.

■ **Line total before discount** This important item specifies how many items you have in stock when you place a new order.

■ **Line total** This specifies how many items you have on hand.

■ **Taxable** If the item is subject to sales tax, check this box.

As you fill out the Unit cost and Unit price fields, the Markup and Line total before discount fields perform calculations and record their contents automatically. When you're done, click OK. Adding each inventory item one at a time can be a time-consuming process. Remember, you're not the only one who has to handle the data entry. Office Live enables you to give multiple users access to your business applications with Editor privileges, so they can also add new information.

NOTE   *At press time, you cannot import inventory information or other data from an Excel spreadsheet or an Access database into an Office Live list.*

Customizing the List

The Products list contains about ten columns that provide a small business with plenty of inventory information. The exact details you need depend on your individual company and services, but you can customize the list just as you can any other in Office Live's business applications.

For instance, many essential pieces of information are missing from the Products list. And, yet, they are important bits of information commonly collected by businesses that keep many inventory items in stock. They include:

■ **Tax information** Here, you record whether tax on the item is collected from the buyer when the inventory item is sold or from the purchaser when you resell the item.

- **Most recent sale**   If you track the date an item was last sold, you can measure how long it typically "sits on the shelf."

- **Sales traffic**   How many items are typically sold at a time? If you track how the item moves in and out of stock; the Sales traffic field can help alert you when it comes time to reorder.

- **Alternate source**   If you can't obtain an inventory stock item from your usual source, the Alternate source can help to write down one or two secondary options. If you're in a hurry and need a stock item soon, having all the supply options recorded can help save you time.

> TIP
> *Microsoft provides an Inventory list template that gives you a head start on tracking your inventory. You can find it on the Work essentials web site (http://office.microsoft.com/en-us/workessentials/HA011230971033.aspx). Importing this list into Office live as a template isn't straightforward. However, you can open the template in Excel and make note of the fields included in the template. You can customize your list and add the fields you want to Product & Service Items.*

Some of the information fields mentioned in the preceding list are somewhat specialized and some of them might be more detailed than a small business needs. But, if you have only a few people managing inventory, having the details recorded in a database can keep everyone in the loop.

> NOTE
> *Once you have your inventory tracking system configured, you need to replenish it manually. A staff person has to monitor what's on hand and reorder when the specified reorder point is reached. You can also configure a "workflow" that causes reorders to be placed automatically. See Chapter 10 for more information.*

Tracking Inventory with a Datasheet

Inventory to sell, assets you use in your company, and other complex information can be easily absorbed in the form of a datasheet. *Datasheets* organize information in the form of rows and columns, and are a way of viewing the contents of a list in rows and columns, much like a web page table or a spreadsheet. Viewing data in the form of a datasheet has another big advantage: it enables you to connect the data to Microsoft Office Access and Excel.

 *To open a list in Access Web Datasheet, you need to have Microsoft Internet Explorer 5.01 with Service Pack 2 or later. Your browser security settings must support running ActiveX controls. Office Live's documentation states you need to have Microsoft Office 2007 installed. However, I was able to work with datasheets with Office 2003 installed.*

Viewing Data in an Access Web Datasheet

Most (though not all) of the lists you create in Office Live can be viewed in the form of an Access Web Datasheet. By default, list data is presented in Standard View. Whenever you want to switch views, click Edit in Datasheet in the Actions menu. As you can see from Figure 9-2, a datasheet gives you a more organized and structured-looking set of information than you get in Standard View.

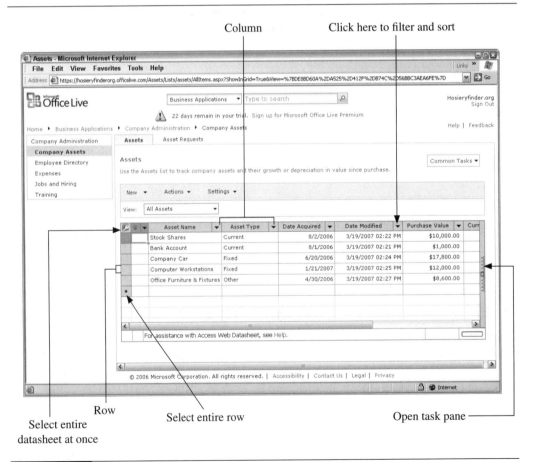

FIGURE 9-2 Choose Edit in Datasheet for a more organized view of inventory and assets.

Entering Data Directly in the Datasheet

Perhaps the single biggest benefit of viewing data in datasheet form is the that you can enter new data directly *in the datasheet itself, rather than using the New asset or New product item form.* I added the italics for emphasis because this is such a significant time-saving feature. Being able to type directly in the datasheet is far faster and more convenient than having to open a form for each list item you need to add. If you're used to working with Excel or Access, you'll take to this feature instantly. You might never use the form, unless you need to customize the list information you capture.

To enter information, open a datasheet by clicking Edit in Datasheet in the Actions menu. Simply click in a cell within the datasheet to position the cursor. Type the information, and then press ENTER when you finish. You can then move on to the next cell.

For some cells, you can't type information. Instead, you have to choose among the options contained in a drop-down list. For instance, in the Assets datasheet list shown in Figure 9-3, if you try to type in the Asset Type field, you are prevented

9

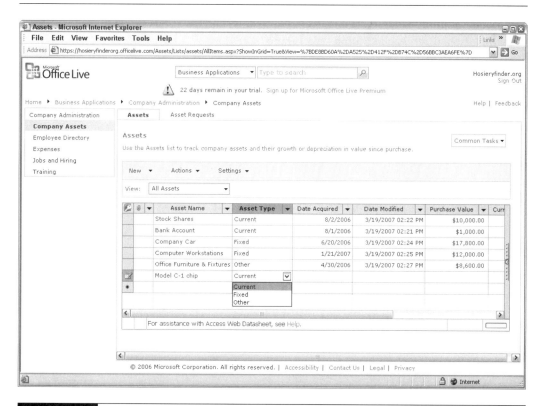

FIGURE 9-3   You can type data in some cells, but others present you with a list of options.

from doing so. A dialog box appears, telling you to choose one of the options from the drop-down list: Fixed, Current, or Other.

 *You can customize fields such as Asset Type by clicking Common Tasks, choosing Modify this application or workspace, clicking Site libraries and lists, and clicking Customize Assets. When the Customize Assets window opens, click Asset Type (or another field you want to customize). When the Edit Column window opens, you can delete options or add more specific ones.*

Other fields in the Assets datasheet can't be edited manually at all. For instance, the Modified field automatically enters the current date and time. You are required to complete all the fields in a row that can be completed manually before you move on to the next row, however.

The way you view data makes it easier for you to understand and work with it. Aside from the data-entry feature just described, another benefit of Datasheet View is visual: the items you record are aligned in neat rows and columns. You can also instantly have the datasheet record the totals of any figures you have displayed in a particular column: Click Action and choose Totals, and the totals are displayed immediately beneath each column (see Figure 9-4).

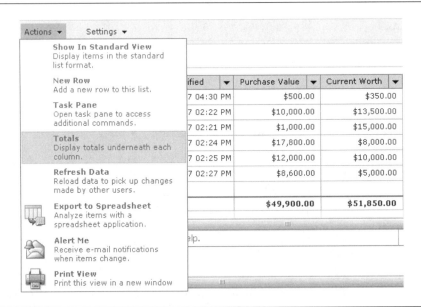

FIGURE 9-4   An Office Live datasheet can instantly calculate totals for you.

NOTE *You won't always see Edit in Datasheet in the Actions menu. Some list types can't be viewed in Datasheet View. These are: discussion board, survey, image gallery, web template library, Web Part Catalog, Data sources, and the Inbox.*

The Assets and Products lists are perfect for viewing in datasheets because of the extensive sorting and filtering functions they provide. If your inventory list includes hundreds, or even thousands, of different items and you're looking for one or two individual pieces, you can focus a search to find them quickly, as the next two sections describe.

TIP *To learn more about working with datasheets, and importing and exporting data, open any list in datasheet form. Then, scroll down to the bottom of the datasheet and click the highlighted word "Help." This opens an Access Web Datasheet Help window. It's more specific than the usual Office Live Help window.*

Sorting a Datasheet

You can sort or rearrange the contents of a datasheet in several different ways so you see the information you need the most. You can rearrange columns by placing the mouse arrow over the vertical line that separates columns. When the pointer turns into a four-headed arrow, click and drag it to the new location. The arrow turns into a pointer only when you pass it over the line just beneath the column name—not the line above it (see Figure 9-5).

9

FIGURE 9-5   Click beneath the column name to select the column, so you can drag it.

To select multiple columns, first select a single column, as previously described. Press SHIFT and select the column adjacent to it to also select the second column. You can move on to select adjacent columns as needed.

The only way to move a row in a datasheet is to sort the datasheet's contents: you need to create a new view. You can create a new view by customizing a list in either Standard or Datasheet View. Click Common Tasks, choose Manage this application or workspace, click Site libraries and lists, and then click Customize Assets. When the Change Field Order window, shown in Figure 9-6, appears, choose options from the drop-down lists to change the current order. You can then position the Asset Type column first in the view and only include the essential information you need, such as the name and value of the equipment.

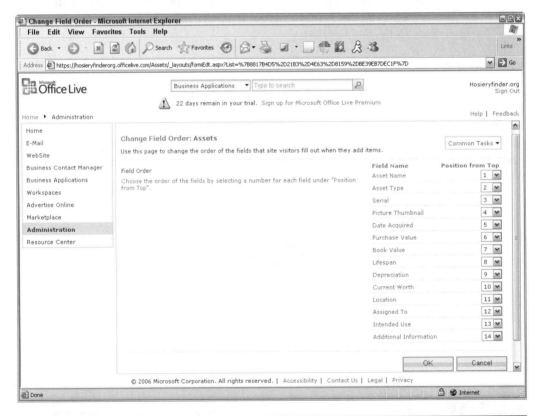

FIGURE 9-6   You can change the order of columns in any Office Live list.

Not only can you change the order of the columns in a datasheet such as Assets, but you can also change the order of the cells within a column. You have two options for sorting datasheet column contents:

- To sort a single column, click the drop-down arrow just to the right of the column's name, and choose Sort Ascending, Sort Descending, or another option from the list.

- To sort multiple columns, you need to open the Task Pane and click the Sort button (see Figure 9-7).

9

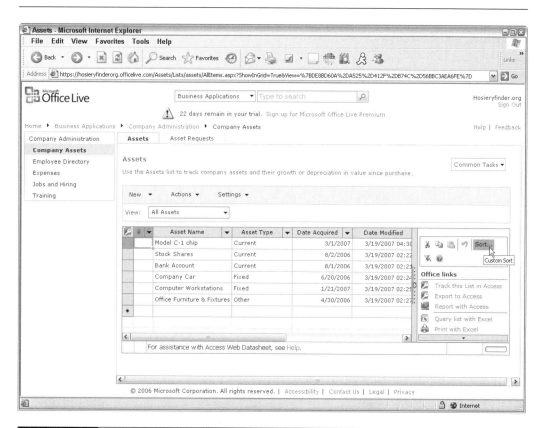

FIGURE 9-7   The Sort button in the Task Pane lets you reorder column contents.

The Task Pane for datasheets opens to the right of the datasheet and is opened by clicking on the arrow just to the right of the rightmost column. Once the Task Pane is open, select the columns you want to sort. Then follow these steps:

1. Click the Sort button.

2. When the Custom Sort dialog box opens, select the sort options you want.

3. Click OK.

You need to choose Ascending or Descending order in the Custom Sort dialog box, shown in Figure 9-8. The option you choose depends on the order in which you selected the columns. If you want to sort by alphabetical order, and one column is called Asset Name and the other is Asset Type, you would choose Asset Name first, and then choose Asset Type.

 *To find Help files that pertain specifically to datasheets, you don't simply enter "datasheet" in the Help window's search box. Enter **Access Web Datasheet** and do a search. Or, better yet, open a datasheet and click the Help link just beneath it.*

Filtering a Datasheet

Filtering is a way to whittle down the data in a datasheet, so you only see what you want. To filter the data, click the down arrow to the right of a column's name. Then, choose the criteria from the list. The list contains standard items, as well as

FIGURE 9-8   You can sort by multiple criteria to get only the data you want.

those specific to the column's contents. First, the column-specific items appear. In a column with items that include Current, Fixed, and Future, you can see these three items at the bottom of the drop-down list. Choose Fixed, and all the Fixed items appear at the top of the column. Click Custom Filter to display the Custom Filter dialog box, where you can specify your own filtering criteria. You can filter for all numbers beginning with 1, for instance.

 *You can't apply filters to columns with multiple-text fields or that include filters.*

Tracking Company Assets

Inventory is merchandise your company purchases or manufactures, and then sells to others. *Assets* are material possessions your business owns and uses to keep the company running. Look around your office and you can see all kinds of assets: computers, printers, toner, paper, phones, water coolers, furniture, and much more. Assets can also be financial holdings: savings you have in the bank or property you own. It's important to keep a list of your assets for taxes, for insurance, and for budgeting—if you know what you have on hand already, you can do a better job of planning what you'll need in the future.

Office Live provides you with two lists for tracking assets: Assets and Asset Requests—and they are examined in the following sections.

Tracking Business Assets

If you created new projects, items, tasks, or other bits of data to add to your Office Live lists, you'll have no problem recording your office assets because the process is the same for all of them: Log in to Office Live, click Business Applications, click Company Administration, click Company Assets, click New, and then choose New Item. Then, you fill out the New Item form with as much detail as you can about the item. A few of the many fields in this form are especially noteworthy:

- **Picture thumbnail**   A photo of the asset can be useful for insurance purposes if you must replace the item.

- **Lifespan and Depreciation**   For tax purposes, you need to estimate the lifespan of the item—how long you will be using it. You then need to state how much the value will be depreciated this year. Your tax preparer can help with this information.

- **Available**   This field indicates whether or not the asset is available for requests. (Asset requests are discussed in the next section.)

As with other types of list information, you can always edit information about an asset by opening the Assets list, clicking the down arrow that appears when you pass your mouse pointer over an item's name, and then choosing Edit Item from the shortcut menu.

Consider grouping your out-of-date and unordered inventory in a category called "charitable items." You can donate your parts or other stock items and get a tax deduction at the same time.

The Assets list is divided into two views: Assets and Asset Requests. *Assets* lets you track the actual property you own—it's a list for describing the pieces of property in detail. *Asset Requests* gives you a place to record and keep track of requests for your assets. This is where your employees can request the use of an asset, whether it's the company car or a camera, so the item doesn't get double-booked. Or, if someone can't find the asset in question, it can be traced to the last person who used it. If you own property that others might need to borrow or make use of, such a list ensures you'll get everything back that was taken. Examples include the company car, the office laptop, a slide projector, a digital camera, or even money taken from "petty cash" to cover immediate expenses.

Tracking and Exporting Lists

Once you have your inventory and asset data saved on Office Live, save a backup for your records. You may also want to perform valuations and estimates, based on the information you recorded. You can achieve both of these goals by making use of Microsoft Access or Microsoft Excel. Of course, Office Live isn't intended to be a "miniature" version of Microsoft Office. In the case of exporting a database, you need to create a link between it and these two applications. You can also save the data in the form of a SharePoint template, so you can create other workspaces or applications based on it. Both options are described in the next section.

Exporting Data from a Datasheet

Entering every asset in your office one object at a time can be time-consuming. If you export the data either to paper or to a Microsoft Office application, you can handle it with the tools these programs provide. You have a number of options. First, you can treat similar items in groups (ten desks as one item instead of ten separate items; a single "office supplies" item instead of breaking them into paper, paper clips, pens, and so on).

Second, you can print a list from within Excel or within Office Live itself. To print from Office Live, click PRINT in the Actions menu on the Task Pane. To print from Excel, have Excel query the list to retrieve the data as the following section describes. When the data is transferred, choose Print from Excel's File menu.

Charting with Excel

You can also express list contents in the form of an Excel Chart. Display the Task Pane, click Chart with Excel to initiate this process, and Excel opens. Dialog boxes appear asking you to confirm you want to make the query, and whether you want to open a new worksheet or new workbook. You may also have to log in with your Office Live User ID and password.

Once you are logged in, the Excel Chart Wizard opens. Follow the steps shown in the wizard to create your chart. When you finish, the data opens, along with the chart itself (see Figure 9-9).

9

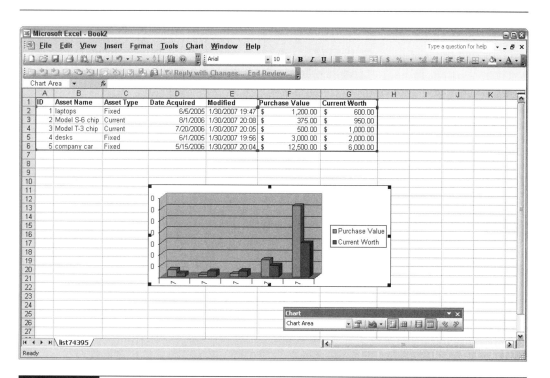

FIGURE 9-9   You can have Excel express your Office Live datasheet in chart form.

Querying the List with Excel

To export Office Live inventory or other list data to Excel 2003 or later, you need to open Excel and have Excel query the list. You do this from within the list itself. First, open the list in Datasheet View. Then, open the Task Pane and click Query list with Excel. If the application isn't running already, Excel opens. The Opening Query dialog box, shown in Figure 9-10, appears. Click Open.

If a login dialog box appears, sign in with the e-mail address and password you use to log in to Office Live. Click OK. The data then opens in the Excel window. Once your list data is open in Excel, you can print it or save it on your file system, as needed.

 *Unfortunately, if you make a change to the Excel data, the changes won't automatically be made on Office Live. The two applications are not synchronized. If you want to maintain the most current data at all times, you need to make changes to the Office Live list and requery the list with Excel.*

Tracking with Access

You can also use Microsoft Access 2003 or later to export Office Live information from Datasheet View. If you export Access, you create a static table; the data in Access isn't synchronized with Office Live. You can open the data in a new database or in an existing database. You can also click Report with Access to create a report that displays all the fields in the Office Live datasheet in the Access table.

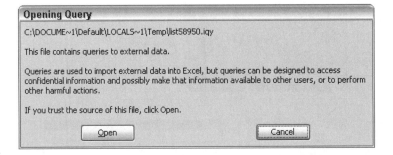

Opening Query

C:\DOCUME~1\Default\LOCALS~1\Temp\list58950.iqy

This file contains queries to external data.

Queries are used to import external data into Excel, but queries can be designed to access confidential information and possibly make that information available to other users, or to perform other harmful actions.

If you trust the source of this file, click Open.

[Open]   [Cancel]

FIGURE 9-10   Before Excel connects to Office Live, you may be prompted to log in.

If, however, you choose to track the data with Access, you can synchronize the datasheet in Office Live with Access. If you make changes in the Office Live datasheet, the changes automatically appears in Access. Display the Task Pane and click the Track this List in Access option to establish the connection.

How to Do It

Track your sales inventory	Click Business Applications, click Dashboard, click Sales, and then click Product & Service Items
Keep track of your equipment and other business assets	Click Business Applications, click Dashboard, click Company, and then click Company Assets
Enter inventory or asset information (or other data) quickly without having to fill out a form	Open the list in Datasheet View and type directly within the datasheet cells
View list contents in rows and columns that can be sorted or filtered	Open the list, and click Edit in Datasheet on the Actions menu (provided the Datasheet option is available)
Open inventory or other information from Office Live in Microsoft Excel	Switch to Datasheet View, open the Task Pane, and then click Query list with Excel or Chart with Excel
Synchronize your Office Live list data with a Microsoft Office application	Open your list in datasheet form, open the Task Pane, and then click Track this List in Access

9

Chapter 10

Creating and Customizing Business Applications

How to...

- Use Office Live Premium's advanced interface to customize your site
- Create a new business application with Office Live Premium
- Use SharePoint Designer to connect to your Office Live site
- Copy an existing business application using Office Live
- Customize a blank application using SharePoint Designer
- Create a workflow to track and replenish inventory
- Save a list as a template

Many software applications have both a "front door" and a "back door." The *front door* is the user-friendly interface that helps you perform tasks by clicking icons, buttons, and other visual clues. If you can get a peek through the back door, however, you can do much more. And, you don't have to look far for an example. You are probably using a version of the Windows operating system. Windows itself, with its Start menu and Desktop, is a front door to your computer. But, when you open a Command Prompt window and start entering command-line instructions, or when you open the Windows Registry with the Registry Editor, you look through the *back door,* where you can troubleshoot, configure applications, and customize the way your system operates.

When you first sign up for Office Live, and start configuring your workspaces and business applications, you enter your web site through the "front door." The Site Designer and Page Manager give everyone a user-friendly way to create and organize web sites and business applications. But, if you want to organize pages into folders, rename them, or add sophisticated content, these tools are limited in what they can do. This chapter introduces some ways in which you can gain more control over your Office Live site with the help of Microsoft SharePoint Designer. This tool is a web editor, as well as a collaboration tool. *Microsoft SharePoint Designer* gives you a look at how your workspaces and web site are organized, so you can both customize and make them work in more efficient and sophisticated ways.

Working with the Office Live Premium Interface

The topics depicted and described in preceding chapters focused on the Essentials version of the Office Live interface. The free Basics version of Office Live is similar, but it contains far less features—primarily you get a web site, domain name, and e-mail. (You can upgrade to more advanced versions at any point.) The Essentials interface lets you work with business applications, workspaces, and a web site.

When you subscribe to Office Live Premium, you discover the interface has a different look and feel than Essentials, though the features (web site, business applications, workspaces, the Member Center, and so on) are the same. When you want to create business applications or customize them, you need to have an Essentials or Premium subscription. The Premium version has a more straightforward interface, which lets you do customization within the Office Live interface itself. The Office Live Premium interface is described in the following sections. The SharePoint Designer application examined in this chapter is a completely separate application from Microsoft Office Live. SharePoint Designer, which is intended for use with SharePoint sites, also works with Office Live, however.

TIP   *If you are curious about Essentials or Premium, you can sign up for a trial account and test them for 30 days. But, to sign up for either account, you need to obtain a unique domain name (a domain name that someone else isn't using as yet or one you own yourself) and you need to submit your credit card number. After the trial period, you are charged for the service unless you cancel your subscription.*

10

Exploring the Office Live Premium Interface

If you are used to Office Live Essentials and move up to the Premium interface, you see much of the same content. The utilities are presented in a different visual format, however. Instead of the column full of buttons on the left side of the Member Center, you see a set of hyperlinks (see Figure 10-1).

NOTE   *The screen shots and examples in this chapter depict the Premium level of service, rather than those of the Essentials level.*

The e-mail service you get with Office Live Premium uses Hotmail, just as Essentials does. You also get access to a shared calendar and instant messaging service (see Chapter 16). The web site interface (shown in Figure 10-2) is graphically different from the one displayed in Essentials and Basics, but it performs many of the same functions.

The most significant differences are in the Business Applications section, and those are described in the next section.

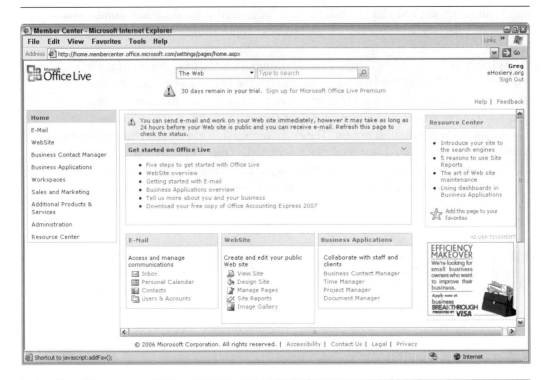

FIGURE 10-1 The Premium interface is similar to Essentials, but it has a different visual presentation.

 *This book was written during the end of the beta (or trial period) of Office Live. I encountered many complications moving from one version of Office Live to another—basically, I had to stop using my previous domain altogether and sign up for a completely new one. By press time, these problems may be resolved. But, it's still a good idea to sign up for the version of Office Live you want in the long run, rather than trying out one version and moving up later.*

Working with Business Applications

Office Live presents you with business applications you can use to compile and share data with other members of your workgroup. But, the selection of applications you get with a Premium subscription is wider than that included with Basics or Essentials. With Premium, you get the additional applications listed in Table 10-1.

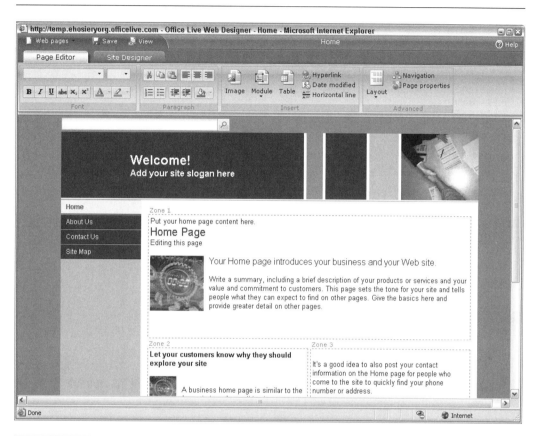

FIGURE 10-2   Office Live's Premium Page Manager interface is similar to that provided by Essentials.

Working with SharePoint Designer

SharePoint Designer is a powerful tool for organizing web sites that use SharePoint technology. Office Live is, itself, one of those sites. You can use SharePoint to open your Office Live web site and edit it as you would with any other standalone web editing program, such as Dreamweaver, FrontPage, or GoLive. When it comes to Office Live, however, SharePoint is the only web authoring tool you have at your disposal. Other applications don't interface with Office Live—not even Microsoft's new web editor, Expression Web.

This chapter can't possibly provide you with a comprehensive look at how SharePoint Designer can help you create a collaborative web site. Instead, it focuses on straightforward tasks everyone can do, whether or not they are interested in

Application	Basics	Essentials	Premium
Web Site	X	X	X
Customer Manager		X	X
Customer Support		X	X
Project Manager		X	X
Sales Applications (Campaigns, Collateral, Competition, Product & Service Items, Estimates)		X	X
Employees (Employee Directory, Expenses, Jobs & Hiring, Training, Work Hours)		X	X
Company (Calendars, Company Assets, To Do, Documents)		X	X
Time Manager			X
Business Contacts Manager			X
Document Manager			X
Company Administration			X

TABLE 10-1   Comparing Office Live Business Applications

being a Webmaster: what SharePoint is, how to get started with it, how to open your Office Live site in SharePoint, how to customize applications, and how to create a Workflow that can automate an Office Live business application.

 *To find out more about SharePoint Designer, consult* How to Do Everything with Microsoft Office SharePoint Designer 2007, *by Ernest Johnson, published by McGraw-Hill.*

Getting Started with SharePoint Designer

SharePoint Designer is a high-powered and somewhat expensive application. You might well wonder why you should consider purchasing the program at all, rather than trying another application, such as Microsoft's own excellent web design program, Expression Web. The answer is simple: if you want to get "underneath the hood" of your Office Live web site, working directly with code or customizing business applications, SharePoint Designer is your only option. No other web editor, including Expression Web, gives you the capability to open an Office Live web site and edit it with complete control. Other editors simply won't be able to open your Office Live site.

Getting started with SharePoint Designer is easier than you might think. Go to the Microsoft Download Center, download the software, install it, and get the application up and running. At press time, you need Windows Server 2003 or Windows XP with Service Pack 1 or later to use the program. Windows Vista was not listed. (This isn't to say that SharePoint Designer doesn't work with Windows Vista, but only that it wasn't listed as a supported operating system.) Once you do this, make sure you are connected to the Internet, and then you can connect to your Office Live site.

> **TIP** *You can download a trial version of SharePoint Designer from the Microsoft Download Center. Go to the Download Center Home page (http://www.microsoft.com/downloads/Search.aspx) and search for the program there. You can open the application 25 times before you are required to purchase a license key. You can purchase SharePoint Designer from outlets where software is sold. At press time, the program was advertised for $261.99 on Amazon.com.*

Touring the Interface

SharePoint Designer represents a step up from popular design programs, such as Microsoft FrontPage. It's a step up because it supports widely supported web standards, such as cascading style sheets (CSS) and Extensible Hypertext Markup Language (XHTML).

At the same time, SharePoint Designer presents users with a familiar interface, especially if you are already familiar with other Microsoft web development products, such as Visual Studio, Visual Web Developer, and Expression Web. The program window, shown in Figure 10-3, is divided into different panes and each pane performs a different function. Many functions are intended to help you apply and manage CSS styles throughout your pages and your site. For Office Live users, the Folder List shown in the upper left-hand corner is of immediate value.

The currently selected web page is displayed in Design View: the large area in the center of the SharePoint Designer workspace. The tabs at the bottom of Design View let you switch among Design View (the way the page looks in a web browser), Code View (the HTML, XML, or other markup code used on the page), and Split View (Design View on the top half, and Code View on the bottom). The other important areas of the SharePoint window are:

- **Folder List**   A hierarchical list of the folders within your Office Live workspace.

- **CSS Properties**   Displays the CSS commands that control the formatting of the contents currently selected in Design View.

10

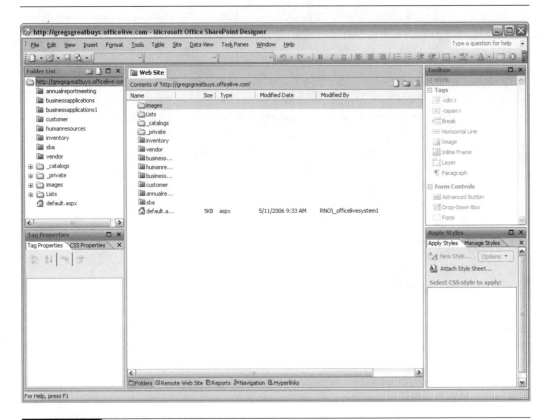

FIGURE 10-3 The SharePoint Designer workspace is divided into task panes.

- **Data Source Library**   Lets you add new SharePoint lists, as well as other sources of data.

- **Apply Styles**   Lets you create new CSS styles or apply ones you already created to content in Design View.

- **Quick Tag Selector**   A list of the HTML, XML, or other commands that control the formatting of the currently selected content.

When you first open SharePoint Designer, all these panes are blank. You either need to create a new web page or web site, or open your existing Office Live page, so you can start viewing and editing content.

Opening Your Office Live Site

As long as SharePoint Designer is installed and your computer is connected to the Internet, connecting to your Office Live web site is straightforward. Start the program and choose Open Site from the File menu. The Open Site dialog box appears. If you have opened your Office Live site in the past, a list of your recently used workspaces and applications, as well as the main URL of your web site on Office Live, appear as shown in Figure 10-4.

You don't need to be limited to Office Live web sites. You can also use SharePoint Designer to open other web sites you created and to which you have user name and password access.

If this is the first time you have connected to your site, enter the URL in the Site name box. Your URL takes the following form:

```
https://[sitename].officelive.com
```

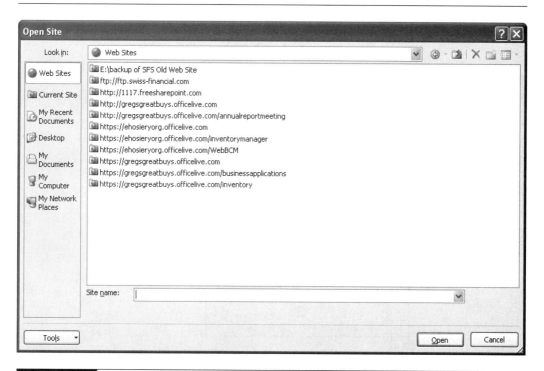

FIGURE 10-4   You can open a remote Office Live site or another site to which you have access.

For instance, because my domain name is gregsgreatbuys.com, I enter https://
gregsgreatbuys.officelive.com in the Site name box.

NOTE   *If your chosen domain name ends in .org or .net, there's a complication.
When you want to log in to your site, you need to append that domain
name extension (.org or .net) to the URL. For instance, if your domain is
ehosiery.org, then you would enter https://ehosieryorg.officelive.com in the
Site name box. The URL you enter always has to end in officelive.com.*

Click Open, and a .NET login screen appears (see Figure 10-5).

Enter the e-mail address and password you usually use to log in to your Office
Live site, and then click OK. The site opens in the Office Live window. Use the
Folder List to navigate through your business applications. You can drag the Folder
list into or out of its "docked" position in the SharePoint Designer workspace to
view its contents more clearly (see Figure 10-6).

The overall contents of your Office Live site appear in Folder List. In the
center of the SharePoint window, in the large pane labeled web site, is the web
site you created with Office Live. You can use SharePoint Designer to do some
professional-level formatting and redesigning of your web site, so you don't have
to use the Office Live Site Designer or Page Editor. You can also customize a
Business Applications page just as you can any other web page, as you see in the
following sections.

FIGURE 10-5   Log in to your Office Live site from within SharePoint Designer.

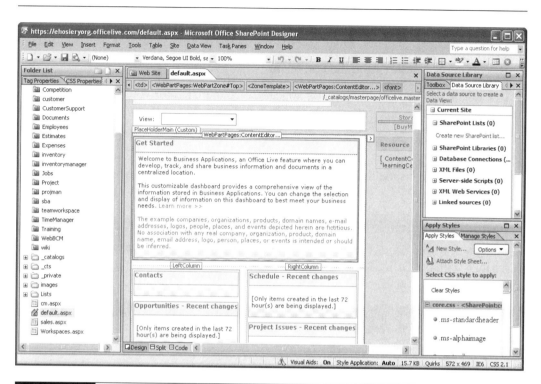

FIGURE 10-6 Your site's files, applications, and workspaces appear in Folder List.

Editing Your Office Live Web Site

One of the biggest advantages of using SharePoint Designer is the capability to control and edit your site using a user-friendly web-editing tool. For those who are creating their first web sites with Office Live, the Page Manager and Site Designer applications you access within Office Live using your web browser are a first choice. However, if you are already used to creating web pages with the help of Adobe Dreamweaver, Microsoft Expression Web, FrontPage, or another tool, you'll find SharePoint Designer familiar. It gives you a way to easily code sites for technologies, such as ASP.NET and CSS. But, SharePoint Designer enables you to interface with Office Live and supports the proprietary code used on the SharePoint platform.

To edit your Office Live web site, you need to open the site in SharePoint Designer. The steps described in the preceding section won't do this; they open your SharePoint business applications. To open your SharePoint web site, follow these steps:

1. Choose Open Site from the File menu.

2. When the Open Site dialog box appears, type the URL for your web site in the Site Name box: http://www.mysite.com.

3. Click Open.

Your Home page should appear in SharePoint Designer's Design View (see Figure 10-7).

Creating New Files

Creating a new web page is easy with SharePoint Designer. The process goes faster than with the Office Live web-based interface, because you don't have to

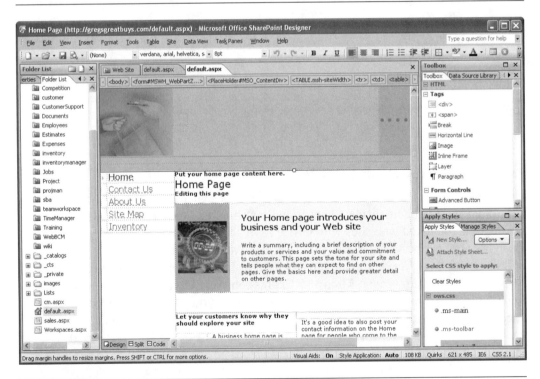

FIGURE 10-7 **FIGURE 10-7** You can open your web site in SharePoint Designer the same way you can open your shared workspaces.

wait for the currently displayed page to refresh each time you choose a command. You can also choose from among many options for new content:

1. Choose New from the File menu.

2. When the New File dialog box opens, select the type of file you want to add.

3. Make sure you check the Add to current Web button to add the file to your Office Live web site.

4. Click OK. The file opens in Design View.

What gives SharePoint Designer so much more power is the range of new-age options you can create. As shown in Figure 10-8, your page options are listed on three tabs: Page, Web Site, and SharePoint Content. You can add single pages or templates and you can also add CSS layouts.

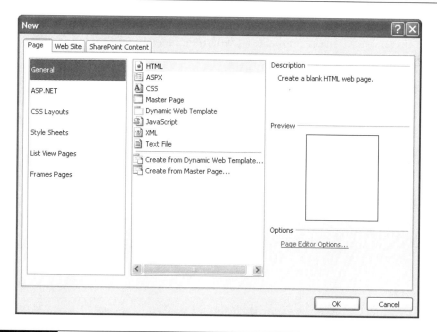

FIGURE 10-8   SharePoint Designer lets you add a wide range of new pages.

Editing Existing Files

Once a file is open in Design View, you can edit it using the controls in Share Point Designer's toolbars. You can format text using the Bold, Italic, and Underline buttons. You can also insert an image from the Insert Image button, and you can add a table using the Table button.

By default, when you open a web site by entering its URL, you open the Home page. Links to other pages appear (they open by default—you can move them) on the left side of the Home page. To open one of these pages, press CTRL and click the link to follow that link. The page opens in Design View, so you can begin editing it.

Creating a New Application

Office Live makes it relatively easy to create your own custom Business Application to fit your needs. The advantage of creating an application from scratch is, you only capture the information you need. For instance, in Chapter 9, you examined how the Products list can help you track inventory. But, the default fields included with this list might not fit the needs of a small-scale company focused on retail or wholesale sales, rather than services. To capture only the data you want, you can create a custom Inventory Manager application, which includes the following views:

- Inventory
- Suppliers
- Order Requests
- Business Documents

Within the Inventory View, you can create the following columns:

- Product Name
- Unit Price
- Items in Stock
- Inventory to Reorder/Reorder Point
- Supplier ID/Supplier Name

The most straightforward way to create such an application is with Office Live Premium, as you can see in the following section. You can also create new business applications with Office Live Essentials. Click Business Applications, and then click Site Settings. When the Site Settings page appears, click Manage Sites and Workspaces under the Administration heading.

Copying an Existing Application with Office Live

If you already subscribe to Office Live Essentials or Premium, you use its interface to create custom applications, as well as installing and using SharePoint Designer. One way to create a new business application is to copy an already existing one, and then customize it. Follow these steps to copy the existing Asset Manager application using the interface provided with Office Live Essentials or Premium:

1. Log in and access the Member Center.

2. Click Business Applications.

3. Click the down arrow next to Common Tasks (see Figure 10-9) and choose Create New from the menu that appears.

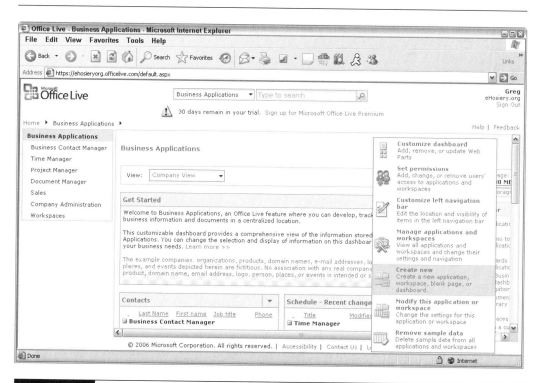

FIGURE 10-9   The Common Tasks menu lets you create and customize business applications.

4. When the Business Applications—Create page appears, pass your mouse pointer over the only option available in the lower half of the screen. A boxed message appears in the upper part of the screen. Now, click Applications and Workspaces.

5. When the Create new application or workspace window appears, choose Business Applications from the Select a category list, and then choose Company Assets from the Select a template list. Company Assets is the closest template to the kind of list you are creating—Inventory Manager. Click OK.

6. When the Site details box opens (see Figure 10-10), enter a title to add to the URL for this application. You don't have to enter the entire URL in the URL box, in other words. If you are creating an Inventory Manager application, you might simply enter Inventory.

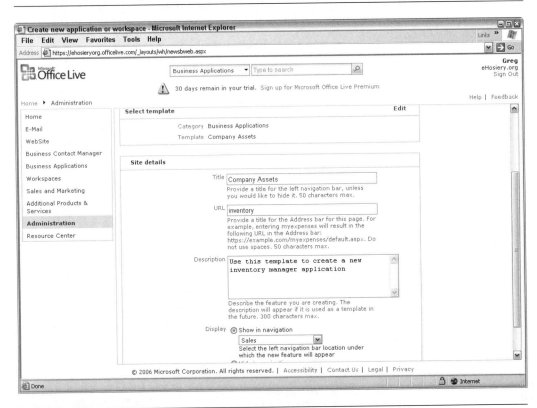

FIGURE 10-10　Enter details about your application in Site Details.

 *You can only type numbers or characters in the URL. You cannot type hyphens or other special characters.*

7. When the Company Assets application opens, you can begin to edit it. Click the drop-down arrows in the application interface. If you click the arrow next to All Assets, you can choose Create View (see Figure 10-11). This enables you to add a new view to the application to accompany the default All Views.

8. Click Datasheet View. The Create Datasheet View: Assets page appears. In the box labeled View Name, enter a name for the view, such as Stock Items. In the Columns section of the page, make sure a check mark is displayed next to the name of the column you want to appear in this view. For a Stock Items View, for instance, you might want to check off Asset Name, Asset Type, Date Acquired, Purchase Value, and Current Worth.

9. When you finish selecting columns, and sort and filter options on the page, click OK. The new application opens, so you can begin entering data.

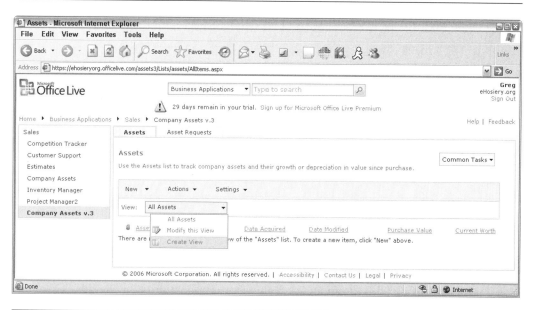

FIGURE 10-11   You can add views or other data to a template you copied.

Creating a New Blank Application

If you copy an existing workspace, such as Asset Manager, you can't change its name to Inventory Manager. To get more control over customizing your application and to start with a "blank slate," you need to start by creating a blank workspace. You can then customize the workspace as needed. Follow these steps:

1. Follow Steps 1 through 4 as presented in the preceding section.

2. Choose Workspaces instead of Applications. The page refreshes.

3. From the Select a template drop-down list, choose Blank Workspace.

4. Click OK. The Site Details box opens. Enter a title (such as Inventory Manager) in the Title box. In the URL box, enter "inventory" or another simple name to be added to the site's URLs. Enter a description in the description box that indicates to visitors what the purpose of the workspace is.

5. In the Display section of Site Details, choose the business application category (Sales, Company Administration, Workspaces, or Top Level) where you want the new workspace to appear in the navigation links on the left side of your Office Live site.

6. Click OK. The page refreshes and you see the Dashboard.

At this point, you can start customizing the site in SharePoint Designer or through the Office Live interface itself. Click Common Tasks and choose Modify this application or workspace. Under Create, click List and libraries. When the Site Libraries and Lists page appears, click Create new content. When the Create page appears, you can choose one of the five types of content for your workspace: Libraries, Communications options, Tracking items, Custom Lists, or Web Pages. When your mouse pointer hovers over an item, an explanation appears. When you click one of the list or library options, enter a name and description on the New page, and then click Create to add the item to your workspace.

Creating a New Application with Office Live Essentials

You don't need Office Live Premium to create a new application. You can do this when you access your Office Live Essentials web site from within your web browser. The steps differ slightly from those in the preceding section.

1. Log in and click Business Applications.

2. Click Administration.

3. Click Manage applications and Workspace

4. Click the New Button.

5. Choose Blank.

6. Give your site a simple one-word name (in my experience a two-word name causes problems either because it has a blank space or doesn't fit the program's requirements in some way).

7. Click Create.

Your site is created and now appears in your list of sites. Click Site Manager to review the list.

If you click this site's name, it opens in a web browser window, but nothing seems to be in it. The window appears to be blank, just as you specified, although it isn't entirely blank. When you open the workspace you just created using SharePoint Designer, you discover some basic "building blocks" are in place that you can customize. You examine the customization process in the following section.

Customizing Your Application

Once you create a blank application, you open it in SharePoint Designer. Double-click the application's name from Folder List. You should see the standard Office Live applications and workspaces: Business Applications, Customer, SBA, Vendor, and so on. You should also see the name of the blank application you created in the preceding section (you may have called it Inventory or Inventory Manager).

> TIP
>
> *You can click-and-drag any pane's title bar, including Folder List, to move it around on the screen. The title bar also contains some important tools: new folder, new file, and the X for closing the pane altogether. If you close a pane, you can make it reappear by choosing its name from the Task Panes menu.*

To start, double-click Inventory. A list of the files contained in this workspace appears in the Web Site pane in the middle of the SharePoint window. Three folders (_private, lists, and images) appear, as well as the Home page, default.aspx.

10

Double-click default.aspx to view the Home page. It opens as a separate tab within the SharePoint Designer window, next to the Web Site tab. What appears is the Dashboard page for the workspace you created. It contains the same contents you're familiar with from the Dashboards you see in Office Live through your web browser: Calendar Events, Opportunities, Customers, and Projects (see Figure 10-12).

You want to begin by creating a list for your workspace:

1. Choose File | New | Page. The New dialog box appears.

2. Click the SharePoint Content tab.

3. Click Lists on the left side of the dialog box, and New List Wizard on the right (see Figure 10-13).

NOTE *The contents of your Office Live site and the level of subscription you have, determine exactly which options appear in SharePoint Content.*

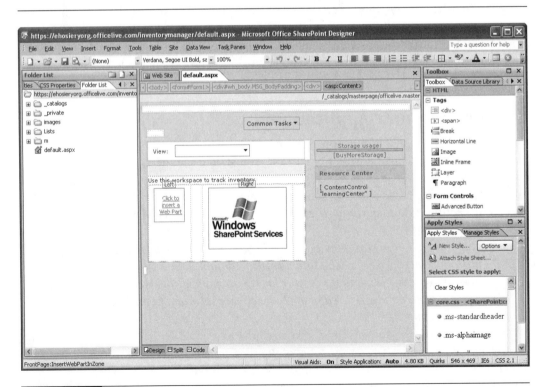

FIGURE 10-12 You first open a Dashboard page for your workspace.

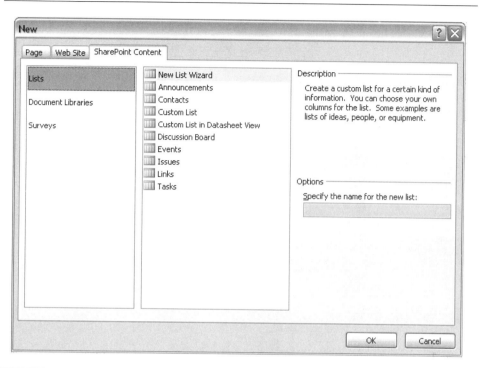

FIGURE 10-13   The contents of the SharePoint Content tab are customized to the type of Office Live site you have.

4. Click OK.

5. The New List Wizard dialog box appears.

6. Click Next.

7. In the first screen (shown in Figure 10-14), enter the name of the list you want to create: Inventory. Click Enable attachments, and then click Next.

8. In the next screen, choose the fields you want this list to have. Select each item in the list, and then choose Modify, Move Up, or Move Down to rename and reorder each one. You want the list to appear as follows:

   ■ Product Name

   ■ Unit Price

10

FIGURE 10-14   Assign a name to your list using this screen of the New List Wizard.

- Units in Stock

- Amount for Reorder

- Supplier ID

Obviously, you can rename these fields or alter them to fit your own company's needs. When you finish, click Next. Follow the steps shown in the remaining screens of the wizard to finish customizing your list. You can also drag lists and other data sources from the Data Source Library Task Pane directly into Design View, where they are added to your page instantly.

Creating an Office Live Workflow

If you lack the personnel or the time to monitor your inventory with the frequency your business requires, you can do some development work and create what Microsoft calls a "workflow." A *workflow* is business logic—a sequence of steps that allows computerized functions to occur automatically when the right conditions are reached.

Creating a workflow requires a special web design tool: Microsoft SharePoint Designer. Because Office Live is built on the SharePoint platform, it only makes sense that this tool should let you open your Office Live site and look inside it. This chapter looks ahead and assumes you have downloaded and installed SharePoint Designer (this is free to use on a trial basis for a limited period) and that you've created a custom business application called Inventory Manager. (You learned how to perform both of these functions in Chapter 10.) Here's a glimpse at how easy it is to do your own web development, even if you lack programming experience. Follow these steps to set up a "trigger point" that tracks inventory levels for you and automatically places product orders when you reach a certain level.

 This section describes an advanced-level process that you may not want to tackle unless you have some programming or web development experience. You need to subscribe to the Essentials or Premium version of Office Live to use these features. And, you also need Windows Workflow Foundation (part of .NET Framework 3.0) installed.

Open Your Site and Create Your Workflow

Once the SharePoint application is up and running, you need to add a custom SharePoint list before you begin to create the workflow.

Adding a SharePoint List

To create a SharePoint list you can work with, follow these steps:

1. Open your Office Live site in SharePoint Designer. Choose Open Site from the File menu, enter the URL for your Office Live site in the Address box, and then click Open.

2. When a .NET dialog box appears, log in with the e-mail address and password you normally enter to access your Office Live site.

3. Open the inventory management business application you want to automatically track. Or, open the blank Inventory Manager application you created earlier in this chapter.

4. First, to create a workflow, you need to add a SharePoint List to your application. Even though your Office Live business application already includes built-in lists, you need to add one from within the SharePoint Designer interface. To add such a list, with your application open in the SharePoint window, click File, and then choose New.

5. When the New dialog box opens, on the General Tab, double-click ASPX. A blank, untitled ASPX page opens.

10

6. Click Insert, choose SharePoint Controls, and then choose Custom List Form. The List or Document Library Form dialog box shown in Figure 10-15 appears.

7. The options you see in the List or Document Library Form dialog box depend on the business application you are using. If you have Asset Manager open, you see Assets and Asset Requests as the two options in the first drop-down list. Choose the options you want, and then click OK.

The list is added to the SharePoint window. Figure 10-16 shows an Asset list added to the current Office Live application, which is called Inventory. Once you create a list, you see it listed in the SharePoint Lists section of the Data Source Library pane.

Adding the Workflow

Once you have a SharePoint list open in the main content pane of the SharePoint Designer window, you can begin to create your workflow. Follow these steps:

1. Choose New from the File menu, and then click SharePoint Content when the New submenu appears. The New dialog box opens.

2. Click the SharePoint Content tab to bring it to the front.

3. As shown in Figure 10-17, choose Workflow, then choose Blank Workflow, and then click OK. Workflow Designer opens. This is the application that lets you create a workflow.

FIGURE 10-15   You create a SharePoint custom list using this dialog box.

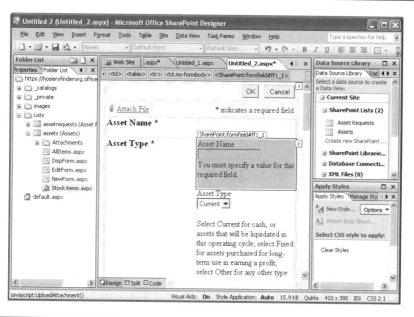

FIGURE 10-16 When you add a custom list, it opens in the main content pane in the SharePoint window.

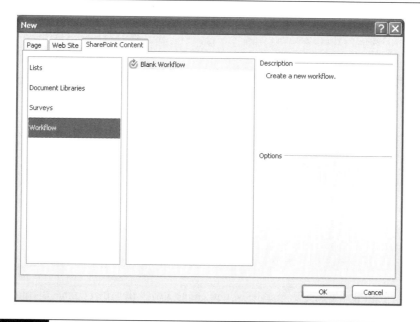

FIGURE 10-17 The Workflow options appear when you work with a SharePoint list.

4. In the box labeled Give a name to this workflow (see Figure 10-18), give a name, such as Reorder Stock, to the workflow.

5. Attach a workflow to a SharePoint list. Choose Inventory from the What SharePoint list should this workflow be attached to drop-down list.

6. Check the box next to Automatically start this workflow whenever an item is changed.

7. Click Next. The Workflow Designer—Reorder Stock screen appears.

In the next section, you assemble the workflow itself.

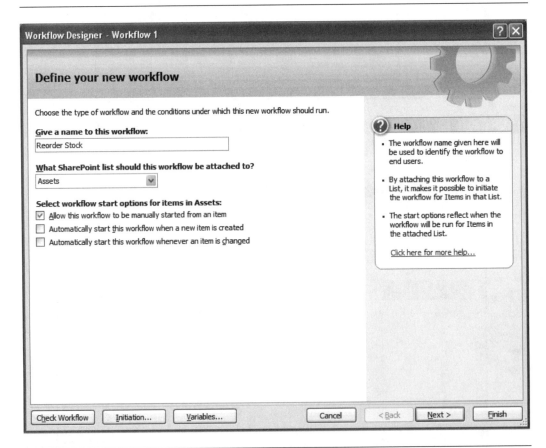

Workflow Designer - Workflow 1   ? X

Define your new workflow

Choose the type of workflow and the conditions under which this new workflow should run.

Give a name to this workflow:

Reorder Stock

What SharePoint list should this workflow be attached to?

Assets

Select workflow start options for items in Assets:
- ☑ Allow this workflow to be manually started from an item
- ☐ Automatically start this workflow when a new item is created
- ☐ Automatically start this workflow whenever an item is changed

❓ **Help**

- The workflow name given here will be used to identify the workflow to end users.

- By attaching this workflow to a List, it makes it possible to initiate the workflow for Items in that List.

- The start options reflect when the workflow will be run for Items in the attached List.

Click here for more help...

Check Workflow | Initiation... | Variables... | Cancel | < Back | Next > | Finish

FIGURE 10-18   Workflow Designer enables you to create a workflow that connects your Office Live data.

Configuring the Workflow

The SharePoint application used to assemble workflows is called (not surprisingly) Workflow Designer. You define the conditions for the workflow to occur, the actions to take, and the fields to be associated with the workflow.

1. In the next Workflow Designer dialog box (see Figure 10-19), you define the conditions under which this workflow will start and the action you want to have happen. Click the Conditions button to define the conditions under which your inventory should be replenished. In the drop-down list that appears, choose Compare Inventory Field. When you choose this option, the following words appear next to conditions: if <u>field</u> <u>equals</u> <u>value</u>.

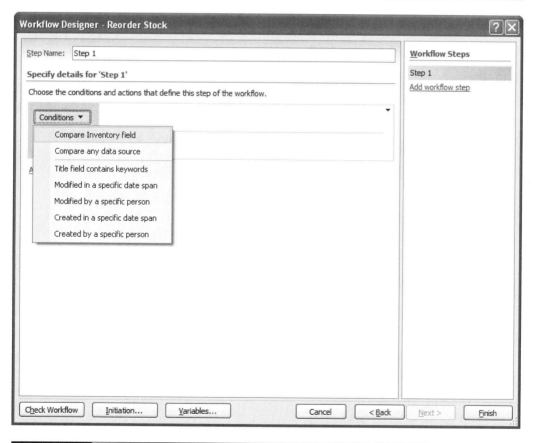

FIGURE 10-19   In Workflow Designer, you set conditions for which your specified action occurs.

10

2. For this example, assume you want the Units in Stock field to hit 6 for the action to be triggered. This means when you have six items in stock, an order is automatically replaced. Click Field, and then click the name of the field you created in Inventory Manager. For this example, the name of the field is Level. Next to the Conditions button, you now see the following:

```
Level equals value
```

3. Click equals, and then choose "is less than" from the drop-down list.

4. Click value, and then type 6 in the box that appears. Now, press ENTER. The Conditions you specified are as follows:

```
Level is less than 6.
```

5. Click Actions, and then choose Create list item in from the drop-down list. This causes a new list item to be created when units in stock drop below six.

6. Click this list (see Figure 10-20).

7. When you click this list, the Create New List Item dialog box appears. Choose Order Requests (see Figure 10-21). This creates a new item in the Order Requests list.

8. The Title (*) field appears because it is the only field in Order Requests. Highlight Title (*), and then click Modify to specify a value for this field. The Value Assignment dialog box appears (see Figure 10-21).

9. Click the Define Workflow Lookup button. This is the button with the abstract-looking symbol (fx). Choose Inventory from the Source list, and choose Asset name from the Field list. Then, choose Inventory: Asset Name from the Field drop-down list (see Figure 10-22). Click OK.

10. When a warning dialog box appears stating you won't be guaranteed to return a single value, click Yes. This associates the Title field in Order Requests with the Asset Name field in the Inventory List. Click OK to close Value assignment and return to Create New List Item.

11. Click OK to close Create New List Item, and then return to Workflow Designer, where the Conditions and Actions statements read:

```
If Level is less than 6
Create item in Order Requests(Output to Variable:create)
```

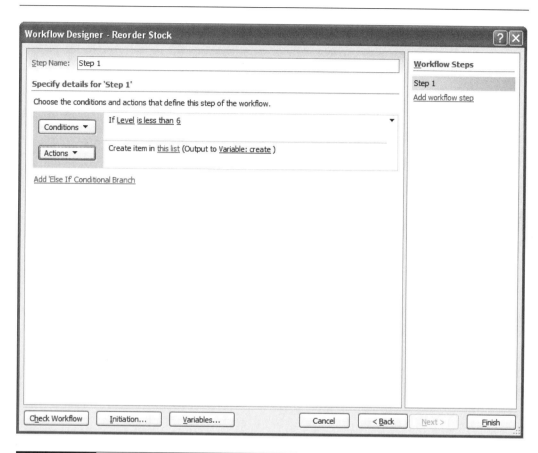

FIGURE 10-20   As you create your workflow, expressions change in the Workflow Designer.

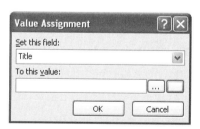

FIGURE 10-21   Set a value for the field you want to associate with your reordering action.

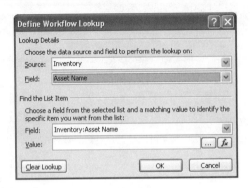

FIGURE 10-22   You associate an item in the Inventory list with a field in Reorder Stock.

What, exactly, do these steps accomplish? They tell Office Live that, when the value of the Units in Stock field in the Inventory list becomes less than six, a new list item is placed in the Order Requests list you're in the process of creating. This identifies the two lists affected by the workflow.

Setting Values for Specific Fields

However, you have to go one step further. You must set a value for the product's ID field:

1. Click Actions, and then click Create List Item.

2. Click this list. When the Create New List Item dialog box appears, click Inventory.

3. Click Add.

4. When the Value Assignment dialog box appears, choose Asset Name from the Set this field drop-down list.

5. Click the Define Workflow Lookup button. When the Define Workflow Lookup dialog box appears, choose ID from the Field drop-down list. This matches the Asset Name field in the Inventory list with the Inventory ID field.

6. Click OK twice to return to Create New List Item.

Specifying the Reorder Amount

Last, you specify the amount to reorder:

1. Click Add.

2. When the Value Assignment dialog box appears, choose Reorder Amount from the drop-down list.

3. Click the Define Workflow Lookup button. When the Define Workflow Lookup dialog box appears, choose Amount to Reorder for the Field, and then click OK twice to return to Create New List Item.

4. Click OK to return to the Workflow Designer dialog box.

5. Finally, click Finish. A dialog box appears, telling you the steps of the workflow are being saved. This assembles the steps of the workflow.

When you're done, test your workflow. Return to SharePoint Designer and modify one of your products: In the Inventory list, click edit next to one of your items, and manually set the value to the inventory for that level to go below six.

How to Do It

Work with specialized business applications, such as Time Manager and Business Contacts Manager	Sign up for Office Live Premium
Download a trial version of SharePoint Designer that you can open for 25 times before purchasing	Go to the Microsoft Download Center (http://www.microsoft.com/downloads/Search.aspx) and search for SharePoint Designer
Add new data sources and apply CSS styles to your Office Live web pages	Use SharePoint Designer to open and edit your site's content
Open an Office Live site in SharePoint Designer that does not end in .com	Add the domain name extension to the first part of the URL. If the extension is .net, the form should be https://mydomainnet.officelive.com

Part IV

Boosting Your Sales and Productivity

Chapter 11

Using Office Live to Sell Your Products

How to...

- Include the essential elements needed to create a sales catalog
- Organize your product sales area with categories
- Add photos to help sell your merchandise
- Create a purchase path for your customers
- Add PayPal Buy Now buttons to your pages
- Add content that builds trust and reassures customers

Office live is a collaborative web-based service that gives workgroup members a place to share files, and do scheduling and other tasks. It isn't primarily intended to give business owners a way to sell to the public. If it were, it would provide shoppers who are looking for merchandise to purchase on Office Live-hosted web sites with a shopping cart and buttons. Those shoppers would then be able to make purchases and transfer payments to you.

Nevertheless, Office Live does provide enterprising individuals like you with the capability to create their own web sites, and if you are an enterprising business entrepreneur, you naturally want to sell your products online. Some business owners who use Office Live sell their products through their site's web pages. But a lot of competition exists among businesses that want to sell online. You have to give your sales catalog the right presentation to inspire trust among your customers and encourage them to buy from you, rather than from a competing web site. In this chapter, you learn what makes a good sales catalog and how to make sure your Office Live site has the right elements.

Creating a Sales Catalog

What makes a commercial, product-oriented, Office Live web site different from a personal site, a site devoted to a club or a cause, or one that advertises professional services? Such a site focuses immediately on products to sell. It also gives online shoppers what they need:

- **Keep it organized** The categories and subcategories within the site and the pages that make them up all enable customers to focus on what's being sold.

- **Grab their attention** Photos, type, and color immediately grab the interest of hurried shoppers.

■ **Make purchasing easy**   Big, clear Buy buttons and straightforward instructions about your payment and shipping options encourage transactions.

Online shoppers aren't looking for you to reinvent the wheel and be "wowed" with lots of technical tricks. They are comfortable with predictability. Convenience and strong content rank higher than technical gimmicks and frills such as animations or video clips.

Organizing Your Sales Catalog

The default category pages you get when you use one of Office Live's web site templates don't include any categories called Products, Services, or Catalog. Creating such a category page, and adding subcategories and individual pages that present the merchandise you have to sell, is up to you.

If your visitors can click into the site and keep finding more information, your chances of making a sale or, at least getting a phone inquiry, go up proportionately. The more information you offer, the "stickier" your site becomes, and the longer customers stay on your site.

Making Your Links Specific

Too many sites include links or buttons that give visitors little or no information about what they gain by clicking them. Make sure your own links are specific and customer-oriented. Your customer has already told you speed is of the essence. Your fickle, harried customer glances at these links, does some head-scratching, and moves somewhere else—maybe to a different site altogether.

You have to guide the visitors, so they quickly find what they want in a flash. What kinds of links do the trick? The following ones are too vague:

```
Products
      Clothing
      Outerwear
      Accessories
```

The following links take up more space because they are separated into several subcategories, but they are also more specific and customer-oriented:

```
Our Original Clothing Lines
      Adult Business Wear
            Suits by Cosmo
            Dress Shoes by Allen-Edmonds
            Italian Silk Ties
      Adult Sportswear
      Children's Casuals
```

Try to guide customers through your site by providing specific information and explaining the benefits of clicking different links.

Dividing Your Sales Catalog into Sections

Consider creating a map of your site that organizes your sales merchandise into as many specific categories and subcategories as possible. It might seem you are giving shoppers more work to do to make a purchase. But you're also giving them a way to explore your site, stay in your domain a little longer than they would otherwise, and find "nooks and crannies" they might not discover without looking around.

By mapping out your site, you also keep a visual record of everything you want to do and organize the site in a way that makes sense and helps customers move from the home page to the checkout area. Your goal is to lead your visitors in, make it easy for them to find what they want, and then guide them to the checkout area.

 *Creating category names and headings is important. But, if you create six different categories—such as Vitamins, Supplements, Sport Drinks, and the like—and for each of those category pages, the title reads simply "Products," you defeat the purpose of organizing your site. And yet, that's what happens with many Office Live sites. Page titles can also improve your search engine placement, especially on Google, which scans keywords in page titles. To change the page title, open Office Live's Page Editor and click Page Properties. When the Page Properties dialog box opens, change the text in the Page title box. You are changing the text that appears in the browser's title bar when the page is viewed.*

Designing a Product Page

A *product page* is where shoppers find out about one or more specific items for sale. You get to a product description page from a category page that contains links to all the products in a specific category. Click a product link, and you get a photo and description of the product. Include a link that lets the customer immediately add the item to a shopping cart.

The typical product description page on the Keni's Nail Art site contains the basics: clear photos, descriptions, prices, and a contact e-mail address. Figure 11-1 shows an example. Also notice the subcategories under the main heading Products in the links on the left-hand side of the page.

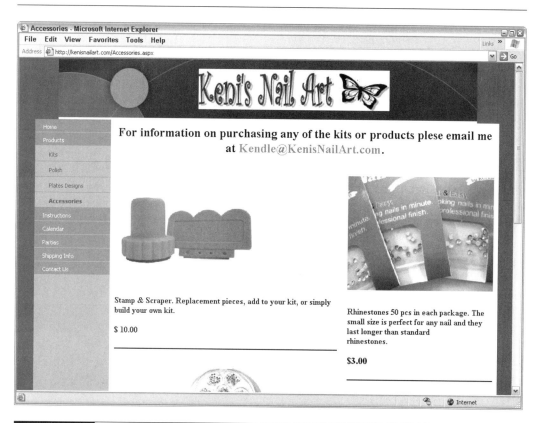

FIGURE 11-1   Include photos, descriptions, and prices in your product pages.

Kendle Marra includes multiple products on one product page. You can also create a separate page for each individual product. That way, you have more space for detailed descriptions.

Adding Photos

The old adage that a picture is worth a thousand words is often cited because it is still relevant. I'm not going to give you an in-depth view of how to take product photos for your Office Live sales listings. It's up to you whether you want to use a digital camera, a scanner, or a conventional camera and have a photo lab or local drugstore save them on CD. You need to follow a few good principles when it comes to lighting, positioning, and selection that can aid your presentation on Office Live or any e-commerce site.

The first principle is less is *not* more. Don't hold back when it comes to taking product photos. Consider the photos of shoes I've taken, shown in Figure 11-2. I always try to take six, seven, or more photos of each item from different angles.

All products don't lend themselves to so many views, of course. If you're only taking a photo of a single bottle of nail polish, a single image is appropriate. But this brings me to the second principle. *Get up close and personal* with your images. Use your camera's macro function to take a single close-up image and, if you need to keep the image in focus, use a tripod. In Figure 11-3, I got as close as possible to show the detail on a signed record album.

The third principle is *light your items from different angles*. Don't use a single incandescent bulb. Point halogen or other photographic lights at the object from two, three, or more directions to reduce shadows. And, be sure you drape a sheet behind the object being photographed that provides contrast and makes your merchandise easy to see. A simple white drape is effective for most purposes.

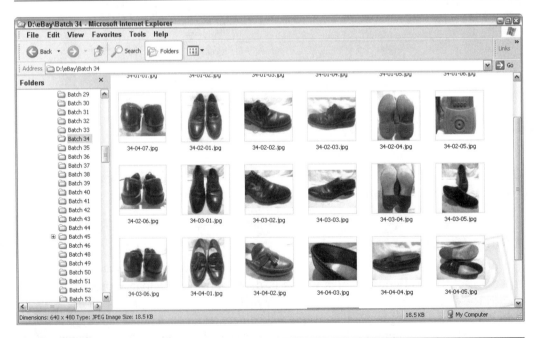

FIGURE 11-2   Multiple photos answer customer questions and encourage purchases.

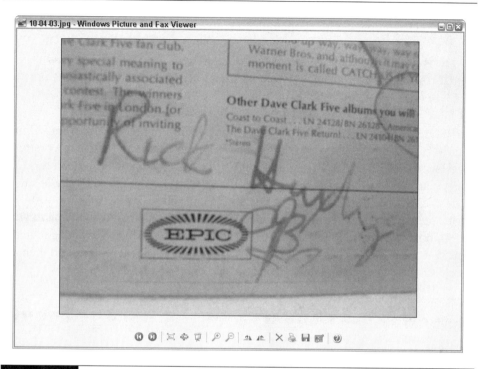

FIGURE 11-3   Get as close as you can and take advantage of your camera's macro function.

11

Creating a Purchase Path

In a customer-driven field, such as e-commerce, the job of the merchant (that's you, of course) is to create an environment that invites interaction and makes it easy to purchase goods and services. An essential part of that environment is providing a way to buy the desired product.

Adding Buy Buttons

Placing a Buy button on every page with a product on it helps the shopper add to their cart. The items the customer selects remain in the cart until they choose to check out or leave the site. You, the merchant, collect payment and shipping information with a check-out system.

The problem: Office Live doesn't come with a catalog or Buy buttons. But some enterprising web page designers have figured out how to add them to an Office Live site. Ma Charina Brooks, who runs the SimplySoy Naturals site profiled in Chapter 3, does not send shoppers directly to PayPal. Brooks uses her

Office Live site to attract shoppers to her products, and then sends them to another site, which is equipped with shopping cart software to enable purchases.

 A shopping cart *is an electronic "holding area" for items chosen from a web sales page. The cart stores the items and totals them at check-out time.*

But there's no reason you can't direct shoppers to PayPal directly from within your web site. For people who sell on eBay, payments through PayPal are pretty much seamless. If you sell through your Office Live web site, you need to direct your shoppers from one of your product description pages to PayPal's site. A graphic icon that looks like a clickable button and sends shoppers there is just what you need. And, as you might expect, PayPal is only too happy to give it to you.

Suppose you log in to Office Live, click Web Site to open Page Manager, and then click New Page. You can choose the Product or Service template, and then give your page the generic name Products (see Figure 11-4).

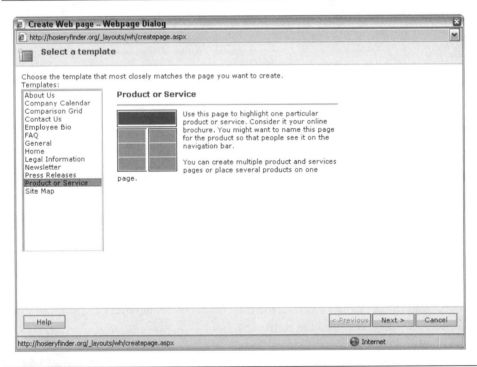

FIGURE 11-4   The Product or Service template gives you standard sales content you can apply to product pages.

Once you have your Products page set up, follow these steps:

1. Go to PayPal, log in, and then navigate to the Buy Now Buttons page (https://www.paypal.com/us/cgi-bin/webscr?cmd=xpt/xclick/request/ SingleitemIntro).

2. Click Get Started.

3. When the Sell Single Items form shown in Figure 11-5 appears, complete it, and leave the standard Buy Now button option displayed at the bottom of the form.

4. Click Create Button Now.

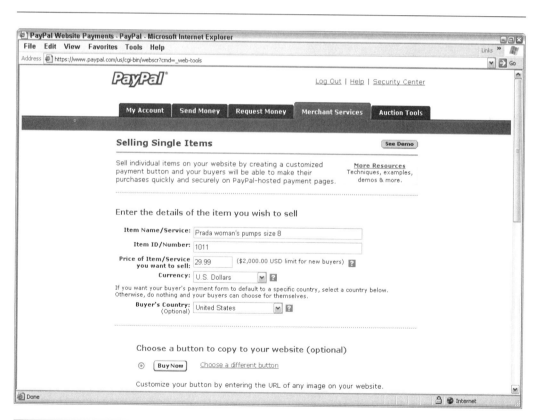

FIGURE 11-5 Complete this form to add a Buy Now button to a single product listing.

5. When the page titled Add a button to your web site appears, copy the text shown in Figure 11-6.

Be sure to copy all the code (it's lengthy) by scrolling all the way through it to the </form> command at the bottom. Once the code is entirely highlighted, press CTRL+C to copy it to your computer clipboard.

6. Return to Office Live, and open the product page you created earlier, if it isn't open already. Position the cursor at the spot on the page where you want to add the Buy Now button.

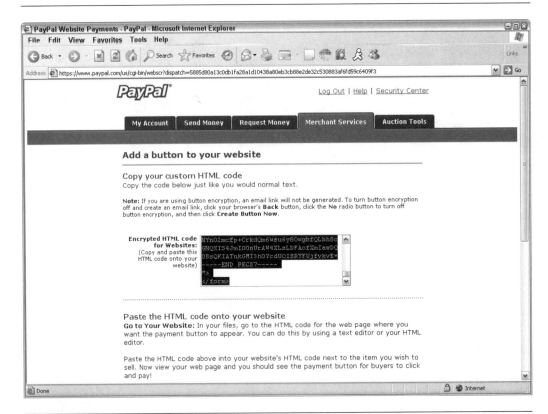

FIGURE 11-6 Copy this HTML code to connect your page to PayPal.

7. Make sure you have positioned the cursor between the <body> and </body> tags, and that the web page has the required <head> and </head> and optional <html> and </html> tags. This tells the browser it is a web page and ensures the code you are adding will appear as a button and not as raw HTML code.

8. Press CTRL+V to paste the button (see Figure 11-7).

Be sure to include some descriptive text along with the Buy Now button, as well as an instruction telling your shopper what will happen when they clicks the button, such as "Click below to complete your transaction securely with PayPal."

> NOTE *PayPal's Web Site Payments Standard and Pro options both have the advantage of phone, fax, mail, or in-person payments from your customers. You don't necessarily have to accept money through PayPal.*

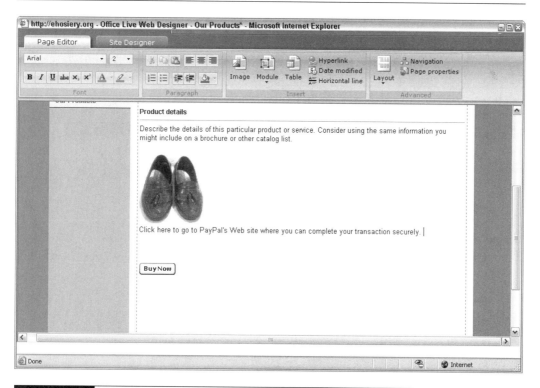

FIGURE 11-7   Copy PayPal's code and paste it on to your page in Site Designer.

11

Finding a Secure Server

Secure Sockets Layer (SSL) is the *de facto* standard for web security and is built into major web servers and browsers. When a web page or site is "secure," that usually means it has implemented SSL on its web server. SSL gives you:

■ Positive ID of your server as yours.

■ Message privacy.

■ Message integrity.

You can often tell a secure page from an unsecured page by looking in the browser status bar for a small lock icon. When you are on the PayPal web site (https://www.paypal.com), the lock icon is "closed" virtually all the time (see Figure 11-8). The https prefix in the site's URL indicates the site uses Secure HyperText Transfer Protocol (HTTPS).

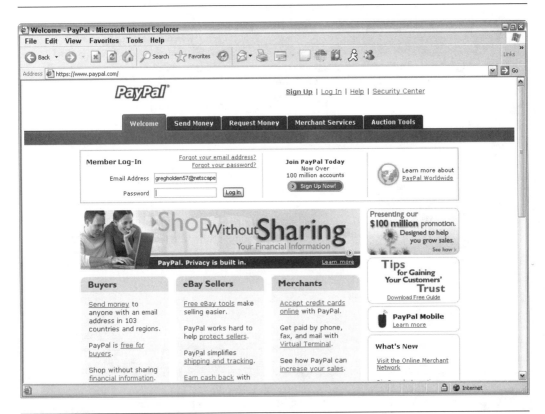

FIGURE 11-8   Shoppers want to see they are on a secure site when they submit payment information.

Most of the secure sites on the Web use SSL. *SSL* prevents hacking of transmissions of sensitive data, such as credit card numbers. It also deters hacking of your site to alter data or gain access to files. The SSL protocol (a widely agreed-upon set of instructions) for data transmission uses a security method called public-private key encryption. *Encryption* is the process of encoding information as it is transferred from one computer to another over the Internet. The sending computer encodes the message and the receiving computer then decodes it.

TIP   *Arrange your site so customers can complete purchases in the fewest clicks possible. Every page on your site should let people view their shopping cart, move to another part of your catalog, or get more information about the buying process.*

Taking Steps to Protect Sensitive Customer Information

If you use PayPal as your payment service, you don't handle customer credit card information directly. If you use a secure server provided by another web-hosting service, or if you obtain a traditional merchant account from a bank or other financial institution, you have to take steps to protect credit card numbers and other critical information. These best practices are good to remember in any case, even if you are "managing" customers' names, addresses, and phone numbers. Here are a few suggestions to remember:

11

- Consider paying outside services for credit card verification. Companies such as Cardservice International, CyberSource (http://www.cybersource .com), or Digital Courier Technologies, Inc. (http://www.dcti.com) verify the credit card data you receive is accurate. Such services might add as much as 22 cents to every transaction.

- Either you or your credit card service should verify the shipping address you receive with an order matches the billing address associated with the card number. If the billing address is in Illinois and the shipping address is in Romania, for instance, you have reason to be suspicious.

- If your web site includes payment forms where you request credit card numbers (something you won't have to do if you use PayPal), ask the customer to submit the four-digit number above the credit card number (if they use American Express) or the three-digit number on the back (if they use Visa, MasterCard, or Discover), as well as the number and expiration date. Only a legitimate customer with the actual card on hand is likely to have the four-digit number.

■ Ask for the three-digit card verification value (CVV) above the signature panel on the back of the card. If you check the CVV, you can substantially reduce fraud.

■ If you are concerned that leaving customer information being stored on Microsoft's computers is potentially insecure, make sure your customer data is held on a computer that is not connected to the Internet, so hackers can't get it. Remove credit card numbers or other customer information you receive from any of your computers connected to the Net.

That last practice is one of the simplest to carry out and also one of the most effective. If customer data is contained on a secure computer protected by passwords, such as Office Live, you provide an even higher level of protection. Use Office Live's Customer Manager to keep your data online, where only you and your coworkers can access it.

Making Your Office Live Site PayPal-Friendly

PayPal is best known as an electronic payment service owned by eBay and used to complete transactions that take place in that marketplace. But, PayPal can be used with any transaction is conducted online. The buyer and seller only need to meet a few conditions:

■ Both parties need to be members of PayPal.

■ The buyer needs to have their PayPal account associated with a checking or credit card account from which payment is drawn.

■ The seller needs to have a PayPal seller's account. The revenue collected from buyers goes into the seller's PayPal account, and PayPal charges the seller a fee.

The seller needs to tell buyers that PayPal is an authorized payment method. This can be done textually, but it can also be done with a Buy button that causes the purchase amount to be transferred to the seller.

PayPal isn't universally liked by all online merchants. They object to the fees it charges, and when online merchants run into a problem with a transaction, they sometimes voice complaints that PayPal is slow to respond. But, for the majority of auction sellers and other online merchants who use the service, PayPal is a trusted service. Even more important, PayPal is trusted and well-known by shoppers, many of whom rely on it as a first choice for transmitting online payments, over sending checks through the mail. PayPal gives customers a way to pay merchants with their credit cards This alleviates the need for you to apply for a merchant account, and then purchase hardware, such as a Point of Sale (POS) terminal, to process credit card transactions.

Setting Up a PayPal Account

Establishing yourself as a PayPal seller is straightforward. You have several options to consider, though. If you are primarily concerned with sending payments through PayPal and also want to accept payments through eBay or your web site, sign up for a Premier or Business account. If you only want to sell through your web site, skip ahead to the sectionson Web Site Payments Standard or Web Site Payments Pro. To get started, go to the site's home page, and click Sign Up Now!

The first decision you need to make when you sign up is to choose the type of account you want to establish. Personal Accounts are mainly for buyers; they limit the number of credit card payments you can receive. Business Accounts are for large, well-established businesses. I suggest you choose the Premier Account option, which enables you to accept payments from eBay or other merchant web sites. After you make this choice, click Continue, and then provide your personal information as requested in subsequent screens.

I highly recommend you obtain a PayPal debit card to go with your accounts. When you receive payments through PayPal, the money goes into your PayPal account. To get access to it, you either need to transfer it to a checking account yourself, or use your debit card. The debit card option is simple, convenient, and works at all Automatic Teller Machines (ATMs), just like bank debit cards.

11

Monitoring Payments

One of the convenient features provided by PayPal is maintenance of your online payment records. You shouldn't depend on PayPal for this, of course. You should use Microsoft Office Accounting or an Office Live application, such as Sales Manager, to keep records or what you sell, how much it sells for, and who buys it. But, if you need to refer to records, they are kept online as part of your account. Once you obtain an account and log in to the site, you see an overview of your recent transactions in the My Account tab (see Figure 11-9).

If you want to go further back in time, PayPal lets you view up to three months of monthly account statements. Click the History tab and specify the number of sales you want to review. The records come up and you can see which ones were paid, and how much of a fee PayPal deducted each time (see Figure 11-10).

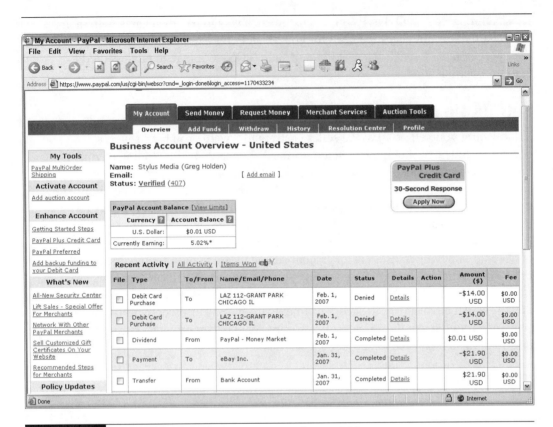

FIGURE 11-9   PayPal lets you view recent transactions quickly.

PayPal isn't your only option when it comes to accepting payments through your web site. Western Union auction payments gives you a different option: buyers pay with a credit card or a debit from their checking account, and Western Union sends a paper money order to the seller by snail mail. Find out more at http://www.bidpay.com.

Adding Extra Information to Support Your Sales

The other areas of your Office Live site, such as the About Us, Site Map, and Contact Us pages, along with other pages you create, promote the trust and incentives online shoppers need to make purchases from you. Presenting your product catalog is your first priority, but talking about yourself is also a good thing.

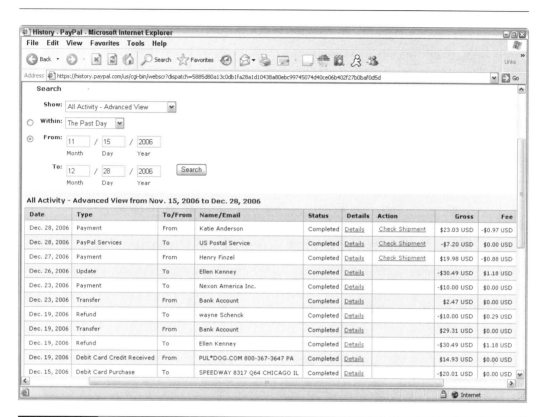

FIGURE 11-10   PayPal keeps a record of recent payments for the past three months.

Use the rest of your Office Live web space to provide essential supplemental information that can boost your sales volume.

Greeting Your Visitors

In most traditional retail stores, someone greets you the moment you come through the door. The "greeter" asks if you need help and directs you to the items you're looking for. You feel, at the least, that the store's employees are paying attention to you and that they'll be available if you need help.

You can't personally greet each customer on a web site, so how do you make the customer feel welcome? One way is to create a look and feel for your site through graphics and personalized content.

11

Another option is to craft a short, personal greeting on your home page to welcome your customers and to invite them to shop with you. Use your standard Office Live About Us page that describes who you are, why you started your online business, and what your goals are for helping your shoppers. Any content that creates a one-to-one relationship with your visitors and makes them feel catered to can set you apart from your competition and encourage customers to further explore your store.

 *You don't have to stick with the standard About Us page name. You might rename this page to About Our Company if you are more comfortable with that. Or, even consider a title such as Our Pledge of Trust or Our Mission, which makes your commitment to customer satisfaction even clearer.*

Describing What Makes You Special or Unique

Online shoppers want to feel they can get some sort of advantage by shopping on your site. Ideally, they can obtain something from you they can't find anywhere else because you made it yourself or it's a hard-to-find item.

 *You'll increase interest in your products if you talk about discounts you offer on the Web or special promotions for return customers. Those are the kinds of things that keep customers returning to your site in the future.*

Building Trust in You as a Seller

Web surfers who are new to shopping online need reassurance that they are doing the right thing. They want you to provide evidence that your products are of good quality and they're getting a good buy. Reassure them by including testimonials from satisfied customers, and even by providing excerpts of product reviews if they're available. Free shipping and money-back, no-hassle return policies also help.

 *The barrier to e-commerce for many prospective shoppers is security. The idea of transmitting credit card or other sensitive information over a worldwide network still keeps many folks from shopping online. Include a Privacy Policy or other statement telling customers you will not sell their personal information and you will take every measure to protect such information.*

How to Do It

Learn how to design an online sales catalog	Consult online publications, such as *CIO WebBusiness Magazine*, and articles such as "Designing Principles," http://www.cio.com/archive/webbusiness/100198_power.html
Take photos for product listings	Buy a digital camera with a macro function and use multiple lights to reduce shadows. The same principles apply for eBay sales photos. See the page at http://cameras.about.com/od/cameratips/ht/auctiontips.htm for more
Obtain a PayPal sellers' account	Go to the PayPal home page (https://www.paypal.com), click Sign Up Now, and then click Sign Now under Premier Account, which is best for beginning sellers. Follow the Create an Account form, which appears on the next page
Add a PayPal Buy Now button to your page	Log in to PayPal, go to the Buy Now Buttons page (https://www.paypal.com/us/cgi-bin/webscr?cmd=xpt/xclick/request/SingleitemIntro), click Get Started, fill out the form to describe your sales item, copy the HTML code provided, and then paste it into the HTML code for your web page
Protect your customers' security, as well as your own	Use good passwords, pay an outside service for credit-card verification, and consider storing especially sensitive data offline

11

Chapter 12

Managing Documents and Sales Collateral

How to...

- Work with the Document Manager

- Create a Document Library

- Establish a Picture Library

- Configure Alerts and Send Library Items

- Use the Sales Collateral Manager

When I worked in a publications office, much of our physical space was consumed by paper. We had an entire room set aside for our archives. Another area held photos, and yet another held file cabinets full of personal and financial records. My coworkers and I spent a considerable amount of time shuffling through files looking for printed documents, photos, forms, and other items we needed to do our work.

Other chapters in this book focus on Office Live's tools for facilitating communication and collaboration in a workgroup setting. In this chapter, you learn how Office Live Premium can help you with document storage and management. You learn how those piles and files full of paper can be stored online, so you can search and find them more easily. You also discover how to share photos and other collateral materials that can be instrumental to your sales activities.

Managing Documents

Office Live gives you several individual tools for managing items that fall under the catch-all term *documents*—any electronic files you work with in your office environment and that more than one person might need to access. Examples include word-processing documents, spreadsheets, images, Portable Document Format (PDF) files, and anything else you need. The following describes the primary tool for working with shared files, the Document Manager.

Working with Document Manager

The capability to store and share documents is an integral part of many different applications in Office Live. And, whenever you create a business application or a workspace for a specific task, you can create a document library for it. The most obvious place to upload and access shared files is the business application called *Document Manager.* But you can find other, similar document-management applications in several other areas within your Office Live site:

- **Document Manager**   Turn to the Document Library in Document Manager for general storage and management of files related to your organization (when those files don't fall into a specific category, such as photos, contact information, customer inquiries, and the like).

- **Business Contact Manager (BCM)**   The Business Documents area is a document library intended for client background and contact information.

- **Customer Support**   This business application, found under the heading Sales, has a feature called Knowledge Base. Use this for information related to customer inquiries.

- **Team Workspace**   If you establish an area for a team project, you can upload and share documents here that are related to that project.

It's worth knowing where all these document storage spaces are, so you don't duplicate files or so you or your coworkers don't have a hard time finding what you need. This is exactly the problem the Document Manager application was intended to alleviate.

> TIP   *When you set up Office Live for your small office, consider issuing a brief explanation to your coworkers of all the various document storage options within Office Live. Tell them to put general business files in the Document Manager's Document Library, customer-related documents in the Business Contact Manager's Document Library, and so on. Or, direct them to the page titled Upload a document to an Office Live document library or workspace at http://office.microsoft.com/en-us/officelive/ FX101997231033.aspx.*

The previous list of document-management workspaces is abstract. You're probably wondering exactly what files can go in each space. Table 12-1 lists some suggestions.

Managing Shared Files with the Document Library

The Document Library within the Document Manager business application is the first location of choice for a place where you can collaborate on, share, store, and monitor the versions of your organization's documents in a central location. You or other users who have Editor or Administrator permissions can upload or

Location	Document Library Name	What to Store There
Document Manager	Document Library	Personnel Manuals, Requisition forms, policies and procedures manuals, human resources files
Business Contact Manager	Business Documents	Client lists, contact information, supplier and partner information
Customer Support application (within the Sales category)	Knowledge Base	An order request from a customer, a complaint, or an inquiry
Team Workspace (within the Workspaces category)	Shared Documents	Schedules, list of team members and duties, or progress reports

TABLE 12-1 Document Library Functions Within Office Live

download documents to or from their individual workstations to the Document Library. In this sense, the Document Library can function much like a central file server. Workgroup members can then open files and work on them individually or contribute separately, and, thus, update the file in a collaborative fashion. By using each library's check-in and check-out features, they can avoid overwriting each other's work.

Getting Started with the Dashboard

The place to start with a Document Library is with the Dashboard. As it does with other parts of Office Live, the *Dashboard* gives you an overview of a Document Library's contents. You can add a library to the dashboard after you create it, so you and your coworkers can access it quickly. You can also call attention to your most important files. To get started with the Dashboard, follow these steps:

1. Log in to Office Live, and Click Business Applications in the set of links on the left-hand side of the page.

2. Click Document Manager.

When the Document Manager opens, the Dashboard is in front (see Figure 12-1).

TIP *Or, you can also log in to Office Live and go to the URL https:// [mydomain].officelive.com/documents to access your Document Manager space. Remember, if your domain ends in .net or.org, that needs to be part of [mydomain], as in https://hosieryfinderorg.officelive.com/documents.*

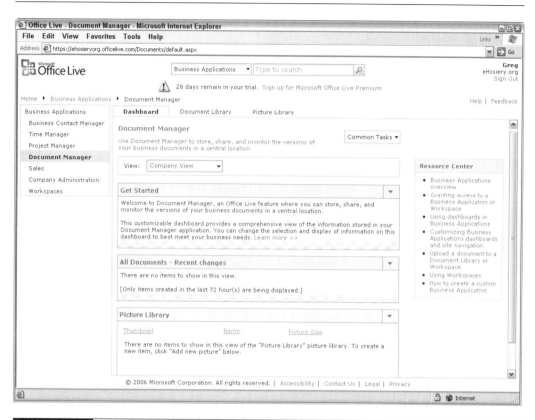

FIGURE 12-1   The Dashboard gives you an overview of your document libraries and the files within them.

Adding Users and Setting Permissions

As with any workspace or application in Office Live, you need to identify the individuals who will have access and define the level of access for each one. The process is much the same as that for other parts of Office Live: you identify the users and assign a permissions level to each one. You do this by:

1. Clicking Administration on the left-hand side of the Office Live window.

2. When the Administration page appears, click Users & Permissions.

3. Choose Document Manager from the View drop-down list. If this is the first time you are assigning permissions to this workspace, you see yourself listed as the only user, as shown in Figure 12-2.

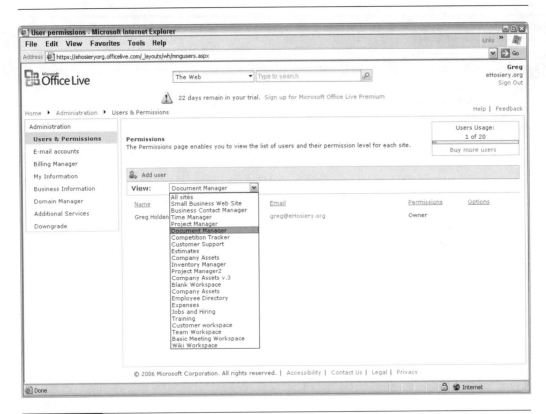

FIGURE 12-2   Use this screen to grant access to your Document Library.

4. Click the inconspicuous Add User link, just above the View link.

5. When the Add User—Web Page Dialog screen appears, enter the user's e-mail address and the screen name they usually use to identify themselves on Office Live or on your company network.

NOTE   *If you try to add a user's e-mail address that does not already exist on Office Live, you see a warning box telling you this. You need to give the user access to Office Live before you give them access to your Document Library or other workspace. You can, however, add a user from another Office Live domain. For instance, if you are giving someone access to the Document Library at www.myofficelivedomain1.com, that person can be a registered user at www.myofficelivedomain2.com.*

6. Click Next.

7. Choose the appropriate level of permissions (Editor, Reader, Administrator) from the drop-down list next to Document Manager, as shown in Figure 12-3.

8. Click Next.

9. In the next screen, compose an e-mail invitation to the user, and then click Send.

10. When the Summary screen appears, click Finish.

When you finish, the Administration screen refreshes and the new user is added to the list of approved individuals.

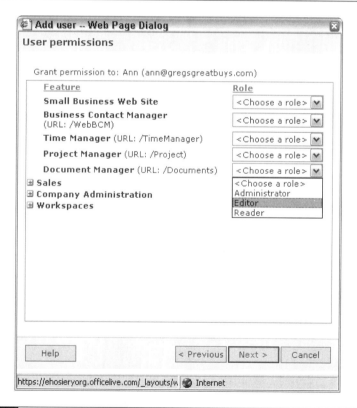

12

FIGURE 12-3   Choose the access level for each user in this screen.

 *You cannot grant users permission while you are in Document Manager or another business application. You can only do so from your home page. Click the Home link at the upper left-hand corner of the Office Live window you are currently viewing to return there if you need to.*

Adding Documents to Your Library

The process of adding items to a document library is similar from one library to another. If you are working with the Knowledge Base in the Customer Support application, for instance, click the New down arrow, and then choose the Knowledge Base Article option. If you are working in the Document Manager, click New and either choose New Document or New Folder from the drop-down menu (see Figure 12-4).

As you can see from the preceding image, the New Document option has a Microsoft Word document icon next to it. The implication is you are going to add a Word file to the Document Library. When you choose New Document, a Word file opens, in which you can type and add to the library. Be aware, though, you aren't

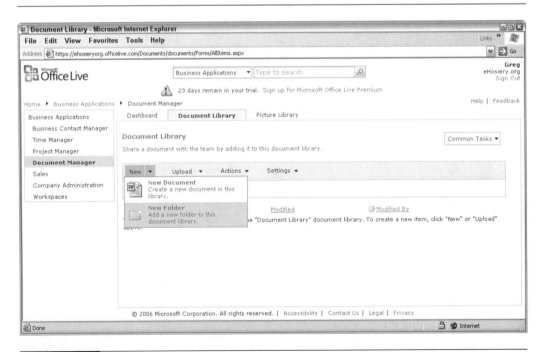

FIGURE 12-4   Choose New to add a new item or folder to the library.

limited to Word files: you can upload images, scanned files, and layouts, as well reduce the paper used by your office.

You can also upload a file from your file system to your Document Library. Click the Upload down arrow, and then choose Upload Document or Upload Multiple Documents. When the Upload Document page appears, click Browse, locate the file you want to upload, and then locate the file in the Open dialog box. Next, click OK to add the file to your document library.

 *If you aren't currently registered as a user who has Administrator or Editor access to the Document Library, you won't be able to upload a new document. You see a Word document stating you do not have access. You need to add yourself as a user to the library or upgrade your permissions.*

Before you add documents, however, you need some organization. You can create folders into which you can organize the files. When you choose New Folder from the New menu, Office Live presents you with the New Folder: Document Library screen. Type a name for the folder in the Name box shown in Figure 12-5, and then click OK.

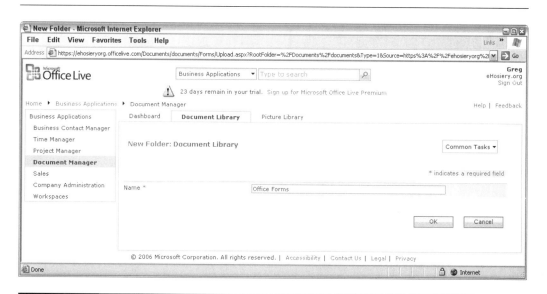

FIGURE 12-5   Creating folders helps you organize a library's contents.

Organizing Your Library

The web-based Document Library interface is cumbersome when it comes to organizing files. If you need to move a group of files all at once, or if you want to move files into or out of a folder, you should open a Windows Explorer window. Click the down arrow next to Actions, and then choose Open with Windows Explorer from the menu that appears. A Windows Explorer window opens with the contents of your library (see Figure 12-6). Notice your document library appears in the Folders pane of Windows Explorer, under the Web Folders heading.

Once you have a Windows Explorer window open, you gain the capability to move files from your file system to a Document Library on Office Live by dragging-and-dropping them. Just display the Windows Explorer toolbar and drag the files from a folder on your computer (or on your network) into the library.

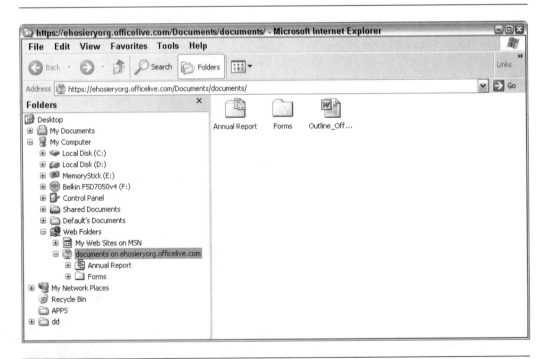

FIGURE 12-6   Use Windows Explorer to organize and move files and folders.

 *You need to be working online (that is connected to the Internet) to open your document library in Windows Explorer and work with it.*

Removing Items from the Library

The Windows Explorer method mentioned in the preceding section works well when you want to add or remove files. Once you have the familiar Windows Explorer interface open, you can select a file or folder, and then choose Delete from Windows Explorer's File menu to remove the object.

Or, you can pass your mouse arrow over the object listed in Office Live to display the down arrow to the right of its name. You can then click the down arrow and choose Delete from the drop-down menu that appears (see Figure 12-7).

Configuring Alerts

You can configure Document Manager to send you alerts when the contents of the library change. Click the down arrow next to the file's name and choose Alert me from the drop-down menu. When the New Alert window appears, choose a name for your alert (be sure to select a name that makes it clear what library was affected), and then enter it. Then, enter a name for the recipient of the alert in the User's box (see Figure 12-8).

12

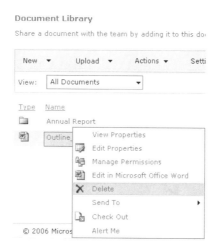

FIGURE 12-7   Click the down arrow next to an item's name to perform actions on it.

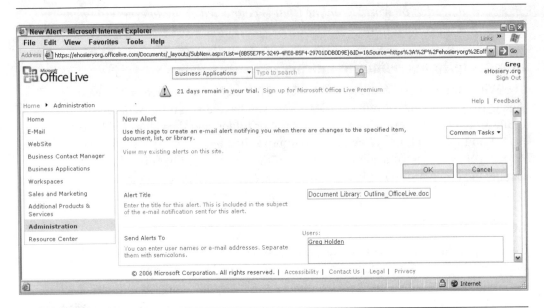

FIGURE 12-8 You can send an alert when the contents of a library change.

Retrieving Files from the Library

This is also known as *downloading*. Once a file is added to a library, you access it by following these steps:

1. Pass your mouse arrow over the file's name.

2. Choose Send to.

3. Pass your mouse to the right and choose Download a Copy from the submenu that appears to the right of Send to.

When you choose Download a Copy, the File Download dialog box appears. Click Open if you want to open a temporary version of the file immediately in Microsoft Word. Click Save if you want to save a copy in a specific location on your file system.

TIP *You can also mail a link to the file by choosing Email a Link from the Send to submenu.*

Checking Library Items In and Out

When you have a library full of documents that can be accessed by multiple users, you don't want two users to access the same file at the same time, with the result that one overwrites the other. To prevent this, you need to check the file out before you start working with it.

Checking out the file is slightly different than downloading it: you pass the mouse arrow over the file's name, click the down arrow to the right of the name, and then choose Check Out. When you do so, a green arrow appears next to the file icon. When another member of your workgroup passes their mouse arrow over the icon, the "checked out" message, shown in Figure 12-9, appears.

Creating a Picture Library

Microsoft calls this shared library a "picture gallery" rather than a "photo gallery" for a reason. A *picture library* is a place where you can store much more than photos. Every company has logos, letterheads, business cards, diagrams, and many other files with a graphics component. By storing such files online, everyone can get access to them. In some organizations, only certain individuals are given access to specific files such as electronic layouts or photos.

Nothing is wrong with designers being the only ones who can change the design of a logo or other image file that contributes to your graphic identity. But, if you need to print a set of business cards in a small quantity for a temporary employee, or a letterhead with a special phone number, there's no reason to submit such requests to your designer, who is busy with more important design work. And, you certainly don't want to have to go to the printer and pay for a print job every time you need a document. Others in your organization can make the changes, provided they have the software in which the file was created.

If your business letterhead is formatted in an application everyone is likely to have, such as Microsoft Word, they can print files on demand. My own business

12

FIGURE 12-9   This message lets other users know they shouldn't open a file.

cards are arranged in the Word file shown in Figure 12-10. Business cards stored in a picture library can be easily customized.

For other documents with more complex design requirements, such as brochures, your graphic designer is the one who should work on them. But, when the design is already completed and the edits you need to make are only typographical, such as business cards, another staff person can be trained in the appropriate design program, such as Quark XPress or Adobe Photoshop, and can make the changes. The point is this: by distributing files via the central repository provided by Office Live, you distribute the work load to save both time and money. Time is saved because more than one person can access and work with files. Money is saved because, for simple editing tasks, you don't always have to send files to the printer.

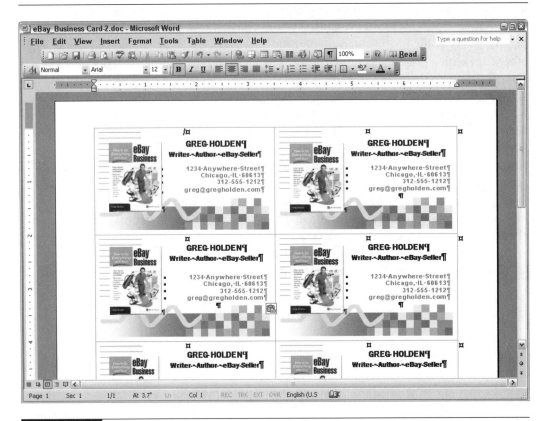

FIGURE 12-10   You can store business files online, so others can print and edit them.

Uploading and Downloading Image Files

To add a file to your Picture Library, click the Picture Library tab to bring it to the front. Then, click Upload and choose either Upload Picture or Upload Multiple Pictures from the menu that appears. When the Add Picture: Picture Library page appears, click Browse. Locate the file on your file system, and then click Open. The Add Picture page reappears with the path to the file entered in the Name box. Click OK to upload the image.

When your images are uploaded, they appear as thumbnails, not only in the Picture Library to which you added them, but also on your Dashboard. The Picture Library thumbnails are shown in Figure 12-11.

The advantage of adding pictures as thumbnails is that, if you want to copy one to your computer, you click it. The thumbnail then appears as a full-size image. A toolbar along the top of the image presents you with five options:

- ■ **Edit Item**   This is potentially misleading. You don't edit the image itself, but you add or change information about it, such as the title and the date it was taken.

- ■ **Delete Item**   This removes the picture from the library.

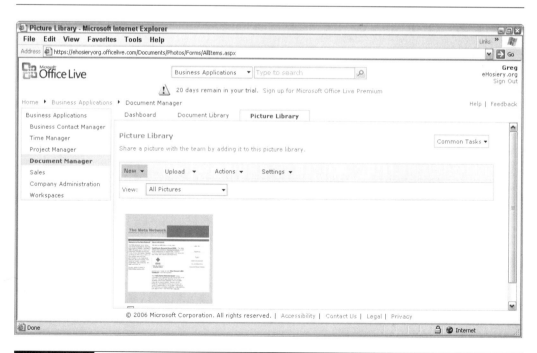

FIGURE 12-11   Pictures stored in a library are shown as thumbnails.

■ **Manage Copies**   This lets you create a copy of the image. If you edit the image and upload it to the library, click Update Copies to refresh the images, so they are identical to the new one.

■ **Check Out**   This adds the green "checked out" arrow to the picture's icon, so others know you are using it.

■ **Alert Me**   This lets you send an alert message to yourself or a coworker when someone changes the contents of the Picture Library.

The Description field that appears when you click Edit Item enables you to provide your workgroup with background information about the picture: when it was created, when it should be used, who added it to the library, and so on.

Performing Additional Actions

The Actions menu in the Picture Library gives you a way to view and work with your stored images. The View Slide Show option lets you "flip" through image files, one after another, in succession in a new window. This window includes play, pause, stop, and other controls (see Figure 12-12).

Other Actions menu options include:

■ **Edit**   This lets you edit the image in an image-editing program.

■ **Download**   This copies the image to your computer.

■ **Send to**   This is the same as the Send to option in the Document Library. It lets you send the file to a coworker.

■ **Open with Windows Explorer**   This lets you drag-and-drop images from your computer or your network directly into the Picture Library.

Be sure to check the inconspicuous check box just beneath a thumbnail version of an image in Picture Library before you perform an action on it. Otherwise, Office Live won't know which image you want to edit or move.

Working with Sales Collateral

Up to this point, the selections have addressed sharing internal documents that can help your office work efficiently. But, you can also store materials in the document

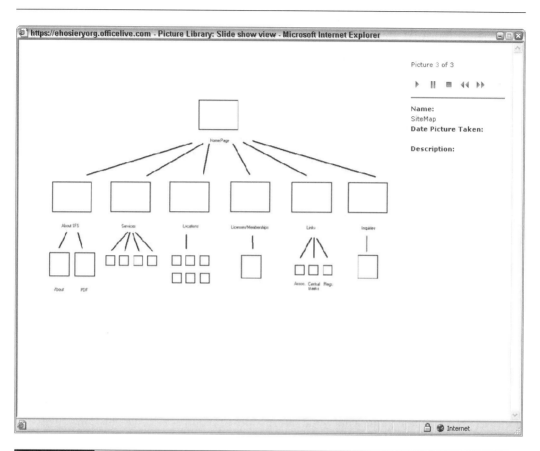

FIGURE 12-12   You can view all your images in a slide-show format.

libraries to support your sales efforts. Some of these files can be for your workgroup members, while others can be for external users, such as your customers.

Creating a Price Sheet

A web-based sales catalog typically presents one sales item at a time. A price sheet can give your vendors and salespeople alike a place where they can get a complete picture of all your products, as well as their current prices. Your own sales catalog might serve the same purpose: it gives you a way to do *upselling*, which is letting shoppers know about other items in which they might be interested.

Of course, most customers won't be able to access your product list in a Document Library. If you want the general public to see your product list, posting it on your web site is better. A price list uploaded to a document library can only be accessed by your wholesale customers or vendors who need access to such internal information.

Producing a Brochure

Near the end of a sales call, it can be helpful to refer a customer to a brochure for more information. Many individuals are more comfortable with reading on their own, rather than taking notes over the phone. Brochures don't have to be printed on paper, of course. You *can* have a printed brochure, but if you want to convert it to electronic format while preserving the layout, you need to convert it to Adobe's Portable Document Format (PDF).

One of the most common applications for converting files from one electronic layout format, such as Adobe Photoshop or PageMaker, to PDF is called Cute PDF (www.cutepdf.com).

Spec Sheets and Fact Sheets

Another type of sales document you can make available to your sales staff and business partners through a document library is a *spec sheet,* which is a file containing physical dimensions, special features, and technical advantages that apply to your products. You want your salespeople to emphasize the right "talking points" that apply to your products. You want them to be able to answer questions immediately. They can download the current spec sheet in a minute or two and have the answers right at hand.

I recently accessed a spec sheet on the web site of one of my personal favorite manufacturers, the Hadley Pottery Company. A spec sheet (an example is shown in Figure 12-13) let me know the sizes of the cup I was interested in, but told me about other pottery in the same pattern that I might also want.

The type of spec sheet information you include in a document library can be far more extensive than what you publish on your web site. You can post brief features or specs online, and then give Office Live users additional "inside information."

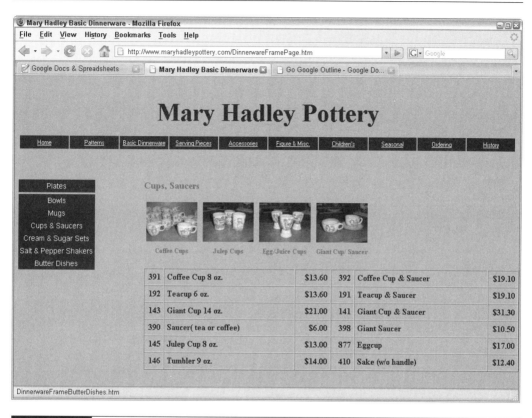

FIGURE 12-13 A spec sheet gives employees and customers an overview of your product line.

How to Do It

Learn how to work with Office Live document libraries	Go to http://office.microsoft.com/en us/officelive/ FX101997231033.aspx
Add users and assign permissions for accessing a library space	Click Administration, click Users & Permissions, choose Document Manager, click Add User, and then enter the information
Add documents to a library	Click New to add a new file, and then click Upload to locate a file on your file system or local network
Adding folders and using drag-and-drop to manage library contents	Click Actions and choose Open with Windows Explorer
Send yourself an alert when the contents of a library change	Pass your mouse arrow over a file's name, click the down arrow, and choose Alert Me. Then enter your own name as the recipient

Chapter 13

Running an eBay Business with Office Live

How to...

- Create a web page for your auction business with Office Live
- Create eBay auctions with Office Accounting 2007
- Configure a Microsoft-hosted eBay Store
- Make dynamic links to your current auctions
- Provide a page full of Frequently Asked Questions
- Record customer contacts with Office Live business applications

"Synergy" is one of those dramatic-sounding words frequently tossed around by people who write about e-commerce. In terms of doing business on the Web, *synergy* simply means making different approaches or business "channels" work in unison toward the same goal. When it comes to online business channels, eBay and Office Live are two of the big players. eBay gives individuals and businesses alike, a way to connect with customers. Office Live gives them a business presence and enables employees to collaborate. If you can bring the two together for your business, you can dramatically increase your potential customer base.

In this chapter, you learn how to make use of your Office Live account to sell your products on eBay. You discover how your Office Live web site tools can support an eBay business. You also explore an innovative new tool for selling on eBay: Office Accounting 2007. And, you learn how to take full advantage of Office Live business applications, which can help you keep better records and track inventory more efficiently—and that can help you be a more efficient eBay seller.

Creating Auction Web Pages with Office Live

In previous chapters, you examined the process of creating a full-fledged business web site with Microsoft Office Live. In particular, you learned that Office Live comes with a wide variety of web site templates that can solve many different business needs. These days, eBay is one of the best places to run an online business. One of the advantages of selling on eBay is you don't specifically need a web site to connect with customers and sell your products.

NOTE
To follow along with the next sections, you need to have an eBay seller's account. Even if you already have an account that lets you bid and buy items offered for auction on eBay, you also need to apply for a seller's account. Go to eBay's home page (http://www.ebay.com), click Sign in, and then sign in with your existing password if you have one. In either case, next click Create a Seller's Account and follow the steps in subsequent screens.

None of the Office Live business templates specifically addresses eBay auction sales, however. A web site for an eBay business may not be absolutely necessary, but it can help you in a number of ways:

- **Product sales**   You can offer products for sale on your Office Live site that supplements what you sell on eBay by giving you another venue where you can advertise yourself and your wares. If you can sell them on your site, you don't have to pay eBay's listing and sales fees.

- **Contact**   A contact page can give customers a way to get in touch with you outside of eBay's communications system.

- **Background**   You can describe your qualifications for sales and build trust in your customers, which is an essential part of developing a sales program on eBay.

The following sections guide you through the process of setting up an eBay-specific web site using Office Live's hosting and design tools.

13

NOTE
Microsoft Office Accounting Express 2007 is a separate program from Office Live. The only real connection between the program and the web service is this: Office Accounting Express is liberally advertised on Office Live, and Microsoft advertises it as a tool that small business owners can use with e-commerce businesses hosted on Office Live or other sites.

Choosing an Auction-Friendly Design

You already know it's easy to create web pages and weave them into a web site using Microsoft Office Live. Is there anything special about creating a site for an eBay business? If anything, you need to relax and have fun when you create your pages. eBay members are all about making personal connections. Personality and liveliness help hold members' attention.

When you're working with Site Designer, choose a lively design (the names are certainly lively enough, including Gecko and Champagne) from the Color drop-down menu shown in Figure 13-1. The six type-font options provided in the Fonts tab in Site Designer all seem restrained and businesslike. The businesslike part is good, but you also want some personality. (Times or Verdana seem a little more lively than the other choices.) The point is you want to create web pages that convey your personality and interests. Don't be afraid to go beyond the standard About Us, Contact Us, and Site Map pages, which create pages that talk about your experience in your field. You can also make links to your current auctions or to your eBay Store. (See the section "Including Essential Web Site Information for Your Shoppers.")

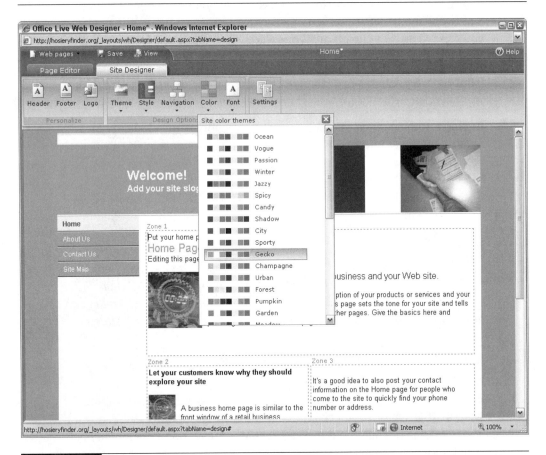

FIGURE 13-1   Site Designer presents you with lively and eye-catching sets of colors.

Listing Products for Sale

eBay enables its members to create retail outlets known as *eBay Stores,* which are sites where members offer fixed-price items for sale. But the marketplace charges a steep hosting fee: eBay Stores start at $15.95 per month. By listing your products or services online, you can boost your sales and save on eBay fees, too. Your web site won't be called an eBay Store, and you have to devise your own systems for accepting payments and completing transactions but, essentially, it serves the same purpose.

Choosing a Look and Feel for Your Catalog

There's no such thing as a "standard" look and feel for an eBay Store. The majority of eBay Stores don't show much design at all, in fact. You get a narrow banner with the name of the store, lots of product pages with as many as ten items per page, and an "About the Seller" page even though many sellers decide not to make use of it. Many eBay Stores don't have logos or photos of their owners, either. They use clip art and the pages focus on the products, rather than the merchants.

To my mind, then, you have a big head start over the competition the moment you start making links to your eBay Store from your site on Office Live. What exactly is an eBay Store? This term is a formal designation for a store set up within eBay itself, using its design tools. I'm talking about a web site on which you offer items for sale that supplement or support your eBay sales. It's up to you to market the site through your eBay About Me page or through invoices and business cards you send to your customers.

As you can see from my own eBay Store, shown in Figure 13-2, most store pages contain a standard set of links on the left, and a single, larger column that provides thumbnail photos and links to sales descriptions.

If you want to emulate this and make your store look like an eBay Store, you can do this easily with Site Designer. Click Layouts from the set of buttons at the top of the Site Designer window and choose the layout that divides a page into a single content web Zone (see Figure 13-3). You already have the default set of navigation buttons in the bar on the left side of the page, so this single area is enough.

You can also customize the layout that divides a web page into two or three columns. A two-column layout is good for presenting a variety of catalog listings in a compact space.

Creating Sales Descriptions

Once you create the general layout for your eBay Store pages, you need to create sales descriptions. In some cases, eBay items sell themselves, as long as you have

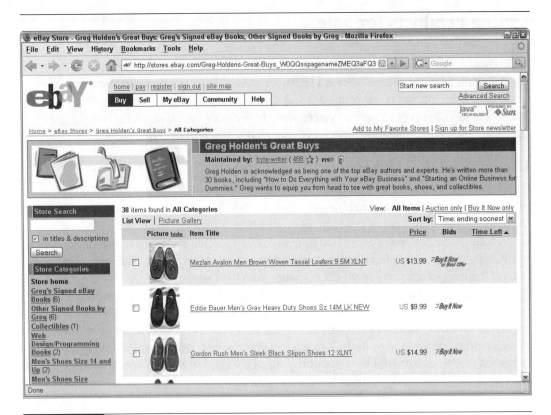

FIGURE 13-2 Most eBay Stores implement this standard layout.

good photos of them. These, though, tend to be rare or expensive objects. For widely available consumer goods offered by more than one seller, descriptions are critical. What makes a good eBay description? It needs to be:

- **Positive** Be sure to talk up the attributes of your items with enthusiasm.

- **Detailed** Include measurements, dimensions, sizes, brand numbers, and any other available pertinent data.

- **Result-oriented** Emphasize what the customer can do with the object, how it would look, how it would make the owner feel, and so on.

- **Backed up with photos** Take as many photos as you can from different angles.

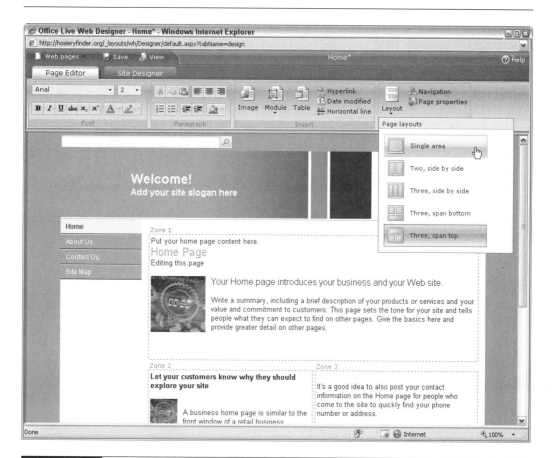

FIGURE 13-3   A single web content area is all you need to contain auction listings.

In my own descriptions (which tend to be a little heavy as far as verbiage), I also use some simple formatting instructions to add visual interest, and I single out names, sizes, and other attributes. An example is shown in Figure 13-4.

> **TIP**   *You can do two simple things to make your auction photos stand out from the crowd. First, use more than one light (preferably one with a halogen or a miniature fluorescent light, rather than an incandescent bulb) pointed at different angles to minimize shadows. (You can also take photos outdoors.) Second, use your digital camera's macro function to take sharp close-ups.*

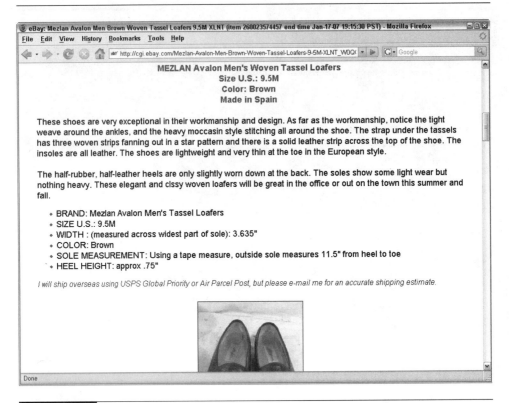

FIGURE 13-4   Simple lists and headings can make descriptions easier to read.

Providing a Purchase Path

Nothing is wrong with accepting checks or money orders from your eBay customers. In fact, all eBay shoppers should provide these payment options for people who are making purchases on eBay. *PayPal* is eBay's official payment service, however (it's owned by eBay, after all), so it also makes sense to sign up for a PayPal seller's account and add some PayPal "Buy" buttons to your pages. Find out more about accepting payments in Chapter 11.

 *You can't direct shoppers from your eBay auctions to your store by including your URL in your listings. You have to mention your business web site in your listings, but you can't make a link from an auction description to any web site outside of eBay. Mention your business name and create a simple About Me page on eBay that directs shoppers to your site.*

Listing on eBay with Office Accounting 2007

You have many ways to list products for sale on eBay without having to be logged in to eBay's web site. If you go through eBay, you use the Sell Your Item form, which is a user-friendly tool, to be sure. The problem is, this form only lets you create a single sales description at a time. The way to build a steady source of income on eBay is to put multiple items for sale each week—as many as 20, 30, or more, if you can. To speed things along, most regular eBay sellers either use special software to create listings or special auction services that give them a way to list on eBay.

> **TIP** *Turbo Lister is a free program I use myself to sell on eBay. You can download and install it at http://pages.ebay.com/turbo_lister/. The program requires storage space and periodic updates. Services, such as SpareDollar (http://www.sparedollar.com) or Vendio (http://www.vendio .com), let you list on eBay and provide other value-added services, but they charge a monthly subscription fee.*

Those special auction services charge a fee for their services. By using Microsoft's own Office Accounting Express 2007 free software package, you can list on eBay, handle accounting chores for your online business, and also connect with Office Live.

> **NOTE** *The following section describes one of two versions of the program— Office Accounting Express—the free version. The other version, Office Accounting Professional, requires you to purchase it. At press time, the price was yet to be determined. You may want to consider purchasing Professional, especially if you want to track your inventory. As you discover in the section "Creating Descriptions," you can only use Express to track "noninventory items."*

Creating an eBay Business with Office Accounting

The first good bit of news about Office Accounting 2007 is you can download and start using it—free. After using the program for 20 uses, you need to register the program, but even then, you don't have to pay for it!

The second good news item is Office Accounting 2007 streamlines the process of creating sales listings on eBay. If you already use Office Live to track your sales inventory, you can connect that inventory to your eBay sales.

13

To start, download the application from Microsoft's IdeaWins web site (http://www.ideawins.com). Once you install the program, you're given the option of registering and activating Office Accounting right away. I suggest you do so early on. You're required to follow through with this step after 20 uses.

Before you install Microsoft Office Accounting 2007, make sure you can meet the program's system requirements. You need 975MB of available hard disk storage space to install the program—that's nearly 1GB just for this single application. You also need to run Windows 2000 with Service Pack 3, Windows XP, or Windows Vista, as well as Microsoft .NET Framework 2.0.

Creating a New Company

Once you install Office Accounting Express 2007, the Start screen shown in Figure 13-5 appears, encouraging you to perform basic functions. Begin by clicking Set up a new Company.

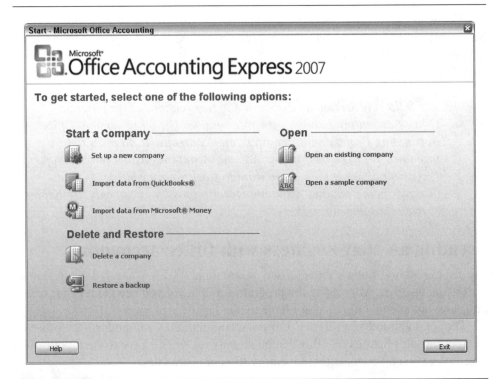

FIGURE 13-5 This initial screen lets you choose the first task you want Office Accounting to perform.

The Company and Preferences screen appears. Click Next. In the Add company details screen, shown in Figure 13-6, add your company's name and location. Follow the information solicited in subsequent screens.

Recording Your Sales Tax

As part of the setup process, you are asked to enter preferences regarding the sales tax you collect. The regulations regarding tax on Internet purchases have been a subject of debate for many years. At the present time, the Internet Tax Freedom Act precludes federal sales tax on interstate commerce conducted over the Net. However, merchants do have to collect sales tax from customers who live in the same state where they do business, as long as that state collects a sales tax.

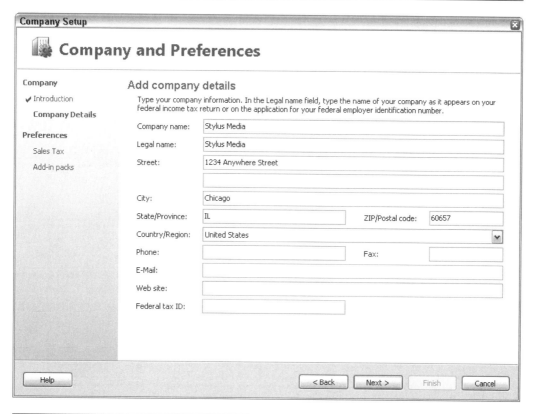

FIGURE 13-6   Fill in details about your company, so Office Accounting can help keep your financial records.

Six U.S. states do not collect sales tax: Alaska, Delaware, Hawaii, Montana, New Hampshire, and Oregon.

Personally, I find collecting sales tax and reporting it to the state a difficult process. Well, the collecting part isn't so difficult. Most of my customers pay through PayPal. When they pay, PayPal calculates the sales tax automatically and adds it to their invoice (see Figure 13-7 for an example).

The problem is not in collecting the sales tax from your customers. It occurs when you have to pay sales tax to your state. The Illinois Department of Revenue sends me a form once a month and I have to fill it out with information on any sales tax I collected in the previous month. Usually, this sends me into a frenzy, looking through copies of old invoices to find any that include sales tax. I find it

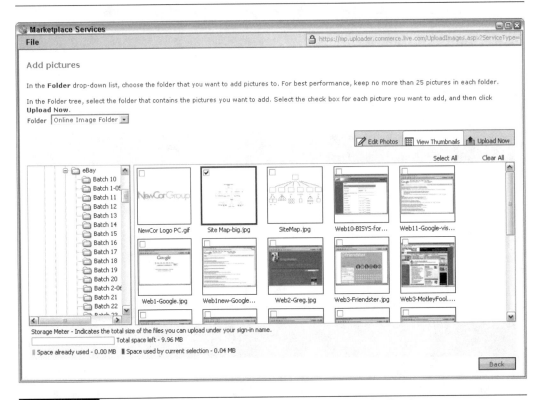

FIGURE 13-7   PayPal and eBay calculate sales tax from buyers who live in your state.

invaluable that Office Accounting keeps track of sales tax I collect, so I can report it easily at tax time. Fill out the form shown in Figure 13-8, which appears during the setup process, to enable this feature. When you finish, click Next to complete the rest of the setup process.

 *You can get your sales tax from your eBay or PayPal invoices. Otherwise, you can look it up at Wikipedia (en.wikipedia.org/wiki/Sales_taxes_in_ the_United_States).*

Configuring eBay Transactions

Once you set up sales tax recording, in the next screen, you select *add-in packs*—software packages that work with Office Accounting to perform specific functions. Be sure to select PayPal Payments. Because PayPal is owned by eBay, it's the system used by many eBay customers to submit electronic payments, so they can receive their articles quickly.

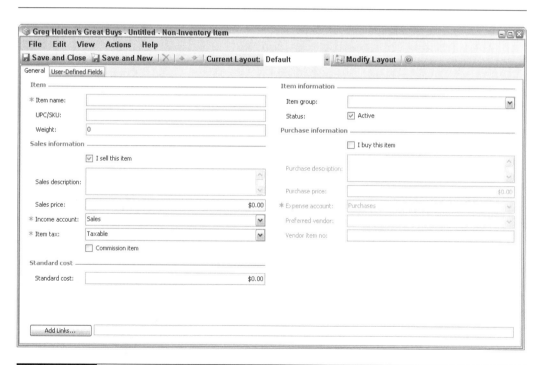

FIGURE 13-8   Complete this form to have Office Accounting record your sales tax revenue.

13

 *When the Select add-in packs screen appears, click Add. A dialog box appears, displaying a group of add-in packs that were installed on your computer, along with Office Accounting 2007. Some let you integrate PayPal payments with Microsoft Word.*

Click Finish to save your company profile on your computer. A dialog box appears to let you know the company data is being saved on your computer. When the main Office Accounting 2007 appears, click the Online Sales button in the row of buttons in the lower left-hand corner. The Start a Task screen appears (see Figure 13-9).

Click the Set Up to Sell Online button. The Marketplace Services window opens. This window contains a series of boxes that provide you with an overview of the process of listing items on eBay. Read the contents, and then click Next. You sign in with your Windows Live ID, which is the same ID you use to sign in to Office Live. The Select a marketplace service plan screen appears. As you read in this screen, you need to choose one of two options for Marketplace Services:

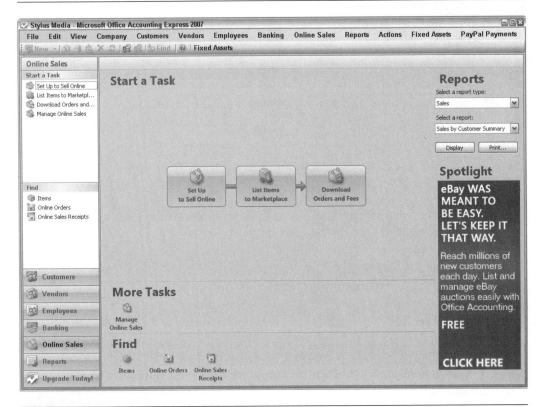

FIGURE 13-9   The Start a Task screen leads you graphically through the process of selling online.

■ **The free option, Marketplace Services Basic**   This option lets you create 20 free listings per month for a year. After a year, you are given the option to upgrade to the Marketplace Services Standard. The screen doesn't make clear whether you can continue with the Basic service, however.

■ **The fee-based option, Marketplace Services Standard**   For a fee of $9.95 per month, you are allowed to list 200 items per month. After 200 listings, you are charged five cents per listing.

For this example, leave the Basic option selected, and click Next. In the next screen, read the terms of service, click I Accept, and then click Next. In the next screen, you need to connect to eBay, and then click Sign Up. In the eBay Download Options screen, you are presented with boxes that summarize a new series of steps: the process of downloading items and processing transactions on eBay. Click Next twice to sign in to eBay. You have to click both Agree and Continue to an explicit warning about sharing your transaction information with Microsoft Corporation that certainly got my attention.

You are asked to manage which orders are to be downloaded from eBay to your computer. I decided to see how many listings would be downloaded, so I specified that all orders since I started selling on eBay should be retrieved. I wasn't sure exactly how many orders would be available. I discovered you can only download the previous three months' worth of orders. You get the capability to track individual customers, so you can offer them rewards or further sales, which builds loyalty. You are also able to track the fees you have to pay to eBay and PayPal without having to wait until you get a statement from eBay. (This process took more than an hour.)

Adding Photos

Office Accounting Express 2007, like Office Live, lets you save digital image files in a special photo repository. You then associate those images with descriptions you create. This book isn't going to delve into every possible detail about capturing photos for auctions or for Office Live web sites. However, a few general principles can help you, no matter how you plan to use your images online:

■ **Resolution**   The term "resolution" refers to the amount of digital information contained in an image file in the form of pixels—tiny rectangles that contain one or more bits of data. The higher the resolution of an image, the sharper it is, and the larger the image file. Smaller files appear more quickly on the Web. And, computer monitors can't display more than 72 dots per inch (Macintosh) or 96 dots per inch (Windows).

13

■ **Format**   Save your images in JPEG format. Remember, though, most digital cameras take JPEG images at very high resolutions such as 2,592 × 1,944, so you can print good-quality paper versions of those images, which you can frame. I capture my images as 640 × 480 TIFF files, and then convert them to JPEG format using my graphics program, Paint Shop Pro. This keeps the file size at 30K or less.

■ **Contrast and brightness**   Keep these two attributes high. Computer monitors aren't the highest-quality display medium around.

■ **Cropping**   Use your graphics program (Paint, Paint Shop Pro, Adobe Photoshop, or Photoshop Elements) to crop an image. *Cropping* is the process of deleting all unessential parts of an image, so only the most important contents appear. Cropping can dramatically reduce file size.

Once you have image files saved on your computer, you add them to Office Accounting Express's Pictures area by following these steps:

1. Choose Manage Online Sales from the Online Sales menu.

2. Log in with your Windows Live ID and password.

3. When the Marketplace Services window opens, click Pictures.

4. Click Add Pictures in the set of links on the left-hand side of the window.

5. The Add Pictures window appears, informing you that you must install the Office Live Image Uploader. Click Install.

6. When the File Download dialog box appears, click Run. When the Security Warning dialog box appears, click Run. Follow the steps shown on subsequent screens to install the uploader. When installation is complete, click Refresh.

7. The Add Pictures window opens and displays the contents of the folder on your local file system, which you identified as your default image folder when you created a web site with Office Live (see Chapter 3). Click one of the folders in the directory tree shown on the left-hand side of Add pictures and select the folder containing the images you want to upload for your eBay auctions.

8. Select the images and click Upload Now to add them to your Pictures folder.

You return to the Pictures window, where the images you uploaded are now displayed. You can then add these images when you fill out the Add Item form to create descriptions of them, as described in the next section.

Creating Descriptions

Next, you return to the Start a Task screen. In the links on the left, under the heading Find, click Item. At this point, you discover you can only create a "service" or "noninventory item" with Office Accounting 2007—you need Office Accounting Professional to create inventory and kit items. This is frustrating, because it means you can't track your inventory using Office Live. I clicked Non-Inventory Item, and then I clicked OK.

In the form that appears (see Figure 13-10), you enter the item name, a brief description, and whether you are selling or buying the item. This is not a sales description for eBay, but a financial description for your accounting records. Once you have the items recorded, you click List Items to Marketplace. Sign in, and select eBay as your marketplace. Any items you created are visible in the next screen, but they aren't ready to be listed. You need to add photos and a description.

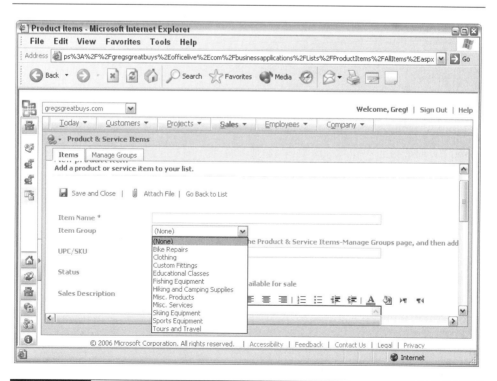

FIGURE 13-10   Create item descriptions using these fields.

This form is basically like eBay's Sell Your Item form, with two glaring exceptions: the capability to format your auction description or do spell-checking. This option may be buried somewhere in the program—or possibly it's available in the Professional version—but I didn't see it.

 *Click User-Defined Fields to set up fields that provide you with important information. For instance, you might create a field called Purchase Price that enables you to record what you paid for the item originally. This is not included in the default fields.*

Downloading Customer Orders

After someone orders an item from you, you can download those things from your Items I've Sold list in My eBay. (This is the page all eBay members receive, which tracks their activity on the site.) Click Download Orders under the heading Online Sales on the left side of the Office Accounting window. When you do this, the dialog box shown in Figure 13-11 appears, so you can track the progress of the download. This can take several minutes, depending on the number of orders you have.

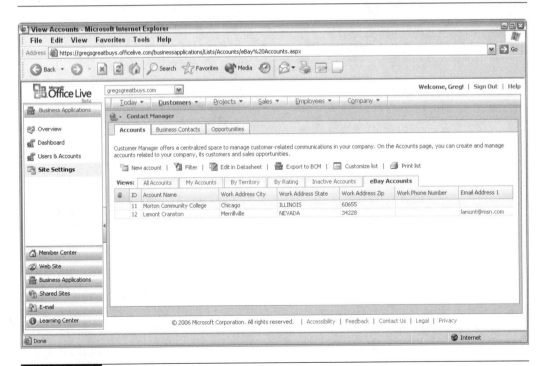

FIGURE 13-11   Office Accounting can download orders placed on eBay.

If the items being downloaded don't match ones you already created as Items in Microsoft Office Accounting, however, they are labeled as Unrecognized Items. You then either have to match them to already existing items or create a new item listing for each one individually—a potentially time-consuming process. Otherwise, the purchases won't be added to your eBay business's database in Office Accounting. In the dialog box shown in Figure 13-12 called Match Unrecognized Items, which appears after you have downloaded orders, click the down arrow across from an item's name and choose Add a new item from the drop-down list.

The steps required for Unrecognized items indicate Office Accounting isn't primarily equipped to track orders your customers placed in the past on eBay, which you listed with Turbo Lister, the Sell Your item form, or another non-Microsoft tool. This is intended to help you list items, create sales listings on eBay, and track orders once they are placed.

As you are recording data for each transaction, you might wonder why you should bother to do this when the same information is recorded in My eBay. The reason is this: My eBay only holds information for a maximum of 60 days. After that, it's gone. Recording it in Office Accounting lets you hold on to it as long as necessary.

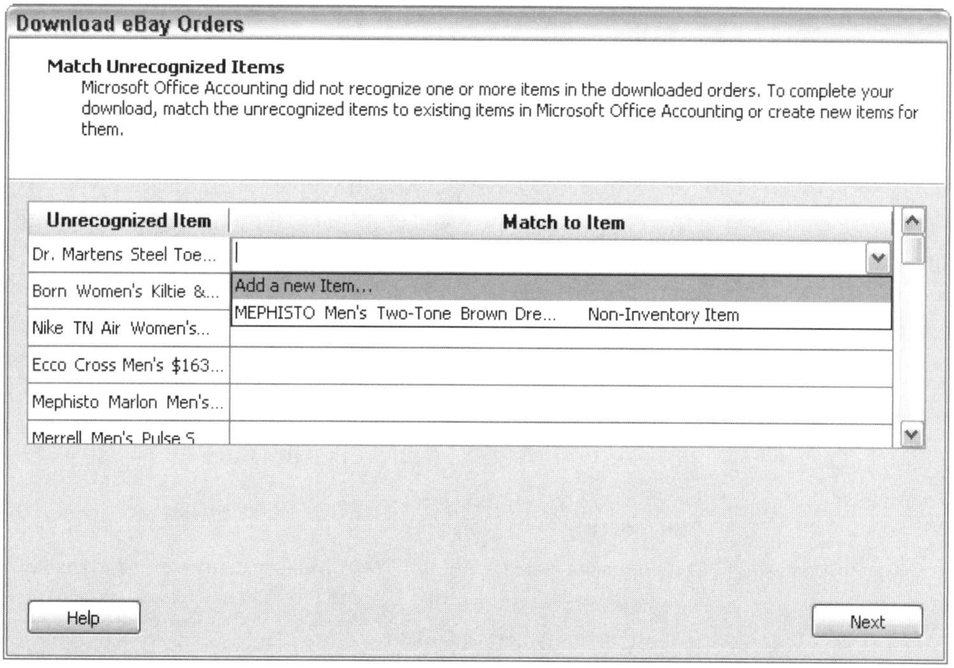

Download eBay Orders

Match Unrecognized Items
Microsoft Office Accounting did not recognize one or more items in the downloaded orders. To complete your download, match the unrecognized items to existing items in Microsoft Office Accounting or create new items for them.

Unrecognized Item	Match to Item
Dr. Martens Steel Toe...	
Born Women's Kiltie &...	Add a new Item...
Nike TN Air Women's...	MEPHISTO Men's Two-Tone Brown Dre... Non-Inventory Item
Ecco Cross Men's $163...	
Mephisto Marlon Men's...	
Merrell Men's Pulse S	

Help   Next

13

FIGURE 13-12   You may need to match sales items labeled as Unrecognized.

You also download tax data for your home state. You need to match that to the sales tax designation you created during the setup process. This information, too, takes a while to synchronize.

Applying Office Live Business Applications to Your eBay Business

I've been selling on eBay for a couple of years now, and while I've done well in some respects, I have to admit that I've fallen short in terms of organization. My inventory has consisted of a huge Microsoft Word table, which I had to update every week and is over 1MB in size. I continually have to search through piles of invoices I print just to find sales tax records or the contact information of customers I want to contact with sales promotions. If I had better records at hand, I would spend less time scrounging and more time conducting business.

Luckily, I now have Office Live at my disposal. I'm using it to streamline many of the recordkeeping functions associated with my own eBay business. Even though I'm pretty much a one-person "shop," by keeping my records online, I can access them when I'm at home or traveling.

Tracking eBay Sales Inventory

You have two options when it comes to tracking your eBay business's sales inventory: you can record it in the Product & Service Items list in the Sales Manager business application or you can use Office Accounting 2007, the separate application you previously examined in this chapter. The pros and cons of each option are summarized in Table 13-1.

	Pros	Cons
Office Live	Don't have to install software	Have to access two web sites for inventory and sales
	Can use familiar eBay tools for listing	No way to export inventory data directly to eBay
	Free with the rest of your Office Live services	
Office Accounting	Basics version is free	Inventory items are only available in Professional version
	Can list inventory items on eBay from within application	

TABLE 13-1   Pros and Cons of Inventory Options

Because recording inventory requires you to pay for the professional version of Office Accounting 2007, this section assumes you want to save money and focuses on Office Live for your inventory-tracking purposes.

Recording Inventory for Auction Sales

You may be used to recording inventory for sales on e-commerce web sites or through brick-and-mortar stores. Typically, you have to record basic information, such as:

- The item's name

- Model and brand numbers

- Purchase price

- Where it was obtained

- When it was obtained

These kinds of details are good, but some additional information can help you create good descriptions on eBay. eBay auction and fixed-price sales on eBay are generally more successful when they contain many details. The kinds of detailed information you need when you create eBay descriptions are different from standard sales items. They need to include:

- **Flaws**   Sometimes, you're selling things on eBay that aren't new. People go to the auction marketplace looking for bargains, and they are opened to used, refurbished, or discontinued merchandise. Just be sure you are upfront about scratches or other flaws. You don't want your customers to be surprised or disappointed and return what you have sold.

- **Dimensions**   Shoppers online can't see what they are buying. They can't touch and feel it. Be as detailed as you can about height, weight, width, or other size measurements.

- **Weight**   You have to ship what you sell on eBay, so make a note of the weight if the item is unusually heavy. You need to make up for the extra shipping cost when you list the item on eBay.

- **Country of origin**   Sometimes, it makes a difference if an item was made in a country known for its quality, such as Italy or France, as opposed to

13

a country known for its capability to make cheap knockoffs. If the item is more desirable because of where it was manufactured, you should charge a higher starting bid.

■ **Item numbers**　You need to keep track of item numbers, so you can assign photos to each one without getting mixed up.

When you are listing 10 or 20 items at a time, once or twice a week, you're talking about taking hundreds of photos. This means it's essential to number and name your items clearly. If you list an item with the wrong photos and don't notice the problem, no one will bid, and you'll have to pay a second relisting fee to post the item with the correct images.

Working with the Products List

Within Office Live's business applications, you don't see an option called Inventory Manager. The closest thing you find to an inventory-tracking tool is the Products list within Business Contacts Manager. Log in to Office live, click Business Contacts Manager, and then click the Product tab. The list appears.

By default, the All Products View contains many of the column headings you need to track inventory of all sorts, including eBay items. The default items include:

■ Title

■ Description

■ Quantity

■ Unit cost

■ Unit price

■ Discount percentage

■ Taxable

Adding a new item to Products View is easy: click New, choose New item, and then complete the New item form. You can, as with other business applications, customize this list to fit the types of eBay details mentioned in the preceding section. You might want to add a starting bid, a reserve price, or information about flaws or the country of manufacture, for instance.

TIP

By default, one of the most important fields for eBay sales—Purchase Price—is positioned on the far right of the list and doesn't appear unless you have a wide monitor or click the arrow on the left that collapses the navigation buttons, which are usually present on the left-hand side of the Office Live window. Purchase price has a bearing on your starting bid: if you purchase something for $6, you might want to ensure you make a $10 profit by setting a starting bid of $16, for instance. You may want to click Customize List, and then click Change the order of the fields to move the Purchase Price over to the left of the column headings.

Recording Customer Contacts

The eBay purchase process is so streamlined that, in many cases, you never have to communicate directly with your customers. If they click on the Instant Purchase option and pay you through eBay's service PayPal, you receive an e-mail telling you the payment has been made. You can then ship out the item without sending any message (though it's considered good form to do so).

However, keeping a record of your customer contacts is a good idea, not only to provide better customer service or maintain a record in case of trouble, but also so you can market to customers who return to you again and again. Often, if you use eBay, you lose track of shoppers who make purchases more than 60 days apart, because their records were deleted from the database. Recording them in Office Live's Contact Manager application gives you a way to keep records for long periods of time and also set up marketing mailings.

Contact Data

Contact information for eBay customers is much the same as it is for other marketplaces, with two additions: the customer's eBay User ID, and whether feedback was left by the user for you. *Feedback* is a system in which eBay members leave comments for one another, based on their experiences in conducting transactions.

13

TIP

If you sell products or services in several venues, including eBay, consider adding a new View to the list called eBay Contacts or something similar. This way, you can sort your eBay customers into one group. You'll need to customize the Contacts list by adding a field/column that specifies in which marketplace the customer purchased from you (eBay, Amazon.com, and so forth).

Questions and Issues

Why maintain a database of questions customers have asked over the years? Personally, referring to such questions in the text I write about eBay is helpful. But, even if you don't write about eBay, having such a database can be useful to record problems people raised and questions that came up, so you can answer them in the future. Just the other day, I had to issue a refund to someone, and I was trying to come up with just the right wording to explain a mistake I made, without making myself look bad. I knew I had performed this function in the past, but scouring my sizeable e-mail records was unwieldy. If I had a record of such communications in place, I could reuse "stock" communications and save time, while simultaneously saving face.

Creating Dedicated E-Mail Service

When you start buying and selling on eBay, prepare to experience a dramatic increase in the number of e-mail messages you receive in a given period of time. Most of these are important communications, telling you when you were outbid, when a sale ended, when you won an auction, and so on.

If you subscribe to one of eBay's many discussion groups, however, you receive a certain number of messages presenting you with that day's communications. The bottom line is simple: if you want to separate your personal or business communications from your eBay messages, it only makes sense to designate one of your available Office Live e-mail accounts to eBay alone. You might even consider different e-mail addresses for different purposes: eBaysales@mysite.com, eBaymessages@mysite.com, and so on.

Including Essential Web Site Information for Your Shoppers

Other areas of the Office Live services can help you with an eBay-oriented web presentation. To make your eBay web site as effective as possible, you should provide links to your current sales descriptions—or even present the actual descriptions in the body of your web pages.

Linking to Your eBay Auctions from Your Web Site

You want to get as much attention for your sales as possible. Web sites and eBay auctions are meant to work together to give you more bang for your buck. When you have auction sales or eBay Store merchandise advertised on the eBay marketplace, you only attract one segment of potential customers (though this is a potential audience of millions).

The *eBay Editor Kit* is a tool that lets you include dynamically generated versions of your eBay auctions (or any other auctions on eBay). *Dynamically generated* means the data is gathered in real-time as a viewer downloads your web page and it begins to appear on their monitor. The information isn't static, as it would be if you simply made hyperlinks to each of your sales. That way, you present the latest bid and "time remaining" information with each of the listings.

To get started with the Editor Kit, open the page on which you want your sales to appear in Site Designer. You might decide to put listings right on the home page of the eBay-related web site you are creating. Then, open a web browser window and connect to the Editor Kit home page (http://affiliates.ebay.com/tools/editor-kit). Click the Get Editor Kit Now button at the bottom of the page, log in, and then fill out the form called Sniplet Creator.

Once you fill out the form and click Continue, your browser displays a chunk of web page code you need to add. The code begins like this:

```
<script language="JavaScript"
src="http://lapi.ebay.com/ws/eBayISAPI.dll?EKServer&ai=behy1knuhyn&
bdrcolor=FFCC00&cid=0&eksize=1&encode=ISO-8859-1&endcolor=FF0000&
endtime=y&fbgcolor=FFFFFF
```

To paste it on to your page, click Edit in the menu bar at the top of the Web Zone where you want your listings to appear.

TIP

As part of the process of setting up the Editor Kit, you need to enter an ID with an affiliate network, such as Commission Junction (www.cj.com). Why? When someone clicks on an eBay auction link you display on your web pages and ends up making a purchase or registering for eBay membership, you earn an affiliate fee for the referral. It's free to sign up, and it might also earn you a few extra dollars.

13

Providing an FAQ

Office Live's frequently asked questions (FAQ) area, which is part of the Customer Service application, is as useful for an eBay sales business as it is for other e-commerce sites you create. The same sorts of questions crop up on eBay, especially when you are selling items. In your FAQ for eBay, you can explain shipping options, describe your returns policy for your customers, tell buyers how to calculate shipping, describe your location and your sales tax rate, and many more bits of useful information.

How to Do It

Create your own eBay "store" hosted by Office Live	Open Site Designer and create a new site that you design for extra merchandise you want to market to eBay shoppers
Customize your catalog page layout	Choose one of the standard layouts by clicking Layouts in Site Designer
Use Office Accounting to record your sales tax	During setup, when you install Office Accounting Express 2007, enter preferences regarding the sales tax you collect
Record product orders your customers have placed on eBay	Choose Marketplace Services Basic, specify eBay download options, and then download product orders from eBay
Upload photos you can add to auction descriptions	Choose Manage Online Sales from the Online Sales menu, install the Office Live Image Uploader, click Add Pictures, and then select files and upload them

Part V

Ramping Up Your Business Processes

Chapter 14

Performing Administrative Services with Office Live

How to...

- Record your business contact information

- Associate contacts with your business accounts

- Export your company's contact list

- Schedule appointments with Time Manager

- Create a basic meeting workspace

- Add agenda information

- Invite meeting attendees to submit preliminary data

For those professionals charged with managing staff and keeping an office running, Office Live can provide valuable time-saving functions. You can manage contacts, keep track of time spent on different tasks, and bring together teams of workers. Simply keeping records of names, job titles, contact information, and the facts and figures can keep an office functioning smoothly. Office Live enables one overburdened employee to handle a heavy work load with grace and efficiency.

While previous chapters focused on specific types of business projects you can handle with Office Live, this chapter examines how the online service can become an integral part of your company's administration. General tasks that help you manage both personnel and business contacts can proceed more smoothly when they are conducted in a shared environment, as this chapter describes.

Working with Business Contacts

Many customers looking for a message are turned off by the impersonal touch of an answering service. Yet, appointments can be hard to set up and confirm quickly. Things can go more quickly with Business Contact Manager (BCM). *BCM* gives you a shared space where you and your fellow employees can look up names, addresses, and phone numbers for your clients and other business contacts. You can also store data sheets, résumés, letters, and other files that provide you with background information on your contacts.

NOTE   *BCM is only available with the Essentials and Premium version of Office Live. Other business applications, such as Time Manager, Project Manager, and Sales Manager, are only available with Office Live Premium.*

Configuring Business Contact Manager

Storing all your contacts in one location gives everyone the background information they need to make personalized connections. Instead of having one sales rep be the only repository of information about Mr. Johnson, for instance, anyone can call and know Mr. Johnson's first name is Tim, his wife's name is Joanne, and he was recently promoted to Midwest Manager for Acme Enterprises. BCM gives you four lists for this information, described in the following sections.

Configuring Accounts

Sometimes, individuals are secondary when it comes to a company's business contacts. Some organizations deal with *companies* as much as they talk to *individuals*. Even if you work with particular people, you need to record what company they work for. This account-related information goes in the *Accounts tab*. Once you have your accounts recorded, you can sort them by address, by the amount of income you receive from them, or other criteria—information that can give you more critical business background on which you can make decisions.

To add a new account, open Business Contacts Manager by logging in to your Office Live account, clicking Business Applications, and then clicking Business Contact Manager. When the BCM screen shown in Figure 14-1 appears, you can start working with the Quick Add dialog box on the Dashboard. If you want to add detailed information, click Accounts.

> NOTE *As you can see in Figure 14-1, you can quickly add a contact by entering their name in the Add Contact box. To add an account, you need to click the Accounts tab, however.*

On the Accounts page, click New, and then choose New Item, as shown in Figure 14-2.

When the Accounts form appears, enter all the information you have about the account. The form is divided into two halves: the top half contains the basics, including the name, phone, fax, and e-mail address. One other item, Account number, is optional—it gives you the chance to assign a number to the company. A numeric designation can help when issuing invoices and other paperwork: instead of always typing the account name, you can include the account number instead.

The bottom half of the New Item form in the Accounts tab gives you the chance to enter more detailed communications information if you have it: you can include a street address, alternate phone or fax numbers, and more detailed information, such as comments. The *Tracking tab* is useful, but it only works if

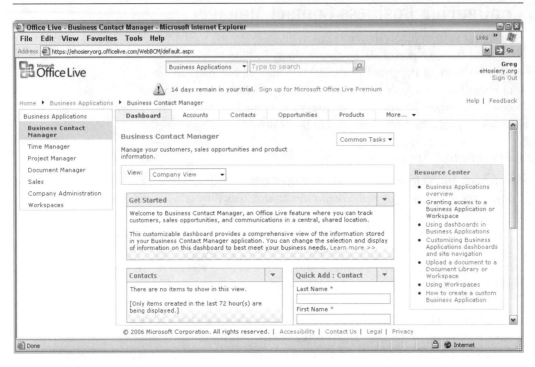

FIGURE 14-1   Business Contact Manager helps you track individuals and organizations you work with.

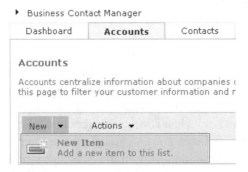

FIGURE 14-2   Choose New Item to add a new account to BCM.

you have already filled out an account name in the Accounts tab and you have at least one contact person in the Contacts tab. If you have done so, Tracking's logging options are enabled. The *Tracking log* lets you and your coworkers record the last time they called the company, or every time the company placed an order. Click Tracking, and then click Add phone log to access the phone logs. A phone log, such as the one shown in Figure 14-3, can tell your staff exactly when an order was placed or a call was made, for instance.

NOTE   *You must fill out the required account name before you add comments or tracking information.*

The various tabs you see when you are in Accounts (Contacts, Tracking, and so on) apply only to the account you are viewing currently. However, overlaps occur between them, as described in the following section.

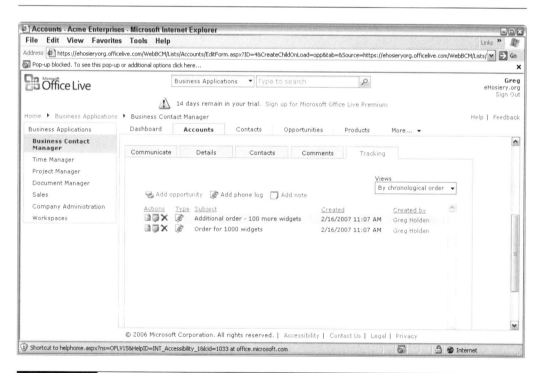

FIGURE 14-3   The Tracking tab lets you create a phone log or list of sales calls.

Adding Contacts

You can make connections between the Contacts list in Business Contact Manager and the Contacts tab in the Acme Enterprises list, for instance. You add a contact the same way you create a new account: by opening Business Contacts Manager, clicking Contacts, clicking New, and then clicking New Item. When the Contacts form appears, you can choose an account name you already created from the Account drop-down list (see Figure 14-4). This lets you sort contacts pertaining to this particular company.

When you associate a contact with an account, the Account name appears as a clickable link in the contact's information. Click the link, and you go to the Accounts sheet for that particular company. Click the Contacts tab in the company's Accounts sheet, and the contact you added also appears there. The person's name appears as a clickable link. You can click it to go to the Contacts list.

As mentioned earlier, you have an even quicker way to add a contact to the Contacts list from the Dashboard. Before you even open the Business Contact Manager application, scroll down to the Add Contact box, as shown in Figure 14-5,

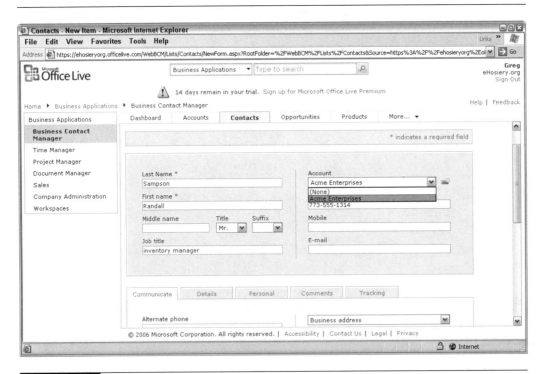

FIGURE 14-4   You can associate contacts with accounts you already created.

FIGURE 14-5 You can add a contact quickly from the Dashboard.

and type the individual's information. Click Save, and that person is added to your Contacts list, which you can also view from the Dashboard. You don't get to add as much detail about the contact as you would in the actual Contacts list. On the other hand, you can enter the person's basic information quickly, and add more details later, if necessary.

Managing Contacts

You can track phone calls or contacts made with a business contact in the Tracking tab in the Contacts list. The Tracking tab in the Contacts New Item form works the same as the one in the Accounts list: it enables you to track phone calls or contacts you made with an individual. Another, perhaps even more important, way to manage a contact is to assign it to a sales representative:

1. Pass your mouse pointer over the person's name in the Contacts list to display the drop-down arrow to the right of their name.

2. Choose Edit Item from the drop-down list.

3. When the Contacts sheet for the individual appears, scroll down to the Communicate section and click the Details tab to bring it to the front.

4. Type the name of the sales rep in the Assigned to box, as shown in Figure 14-6.

5. Click OK to save your changes.

You can then create an e-mail alert, which is automatically sent to a sales rep when you assign the contact to them. You do this by entering the sales rep's e-mail

14

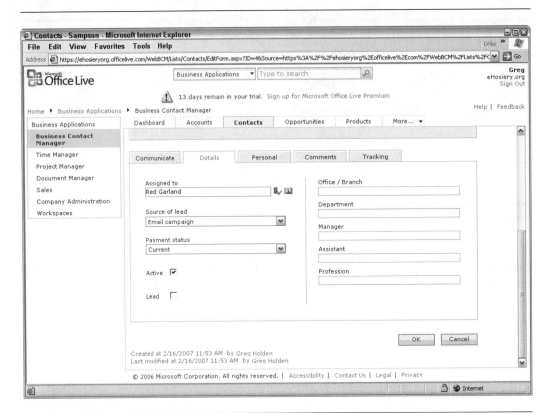

You can assign a contact to a staff person, and then alert the employee.

address in the Assigned to box in the Details tab. To send such an alert, the recipient must have an e-mail address in your Office Live domain. If you attempt to send an alert to someone outside your domain, you see an error message—but only in the Details tab. If you don't look at Details on a regular basis, the sales rep won't be contacted, and neither will the contact.

Once such an address is created, pass your mouse arrow over the contact's name in the Contacts list. Choose Send Alert from the drop-down list that appears, and then enter the recipient's e-mail address in the form that appears.

TIP

A good idea is to give each of your sales reps an address within your office Live domain, even if they already use another e-mail address. It gets your employees in the habit of using Office Live, and it enables you to track phone calls using the Tracking tab.

Updating Contact Information

The advantage of having business contact information online is you gain access to the latest details immediately. But, for the system to work, you need to edit the contact information as needed. Luckily, updating contact data is easy with Office Live. You can edit the contact either by filling out a form (the same kind of form you use to add a contact) or as part of a datasheet. If you want to edit the data by filling out a form, follow these steps:

1. Log on to Office Live, and then click Business Contact Manager.

2. Click the Contacts tab.

3. Pass your mouse arrow over the contact you want to update. When the down arrow appears, click it.

4. Choose Edit Item from the list that drops down. (Or, you could click Edit Item above the individual contact entry.)

5. When the Contacts form appears, make your changes there, and then click OK to save them.

Personally, I find opening a form and making changes time-consuming, especially when I only need to repair a typographical error or change a phone number. When the information you need to change is simple, consider viewing your contacts in datasheet form and making changes as follows:

1. Open Business Contacts Manager and click the Contacts tab as previously described.

2. Click Actions, and then choose Edit in Datasheet from the drop-down list that appears.

3. Click directly in the cell and edit the cell contacts by typing the new information (see Figure 14-7).

TIP   *If you think others have made changes to the Contacts list recently, choose Refresh Data from the Actions drop-down list to make sure you are editing the most recent information.*

14

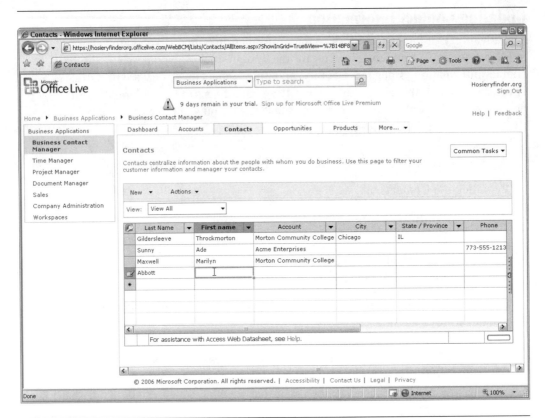

FIGURE 14-7 It's easy to edit or create contact information by typing directly in a datasheet.

Deleting a Contact

Business contacts come and go as frequently as people change jobs and employers. Deleting a contact from Business Contact Manager is easy. But, you need to be aware of some implications.

Deleting a contact is easy: open Business Contact Manager, click Contacts, and then pass your mouse arrow over the contact's name. Click the down arrow and choose Delete Item. When you delete a contact, however, you also delete any items linked to it, such as a tracking item or a file. Just because a contact has left a company, that doesn't mean you're no longer going to pursue any sales opportunities associated with that company. Before you choose Delete Item, make sure you save the opportunity by associating it with another item, such as an account or a business contact, which you're *not* planning to delete.

TIP

When you delete a contact or other item from a list in Office Live, it doesn't go away immediately. It goes into a Recycle Bin of the same sort you have in Windows. These items remain in the Recycle Bin for 30 days. You can restore an item if you have Administrator privileges to the application or workspace from which they were deleted. Open the application or workspace, and then click Common Tasks. Click Modify this application or workspace, then click Deleted Items. Select the items click Restore Selection, and then click OK.

Exporting a Business Contact Manager List

Maintaining a list of contacts in your Office Live Contacts application is useful. But, if one or more of your sales reps doesn't have access to the Internet for some reason, you need to export or print the data. Exporting has the added advantage of giving you an electronic copy of your contact information, which you can edit conveniently on your computer.

You can export any list to either a Microsoft Access or a Microsoft Excel file. The options are the same as those explained in the section "Tracking and Exporting Lists" in Chapter 9. Here are a few examples:

- Choose Export to Spreadsheet from the Actions menu to link any Office Live list view with an Excel worksheet.

- Choose Query list with Excel from the Datasheet task pane to link an Office Live list view with an Excel worksheet.

- Choose Export to Access from the Datasheet task pane to create an Access 2007 table (it isn't linked to the Office Live list).

NOTE

See the topic "About exporting lists" in Office Live Help for a complete set of options for exporting List Views. The Help file says the List View must be exported to Access 2007 or Excel 2007, but I was also able to export data to Excel 2003.

14

Contact Manager has a special option for exporting list data. You can export one view (My View or Company View, for instance) of your Contacts or Employees lists to a Contacts folder in Outlook 2007.

Administering Your Company

To be an effective administrator, you need to have access to a wide variety of business information at your fingertips. You have to manage three primary factors: time, money, and human resources. The business applications that come with Office Live Premium enable you to perform all these functions, and they are described in the following sections.

Managing Your Time

Time is money, or so the old saying goes. Usually, this means managing your time well or saving time in some other way. But, this also means keeping track of your office resources, such as meeting rooms, projectors, or other equipment, as well as managing your meeting schedules, so you don't run into conflicts. By giving your employees the ability to set up meetings or reserve resources themselves, you not only save your office managers some work, you also track resources more efficiently.

Reserving Time for Meetings and Resources

In a traditional business environment, meetings are scheduled and resources are reserved the old-fashioned way. Staff enter their appointments into a database or send a message by e-mail or (shudder) paper to the accounting staff. In any case, the data goes to a single point in a sort of information funnel: The burden of recording meetings and reservations falls to an administrator. No matter what job title this person goes by—bookkeeper, accountant, fiscal assistant—this person has a lot of work to do. By giving anyone in your office the capability to perform these time-related functions, you gain several advantages:

- Employees submit data from wherever they are, whenever they need to. They don't have an excuse for "losing" information.

- Time-related data can be entered using a web browser, rather than proprietary software.

- Using an online service frees your fiscal person for other duties.

- Administrators can access appointments and reservations data easily from any location.

To record time information in Time Manager's interface, follow these steps:

1. Make sure you establish user accounts for all the staff who will enter timesheet data. The value of using Time Manager comes from enabling multiple data entry points, so all the work doesn't fall on you.

2. Log into Office Live, click Business Applications, and then click the Time Manager link on the left-hand side of the Office Live screen.

3. When the Dashboard appears, scroll down to the section labeled Schedule and Reservations, and then click the date for the day you want to set an appointment. Click the number for the day. Don't click in the calendar cell.

4. The Schedule and Reservations screen changes from a one-month view to a single-day view, with the hours of the day displayed in rows. Click on the number of the hour when the appointment needs to occur.

5. When the New Appointment form, shown in Figure 14-8 appears, select the workgroup members who need to meet with you in the top-half of the form. Click Add to move their names to the right side of the form.

6. Scroll down to the second half of the form and identify any resources, such as equipment and meeting rooms, that you need. Click Add to move them from the left side of the screen to the right.

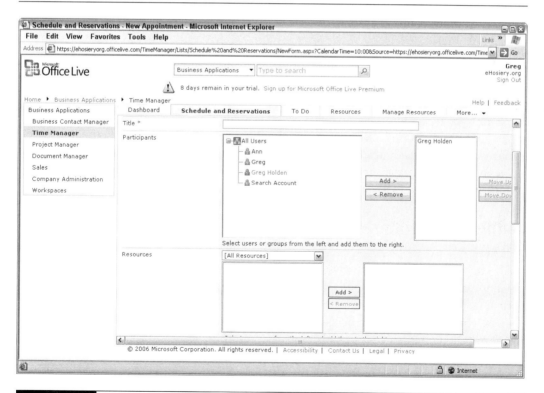

FIGURE 14-8 Use this form to make appointments and identify the resources you need.

7. Scroll down to the Begin and End fields, and then specify the start and end times for your appointment.

8. Click the Check button farther down on the form to have Office Live check to make sure no other appointments are set up during that time.

9. When you're done, click OK.

This kind of sophisticated online scheduling is especially useful when your workgroup members are in different locations. For your own small business, Office Live might be just the trick for getting your team together.

Best Practices for Online Time Management

Before you start using Time Manager, make sure you have granted access only to the approved personnel and that they have password protection. In addition, when you measure the cost of having your scheduling done online, remember two things:

■ You may not want your systems staff knowing all the information you keep in a time-reporting system.

■ When you have Office Live host your Time Manager application, you have 100 percent full functionality immediately with complete knowledgeable support.

Web-based scheduling, like other types of hosted applications, works best when your organization lacks the personnel or time to accomplish the specified services in-house, and multiple users have to coordinate activities. It also comes in handy when you and your coworkers work in different locations. They can then use the web resource as a virtual gathering place to share information.

Gathering Estimates and RFPs

The *Estimates list,* under the Sales application, gives you a place to record quotations you gave out to customers. Often, estimates for complex projects have multiple components that need to come from separate staff. One person might do the design component, another person the writing, and another the technical aspects of the project. The Estimates list can be used to give those employees a place to submit their separate figures, so your organization can present an accurate proposal.

You, the administrator, can add the quotation to the Estimates list by filling out the New Item form. You can then ask the staff involved in creating the estimate to add their figures in the Notes field. You also have the capability to attach files with

Time Manager, so you can attach the final presentation, giving everyone a record of it. Just click the Attach File link at the top of the New Item form to locate the file you want to attach.

When all the components are submitted, you can add them. You could do the same thing by e-mail, but having a formal record stored in your Estimates area can help you in the future when you need to submit similar proposals to this or other customers.

Fostering Employee Collaboration

When I worked full-time in an office, we had a weekly meeting to go over ongoing jobs—or at least we tried to hold such a meeting. More often than not, one or more people were absent because of business trips or conflicting meetings, not to mention illnesses and vacations. While you can't do anything about the latter two options, you can certainly facilitate bringing people together by creating workspaces and setting up appointments with Office Live—appointments you can set up with Time Manager as described earlier in this chapter, by the way. Setting up virtual workspaces on Office Live can be more convenient than reserving a physical meeting space in your real-world office.

Office Live workspaces enable you to exchange information with a discrete group of employees, vendors, or customers. You can upload or download files or images from a document library, for instance. You can schedule meetings using the Dashboard (see Figure 14-9).

Three workspaces are described in this chapter. A fourth workspace—the customer workspace—is intended for you and your customers to "get together" virtually. See Chapter 7 for more information.

14

Giving Your Employees Access

One of the primary advantages of workspaces is, they give a group of colleagues (a workgroup, in other words) a place to share files, as well as to view schedules and other information. Granting permission to enter a workspace is basically the same as adding user accounts to other parts of Office Live.

1. Click Administration in the list of links on the left side of the page. (If you don't see Administration, click Home, and then click Administration.)

2. Click Users & Permissions.

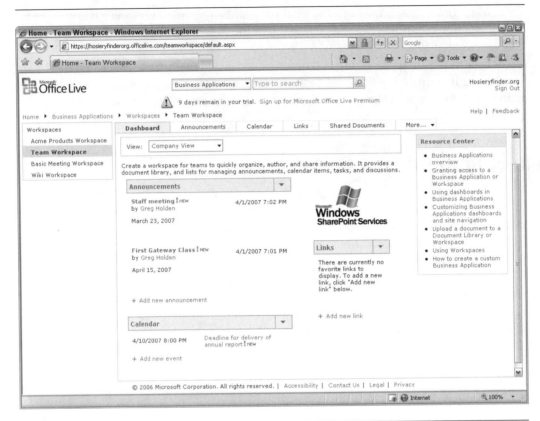

FIGURE 14-9   The Team Workspace lets you manage projects being conducted by a workgroup.

3. When the permissions page appears, scan the list of users for your Office Live site. If any new users need to be added so they can access the workspace you are about to create, you can add them now. To find out which of the current users has permission to access your workspace, choose the workspace from the View drop-down list.

4. Click Add User to add the individual to your workspace, if needed. If the individual you want to add is already on the list, click Edit next to their name.

5. When the Edit user information screen shown in Figure 14-10 appears, give the person access to the workspace(s) you want to create. The user can be given Administrator, Editor, or Reader permissions.

6. When you're done, click Save.

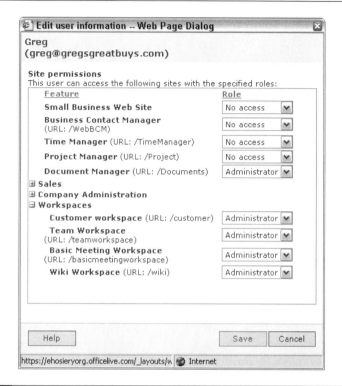

FIGURE 14-10 Add users to a workspace by assigning them a permisssion level.

Using the Basic Meeting Workspace

The *Basic Meeting Workspace* contains all the elements needed to plan and organize a meeting. When you first connect to the Basic Meeting Workspace, you see these elements grouped in the Dashboard. Before the meeting takes place, you can use them to add essential information for your participants:

- **Objectives**   Click Add New item to set specific goals and objectives you want to accomplish in your meeting.

- **Agenda**   This isn't the same as goals and objectives. This is a list of topics you need to cover.

14

- **Attendees**   You can add the names of the staff who will attend the meeting. Names must match those who are already signed up for Office Live.

- **Document Library**   Almost every meeting has some printed material that everyone in attendance needs to review or discuss. You can save some toner and paper by uploading electronic versions to the Document Library, so everyone can access them beforehand.

Adding Attendees

By adding attendees, you not only give everyone an idea of who is participating, but you also provide important secondary information: Comments, Response, and Attendance. You complete each of these fields by clicking Add Item and filling out the Attendees: New Item form, as shown in Figure 14-11.

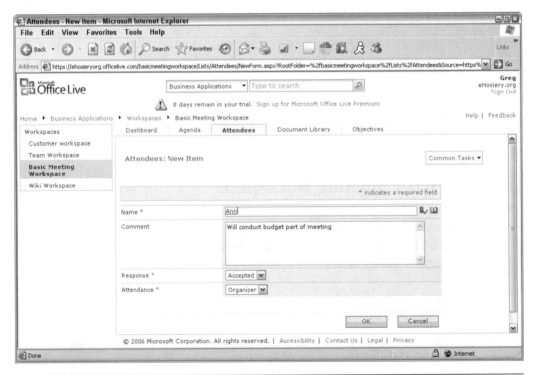

FIGURE 14-11   You can add comments and other information about attendees.

Before the meeting takes place, you can help those in attendance learn all they need to know by completing three secondary, but important, bits of information:

- **Comment** Is the attendee expected to conduct part of the meeting or be responsible for a topic of discussion? If so, this is the place to make note of it.

- **Response** Was someone in the office invited? Did they turn down the invitation? Is a critical staff member coming? You can choose one of three options (Accepted, Tentative, Declined) to indicate what's happening.

- **Attendance** What role will this person play in the meeting? Do they have to attend? Each person's attendance can be designated as Organizer, Required, or Optional.

You can save yourself some e-mail communications with your colleagues by choosing options, such as Required from the Attendance menu, and sending e-mail notifications to them automatically via Office Live. This way, you won't need back-and-forth discussions with them trying to determine whether they must attend.

NOTE *If your attendees have Editor or Administrator permissions in your workspace, they can add their own comments to the Attendee: New Item form. They can voice their concerns or report some preliminary information before the actual meeting takes place.*

Setting the Agenda

For most meetings, an *agenda* is a simple list of subjects to cover. The Basic Meeting Workspace gives you the chance to add additional information. When you click Add new item in the Agenda box in the Dashboard, you go to the Agenda: New Item form where you can not only add the Subject (the agenda item itself), but also the Owner (the person primarily responsible for this item), the Time (the time to be allotted for discussion during the meeting), plus any Notes you want to add. You can even format the agenda item in boldface, italic, and bulleted or numbered lists if you want to make it more readable to your viewers or call attention to a particularly noteworthy topic, such as the one shown in Figure 14-12.

NOTE *The formatting options in the Notes field are "grayed out" and inactive until you click inside the field itself. Then, they "light up" and you can work with them. Make sure you select a block of text before you attempt to apply the formatting.*

14

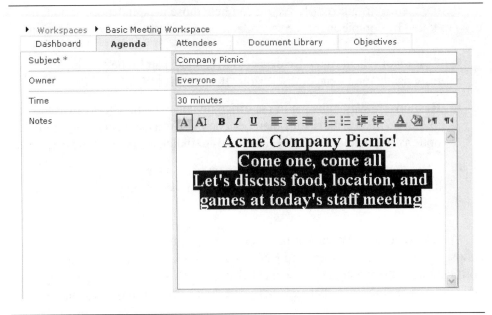

FIGURE 14-12   You can add notes to agenda items and then add formatting to them.

Creating a Team Workspace

At first glance, you might ask yourself, what's the difference between a meeting workspace and a team workspace? Our team is holding the meeting, so why would we choose one workspace instead of the other?" This is a reasonable question, and the answer becomes clear when you click Team Workspace and look at the tools Office Live gives you. Instead of Agenda, Attendees, Objectives, and Document Library, you have:

- **Calendar**   Use this to post upcoming events or deadlines.
- **Announcements**   Sales, gatherings, projects, or events can all go here.
- **Links**   Photos of the office party or diagrams related to a design project you're working on are suitable for this area.

It's clear this workspace is suitable for a less formal "gathering" than the Basic Meeting Workspace. You might use the Team Workspace as a central storage place for information about your team, including guidelines, schedules, and announcements. This is like a reference library you can fill with background information that any member of your team can access, whether or not a meeting has been scheduled.

Exploring Wiki Workspaces

The term "wiki," like "blog," has cropped up and become popular thanks to the Web. A *wiki* is a forum that provides information online and to which multiple individuals can contribute. Use this workspace to create any set of information that many people can add to. For example, you could brainstorm ideas, collaborate on designs, or build an encyclopedia of knowledge.

The classic wiki is the online encyclopedia Wikipedia (www.wikipedia.org). Many hands contribute bits of knowledge, which can then be edited and "corrected" by other hands. The problem with wikis is not getting people to contribute, but in ensuring that what is written is valuable, as well as accurate. In a corporate environment, it's important to edit your employees closely and provide them with strict guidelines, so they are aware of what constitutes suitable and unsuitable content.

How to Do It

Add information about one of your business accounts	Open Business Applications, click Business Contact Manager, click Accounts, click New, and then choose New Item
Record your most recent phone call or order from a client	Open Business Contact Manager, click Tracking, and then add the information
Associate a contact with an account	Open Business Contacts Manager, click Contacts, click New, click New Item, and then choose the account name from the Account drop-down list
Export your Business Contact Manager list	Choose Export to Spreadsheet from the Actions menu in any Office Live list, or choose Query list with Excel or Export to Access from the Datasheet task pane
Set up an appointment or reserve a resource	Open Time Manager, click a date under Schedule and Reservations, and then move the names of participants from the left side to the right side of the window

14

Chapter 15

Accounting with Office Live

How to...

- ■ Follow good accounting principles for your small business

- ■ Settle on an accounting period and accounting method

- ■ Record income, expenses, and assets with Office Live

- ■ Create a custom Income business application

- ■ Establish a connection between Office Accounting and your accountant

- ■ Transfer financial files manually to and from your accountant

- ■ Use Office Live to facilitate data transfers

If you operate a small business with only a handful of employees, chances are you can't afford the luxury of assigning one of those employees to performing accounting and bookkeeping functions full-time. Your primary concern is to find salespeople, inventory managers, and people to fulfill orders. Those functions put money in your accounts and keep your business running.

Simply putting money in your accounts is only the beginning, of course. You need to know, at any given moment, how much money you have available and how to spend it wisely. If you don't keep track of income and expenses, and the amount of money you have available to make purchases, both your profit margin and the future of your business might suffer. I hope you have someone on staff who can help you balance the books. If you don't, you can use Office Live and a related program, Microsoft Office Accounting, to keep track of your business finances. Even if you work with a professional accountant on a contract basis to prepare your taxes or run reports, you can use either application to transfer your "books" back and forth. Office Accounting is especially streamlined for conducting such transfers. This chapter examines the kinds of accounting information you need to record, how to use Office Live business applications to record them, and how to use Office Accounting to transfer financial data files between you and your accountant, using Office Live to facilitate communication.

Following General Accounting Principles

You don't have to be a fiscal genius to keep track of income and expenses as well as other important aspects of your small business's operation. You only have to do the basics, so either you or your tax preparer can file the appropriate paperwork smoothly at tax time. At the very least, you need to know whether your business

Accounting Terms You Can Count On

Accountants and tax professionals often seem to speak a different language than "the rest of us." Luckily, the specialized terms they use aren't difficult to understand. Here are a few basics:

- **Account**   A type of financial record related to an activity or subject, such as an equipment account or income account.

- **Accounting period**   An arbitrary period of time over which profits or losses are calculated, such as a month or a year.

- **Accrual method**   A method of accounting in which revenues and expenses are recorded at the time the transaction takes place—not when cash is transferred.

- **Amortization**   The change of the value of an expenditure over a period of time.

- **Asset**   A piece of property or equipment owned by a business.

- **Credit**   An accounting entry that records an increase in assets or goods sold that results in an increase in revenue.

- **Debit**   An accounting entry that records an expense.

- **Expense**   An expenditure that results in a reduction in your revenue in a given accounting period. If you buy a copy machine for cash, that is an expenditure, but not an expense. The expense occurs as the machine depreciates over time, and you have a reduction in revenue.

- **Liability**   The amount your company owes to someone else. A *long-term liability* is the amount of a mortgage or a similar loan. A *current liability* is an amount due within a year.

These aren't just abstract accounting terms, of course. Even if you don't throw them around in everyday conversation, they do have a practical value because some of them show up in the Office Accounting interface or in the program's Help files. They also come in handy when you talk to your accountant or tax professional.

15

is successful, and accounting can help you measure your level of success. You do so by maintaining a daily record of your company finances, as described in the following sections.

Choosing an Accounting Period

To know how your business is doing, you need to compare your income and expenses during one period with another period. This period doesn't necessarily need to be a 12-month calendar year, and it doesn't necessarily need to begin on January 1. It's up to you. You might track your performance on a month-to-month basis or from April 1 to March 31 the following year.

In any case, to use the numbers you gather by accounting, you need to identify an accounting period. Many large corporations have a 12-month accounting period, but they choose a date such as June 1 as the beginning. In that case, May 31 is the date they "close the books." The accounting period chosen isn't arbitrary. In most cases, the dates chosen match the dates by which a business has to pay quarterly taxes or when it needs to pay bills to suppliers.

 *You can find a good introduction to accounting principles for nonaccountants at www.alpineguild.com/how_to_keep_score_in_business.htm. It likens accounting to "keeping score" in an athletic contest or other event in which numbers and totals play an important role.*

Choosing an Accounting Method

In practically every analysis of accounting for nonaccountants, you see the terms "cash-based" and "accrual-based" accounting. You're told to choose one or the other method when you keep your books. It's not always clear what these terms mean. In the *cash-based* method of accounting, a business keeps track of cash receipts and payments as they occur. But, in the *accrual* method of accounting, you record an expense when a service is rendered, even if you haven't yet paid for it. If you buy 1,000 inventory items on June 15, but payment isn't due until July 15, for example, you record the bill as having been paid on June 15.

Even though the cash-based method is the simplest and most straightforward, if your business maintains inventory that you sell either online or through a brick-and-mortar store, you have to use the accrual-basis method.

Keeping Basic Financial Records

In the long-ago days, when men wearing green eyeshades wrote down accounting data in a ledger book, they kept track of two kinds of records: debits and credits.

This is still basically what accounting boils down to. But, you need to know about some refinements and distinctions.

Recording Income

As far as income, you should be aware that some of your income is taxable, and some is not. Your revenue—which is the type of income you receive from sales—is taxable. But, when you apply for or receive a loan, the income you receive is not. You need to record both types of income. If you don't, it is labeled unreported income and you'll probably have to pay taxes on it later.

 *When you record revenue, whether you use Office Accounting or Office Live, be sure to mark down not only the amount you receive, but also the date of the transaction, the form of the payment, the client or company that paid you, and what was purchased from you.*

Recording Assets

An *asset* is a piece of property or equipment owned by your company, such as your furnishings, computers, and pens and pencils. After you pay your creditors, what remains is your *equity* (the part of your home you don't owe to the bank is your equity, for instance).

Assets, like income, needs to be recorded in some detail. You should record not only the name, model number, and description, but also the purchase price, the date the item was acquired, and so on. Office Live Premium has a Company Assets application under the Company Administration heading. It asks for this basic information, and it also gives you a space in which you can record the serial number. You can even upload an image of the asset, as shown in Figure 15-1. The New Item form in the Company Assets application also includes the following:

- Book Value (the original cost minus depreciation)
- Lifespan (the period of time over which you expect to own the item)
- Depreciation (the amount the value of the item changes each year)
- Location (where the item is physically located)
- Assigned to (the staff person who has responsibility for the item)
- Intended use (how your company will use the item)

Company Assets also has an Asset Request tab, which lets your office track who has physical possession of an item (such as a cell phone, camera, or company car) at any given time.

15

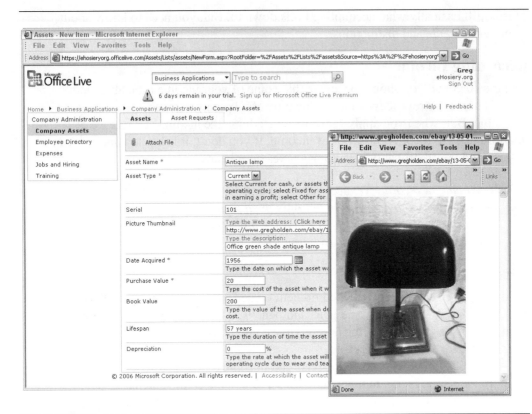

FIGURE 15-1 Company Assets lets you record extensive information and include images.

Recording Expenses

Business expenses can take many forms. You need to buy tangible goods and services. You also have to record travel expenses, business lunches, advertising costs, and postage and transportation. When tax time comes, recording what the expense was for becomes important. If you use Office Live's Expenses application (which, like Company Assets, is found under Company Administration), you record the Expense Type (Travel, Training, Entertaining, Equipment, Morale, and Other), as shown in Figure 15-2. You also identify the related employee, the date the expense was incurred, and the date the expense was paid. If you order supplies, the expense is incurred on that date; but you may not pay for the items purchased until 30, 60, or 90 days later.

Creating an Income Application

The preceding sections briefly described Office Live business applications that let you record two of the three basic types of accounting information: assets and expenses.

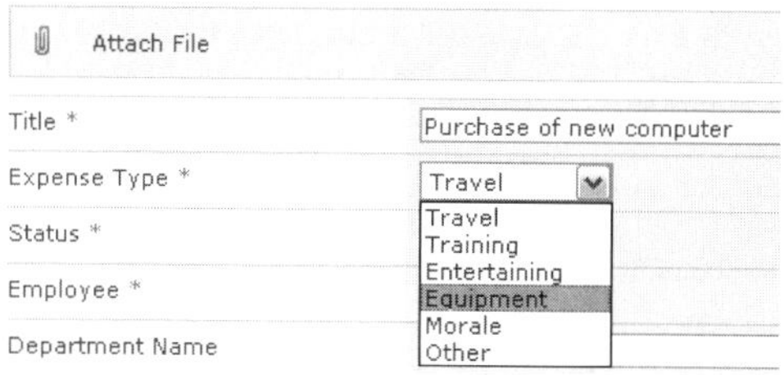

⏚	Attach File	
	Title *	Purchase of new computer
	Expense Type *	Travel ⌄
	Status *	Travel / Training / Entertaining / Equipment / Morale / Other
	Employee *	
	Department Name	

FIGURE 15-2 Office Live's Expenses application lets you record an expense type and other information.

What about the third type of information? You won't find an application called Income or Revenue under Company Administration. You can, however, create such an application yourself. Because both the Company Assets and the Expenses applications ask for the basic types of accounting information (date, type, employee, and amount), it makes sense to copy one of these applications and turn it into your own custom Income application. Follow these steps to create this third essential accounting component:

1. Click Business Applications to view the Dashboard for this part of Office Live.

2. Click Common Tasks, near the upper right-hand corner of the Dashboard, and then click Create new from the menu that appears.

3. Click Applications and Workspaces.

4. When the Create new application or workspace screen appears, click Business Applications from the Select a category list, and choose Company Assets from the Select a template list. Then click OK.

5. When the Site Details form appears, enter Income as the title. Enter the title you want to appear in the URL for the Income application. The obvious choice would be the single word "income," which would result in the URL https://[yoursite.com]/income/default.aspx.

6. Enter a Description for your site.

7. In the Display section, choose Company Administration as the category. Then click OK.

15

The application is created, and the title Income is added to the list of applications on the left side of the window. But, as you can see, the application is called Assets because you used Assets as the template. To change the name, follow these additional steps:

1. Click Common Tasks, which appears on the Dashboard or virtually any page in Office Live.

2. Choose Modify this Application or Workspace from the Common Tasks drop-down list.

3. Click List and Libraries under the heading Create.

4. When the Site Libraries and Lists page appears, click Customize "Assets."

5. When the Customize Assets page appears, click Title, Description, and Navigation under General Settings.

6. Change the contents of the Name box to Income. Optionally, you can also change the description in the Description box.

7. Click Save to save your changes.

You return to the Customize page, which is now called Customize Income. You also need to click on each of the column names in turn to customize them. For instance, if you click Asset Name, you can change the name to Income Name. Click Asset Type to change the column to Income Type. You need to perform a variety of other customization tasks as well, but after you change some column titles and list view names, you have a place to record your income, as shown in Figure 15-3.

Although you can create your own Income application by customizing one of the existing Office Live applications, you gain more power and flexibility by using Office Accounting.

Connecting Office Accounting with Your Office Live Site

In Chapter 13, you learned how to obtain and start using Microsoft Office Accounting Express. When you first configure an Office Live site and start using Office Accounting, establishing a connection between the two programs

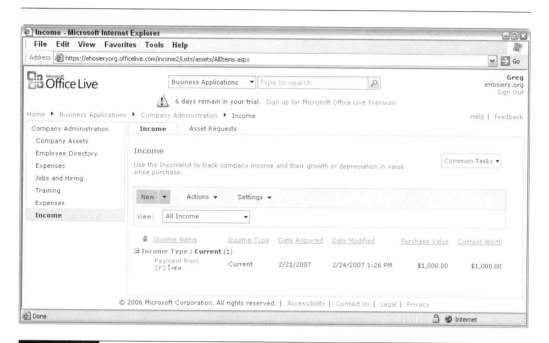

FIGURE 15-3   You can create a custom application to record income in Office Live.

is helpful. You want to be able to export expenses to Office Live to Office Accounting, and to import data from your accounting software to Office Live. You can use Office Live and Office Accounting to transfer a data file called an Accountant File from one individual's computer to another. The process basically uses your Office Live web site as a transfer point: you send your data to your Office Live site, and your accountant retrieves it from Office Live. If both you and your accountant are connected to Office Live, you both know when the transfer is initiated and when it is completed, because of special notifications that appear in the Office Accounting interface.

This chapter isn't meant to be an examination of every feature you can perform with Office Accounting; a detailed examination would require several chapters and possibly a book of its own. Suffice it to say that you can perform the basic income, expense, and asset accounting with Office Live that you reviewed earlier in this chapter. The sections that follow discuss how to transfer your financial data from one user to another using your Office Live site.

15

 *Microsoft Office Accounting Express 2007 is a free tool. It's not part of any of the three Office Live packages. The Premium version is, as you would expect, more full featured than the Basics version. But it also carries a purchase price. At the time of writing, I saw it available for $149.95. You can download the free version of Office Accounting Express 2007 at http://office.microsoft.com/en-us/officelive/FX102036301033.aspx. Both versions work on Windows XP, 2003 Server, or Vista. The Macintosh OS is not supported.*

Creating an "Accountant" Account

The first step in transferring your "books" using Office Live is to set up an account for your accountant to receive the information. Office Accounting requires you to set up an account for your accountant because you use Office Live to send them your information when you need to file your taxes.

 it's reasonable to ask why you should go through the process that follows to set up a data transfer procedure using Office Live. You could, of course, e-mail your financial information to your accountant. E-mail is notoriously insecure, however. Transferring an accountant file using Office Live is more secure and it's convenient. And, it sets up a direct, quick means of transferring information between two individuals. Office Live is much like a secure connection over the Internet that's commonly called a virtual private network (VPN).

Just because it's called an "Accountant" account doesn't mean the other person needs to be an actual bookkeeper, however. You can set up such an account to send your data to anyone in your office who needs to work with financial information. You can even send it to yourself, so you can keep a backup of your information. No matter who the recipient is, the preliminary steps are the same. The following steps assume you have downloaded and installed Office Accounting Express, as previously described in Chapter 13:

1. Click Company and choose Company Information. The Company Information dialog box opens (see Figure 15-4).

2. Enter the basic information about your company in the Company Information dialog box. Be sure to enter your own e-mail—the one you plan to use when your accountant invites you to transmit your data.

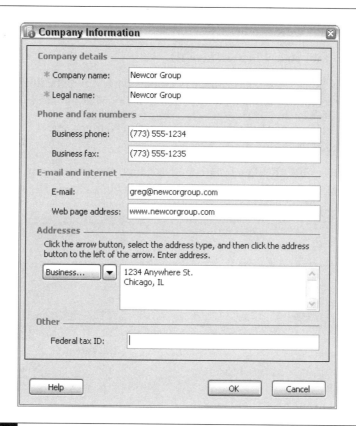

FIGURE 15-4   Record your own and your accountant's e-mail addresses in this dialog box.

Configuring Accountant View

Before you can transmit a file to your accountant, you need to configure Office
Accounting's Accountant View. Follow these steps:

1. Choose Start, click All Programs, click Microsoft Office, click Office
Accounting 2007 Tools, and then click Accountant View.

2. When the Accountant View window opens, click Sign up for Online
Transfer in the My Clients pane in the center of the window.

3. When your default browser launches and the Office Live Premium window
is displayed, click Sign in, and then sign in to your account.

15

4. Once your web site is open in Internet Explorer (IE), switch back to the Accountant View window. Now, click Sign in.

5. Sign in with your Windows Live ID.

6. Choose the client's name in the My Clients pane. Click the down arrow in the Actions column, and then choose Enable online sharing (see Figure 15-5).

7. Select a client, click the down arrow next to Actions, select Send Invitation, and then choose Go.

8. When the Select E-Mail Template dialog box, shown in Figure 15-6, appears, click Invite for Online Sharing.txt, and then click Open. The message Invitation Sent appears in the Status column.

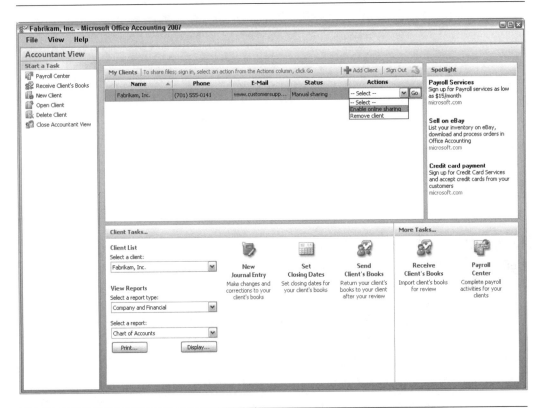

FIGURE 15-5   Once you manually transfer a file, the client is added to My Clients.

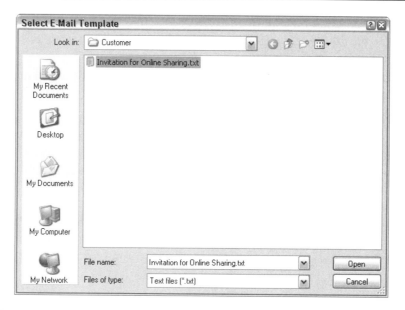

FIGURE 15-6   Send a standard e-mail invitation to your "client" to receive financial data online.

9. Open the e-mail you receive from the "accountant" or other person in your office using your Office Live e-mail interface. Click the link contained in the body of the e-mail message. Sign in to Windows Live, if necessary.

10. When the web site opens, switch back to Office Accounting 2007. Click File, choose Accountant Transfer, and then click Sign in for Online Transfer.

At this point, the Online Transfer is set up. To transfer files, the accountant needs to request the files be sent.

Manually Transferring Financial Data

Once you establish a connection between your copy of Office Accounting and that of your accountant, they only have to choose an option from a drop-down list to send you a file or to receive one from you. You appear in your accountant's list of clients.

To get on the list of clients, you need to send a financial file, called an "accountant review file," to your accountant using a manual transfer. You can transfer it using a CD, a USB drive, or an MSN Hotmail account.

15

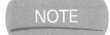 *The preceding steps work if you and your accountant both work on the
same computer. If you are in different locations, then you need to transfer
the .ate file using a CD or memory stick, or a Hotmail e-mail account.*

1. Choose Accountant Transfer from the File menu, and then click Send
   Books from the submenu that appears.

2. When the Welcome to Accountant Transfer: Send screen, as shown in
   Figure 15-7, appears, leave the Send books manually option selected, and
   then click Next. Follow the instructions on subsequent screens to configure
   the data you want to send. You may want to add a password to protect the
   data file itself or the backup file Office Accounting automatically creates.

*You may want to write down the location of the .ate data file that Office
Accounting creates. You or your accountant need to locate the file. The
path leading to the file is complicated, and it can be hard to remember.*

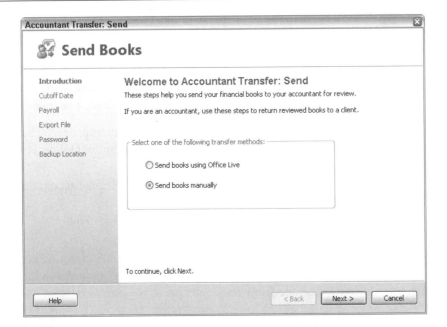

FIGURE 15-7   Send your "books" manually, so you can send them using Office Live.

3. Once the file is sent, you or your accountant should switch to Accountant View. Click the Windows Start button, and then click All Programs, Microsoft Office, Office Accounting 2007 Tools, and, last, Accountant View.

4. Click Receive Client's Books.

5. Leave the Manual transfer option selected and click Next.

6. Click Browse and locate the file on your file system. (You may need to refer to the path you wrote down earlier.)

7. Click Import. The Receive Books screen appears to keep you apprised of the file transfer (see Figure 15-8). When the transfer is complete, a message appears in Receive Books entitled Receiving financial data file complete.

8. Click Finish.

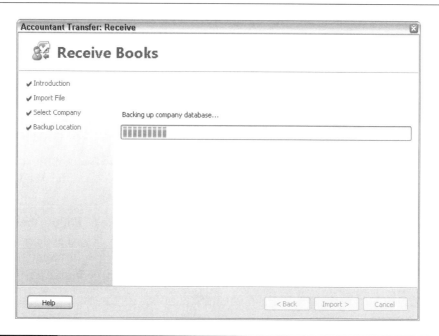

FIGURE 15-8   It can take several minutes to manually transfer a file, and this dialog box notifies you of the progress.

Transferring the Data

When you establish a connection between yourself and your client, and your name appears in the My Client Pane in Office Accounting's Accountant View, you can then transfer the files. The person designated as "accountant" needs to initiate the transfer by requesting the files be sent, rather than you sending the data yourself.

This one-way method of data transfer might seem inconvenient, but you already know you can manually send your files to your accountant, as previously described. Having the accountant make the request lets the accountant work on the files when they are ready. This enables you, in turn, to keep working and updating your financial information up to the last minute. This also gives the accountant the ability to request a cutoff date, so they get only the data they need.

If you use Accounting Professional 2007, rather than Express 2007, the accountant automatically sends a reminder to send them your information. The reminder goes to the client's Company home page. Express doesn't have this reminder feature.

To initiate the transfer, follow these steps:

1. Open Accountant View, and then click the name of the client (the one who has the data you want) in My Clients.

2. Click the down arrow under Actions, choose Request Books, and then choose Go.

3. When the Request Books dialog box appears, enter the cutoff date you want.

4. Once the request is made, the client switches to Office Accounting and chooses File, Accountant Transfer, and Send Books to open the Accountant Transfer: Send screen.

5. Click Send books using Office Live, and then click Next. Follow the steps shown on subsequent screens to create an optional password and send the file. When the file is sent, the parenthetical phrase (Books Sent To Accountant) appears in Office Accounting's title bar (see Figure 15-9).

Fabrikam, Inc. - Microsoft Office Accounting Professional 2007 (Books Sent To Accountant)

| File | Edit | View | Company | Customers | Vendors | Employees | Banking | Online Sales |

FIGURE 15-9   Look in the title bar for confirmation that the data file was sent.

6. Once the file is sent, you or your accountant switches to Accountant View, and then clicks the client's name in My Clients. Then, click the down arrow under Actions and choose Receive Books.

7. When the file is transferred and you are ready to open it, click the client's name in My Clients. The message Reviewing Client's Books appears in the toolbar.

Once you finish reviewing the files, you can send them back by opening Accountant View, clicking the client's name, clicking the down arrow under Actions, and then clicking Send Books.

How to Do It

Establish a foundation for good accounting practices	Settle on an accounting period, such as July 1 to June 30, and then choose between cash-based or accrual-based accounting
Create a list of your company's equipment and other assets	Use the Company Assets business application in Office Live Premium to record value and to depreciate the item over time, and even to point to a thumbnail image
Keep a record of your business expenses	Open Business Applications, and then click Company Administration. Next, click Expenses, then click New, choose New Item, and then fill out the New Item form
Record business income in an Office Live application	Copy Assets or Expenses as a template, and then customize the application
Set up company information for Office Accounting	Click Company and choose Company Information in the Office Accounting toolbar. Enter your e-mail address and other company information
Manually send a data file to your accountant	Click File, choose Accountant Transfer, and then click Send Books

Chapter 16

Advanced Productivity Tools

How to...

- Collaborate by creating a workgroup on your desktop

- Communicate in real-time with Office Live Meeting

- Take your act on the road with Office Live Communicator

- Schedule meetings and other events with Office Live

- Conduct instant messaging with Windows Live Messenger

- Publicize your Office Live business with adManager

Office Live is all about maximizing your productivity. Most of this book's chapters, in fact, focus on creating a web site, setting up shared workspaces, and taking full advantage of the online service's business applications either to get more work done or to get done as much as you need with limited personnel resources.

Once you get used to Office Live, you'll naturally turn to other related services and products to help boost your business performance to an even higher level. This chapter examines some of the Office- and Office Live-related products you may want to explore after you begin to move some of your business communication and file sharing functions online. Once you integrate Office Live into your business you should find it relatively straightforward to move to the services described in this chapter and integrate them with your new online business operations.

Connecting with Your Peers: Office Live Groove

Office Live Groove is an application that takes advantage of peer-to-peer technology to let individuals share designated files. At first glance, Office Live seems similar to Office Live Groove in more than name only. Both programs allow networked individuals to share files on their computers. Both are accessed online, rather than software installed on a file system.

> **NOTE** *Office Live Groove is related to a similar program simply called Office Groove. Office Live Groove isn't software you have to install and maintain. You try it, you are up and running quickly, and you subscribe if you find the service useful. It's ideal for small businesses that don't have extensive IT support. Office Groove, on the other hand, needs to be deployed on each of the computers in a company network. Not only that, but you also need to run a server program called Office Groove Server to make Office Groove work on your internal network.*

The obvious question is, what is the difference between the two "live" services? Should you consider Office Live Groove if you already use Office Live? In fact, a big difference does exist: Office Live is built on Windows SharePoint technology, as described in Chapter 10. Somewhere in Microsoft's facilities, when you connect to your Office Live site, you are making use of a SharePoint server.

With Groove, you don't need a server. Members of a workgroup connect directly to one another's computers using peer-to-peer networking. Each computer on the network can be a server on the network, and each can be a client. You don't necessarily need to be able to share the entire contents of any one individual's file system, of course. Instead, you set up a directory for sharing files and you make available only the ones you want to provide. Groove should work faster on a local network than Office Live because it doesn't use an Internet connection at all. It uses only your local network's Ethernet connection, which is extremely fast. Groove is a good option for file sharing when your Internet connection goes down, for instance.

Office Live Groove 2007 originally went by the name Groove Virtual Office. It's offered as part of Office Enterprise 2007, which also includes Office OneNote 2007 and Office Professional Plus 2007.

Understanding Peer-to-Peer Collaboration

If you ever used the services of Napster or one of the other well-known (and infamous) file-sharing networks, you're familiar with peer-to-peer technology, which is what Office Live Groove provides.

Napster enabled computers to set themselves up as servers and share music with other users (or peers) on the network. In this peer-to-peer setup, you were able to download any music in a folder the Napster member had set up for file sharing. The downside was this: transferring the files depended on the speed of the user's Internet connections, the speed of the computer, and whether the user was available on the Internet at a given time. The same downside applies to Office Live Groove. If a user isn't online, you can't retrieve their files using Office Live Groove. That's why Groove users may want to set up an Office Live Essentials or Premium workspace as a backup, so they can access files on a 24/7 basis.

16

You'll find the Office Live Groove home page at http://office.microsoft
.com/en-us/groove/default.aspx. You can download a trial version of the
program there and launch it 25 times. Then, you are required to pay a
$79.95 yearly subscription to keep using it—for each user.

Creating a Workspace

A blog devoted to Microsoft Office Live Groove (http://blogs.msdn.com/marco/
archive/2006/02/23/538047.aspx) states this application is being used internally at
Microsoft itself. That's a reason why it's so easy and practical to use. In particular,
it's easy and fast to create a workspace.

Once you use Office Live for a while, you get used to working on the server.
If you've been away for a while, you might have to log in again. When you want
to view a new page, you need to wait for it to reload. If you want to upload a
document or image to your Office Live space, it might take a minute or two as the
Image Manager opens.

With Groove, your own computer is the server. You set up your workspace
right on your own file system with just a couple of mouse clicks. You don't need
to set up a server. You don't even need an internal network. As long as your
computers are on the Internet, you can set up a shared workspace and invite
selected individuals to use it. And a measure of security comes from assigning user
names and passwords, too.

What makes Groove unique is a peer-to-peer architecture that lets individuals
in an enterprise collaborate directly with one another, rather than through a server.
In the sample image provided by Microsoft and shown in Figure 16-1, you see, in
the window on the right, a group of workspaces set up on one computer. Clicking
the New Workspace link near the top of this window opens the dialog box on the
left, which lets you specify the kind of workspace you want to create. You can
choose from a set of predefined templates—an option that should be familiar to
Office Live customers.

On the downside, Office Groove is expensive. And it doesn't include web site
and e-mail capability. Office Live, at the same time, can enable your office to
create a web site and get a free domain name, not to mention business applications.

Synchronizing with Other Users

Office Live Groove gives new speed and convenience to the concept of shared
workspaces. You can see who is working on a file at any given time through alerts,
and Read and Unread designations tell which files have been viewed. If you make
a change to a file in a shared workspace, even when you are offline, Office Live

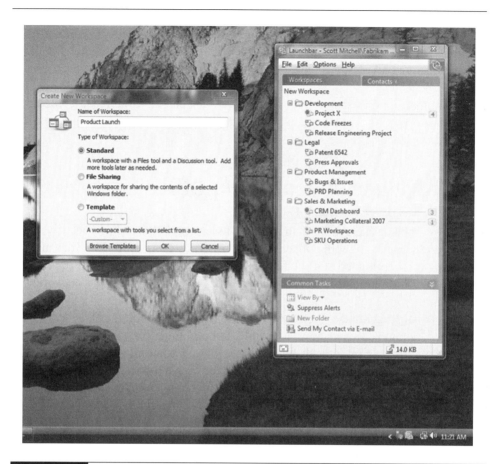

FIGURE 16-1   Office Live Groove lets you create shared workspaces on your computer, rather than a remote server.

Groove can send (or, in computerspeak, *push*) the new versions right to the shared workspaces of the coworkers you identified for file sharing.

Integration with Office Live

Groove and Office Live give a workgroup two different ways to collaborate but one point of connection is between them. You can use Groove to download document libraries from your Office Live workspace. You can work with them offline, and then synchronize changes back to the site when you're online again.

16

Groove users could also use Office Live workspaces as backup repositories of important business information. Uploading the files you share on your computer to Office Live ensures someone can access updates to critical documents, even if no other team members are online. Office Live can be a useful backup because of Groove's dependence on individual workstations for file sharing. To use Groove and access another person's shared files, that person must be online, and their computer needs to be operating correctly. You can use Office Live as a sort of storage area, so anyone can get access to the shared files at any time.

Getting Together in Real Time: Office Live Meeting

By now, you've probably figured out that one of the keys to Microsoft's success is giving computer users more than one way to accomplish a task. Office Live and Office Live Groove are both collaboration tools. They let people share files and data using their computers. Office Live isn't always fast. Office Live Groove can be faster, depending on the performance of your workstation and your network connection.

Long-distance phone calls can be expensive and, depending on the service available, communication is always reliable. For real immediacy and collaborative features, and to save on long-distance phone bills, it's hard to beat *Office Live Meeting*, which lets you communicate with others on a network in real-time. Office Live Meeting is a web conferencing tool. It can function as a teleconferencing or videoconferencing tool, depending on whether your computer is equipped with a camera, as well as a microphone and speakers.

Live Meeting, like other web conferencing tools, is intended to help small businesses save on travel expenses. Rather than having staff people travel to meetings, they can videoconference by speaking online using their computers' built-in audio systems. With Live Meeting, everyone can connect to the same web site to conduct an online meeting. Live meeting also includes a whiteboard tool that lets participants in a conference create diagrams. Office files, such as PowerPoint presentations, can also be shown during a conference.

TIP   *The quality of the communication you conduct with others on the Internet depends on the speed of your Internet connection and the processing power of your computer. Supposedly, Office Live Meeting only requires a 56 Kbps or faster connection but, certainly, a DSL or cable modem connection would be better. It also requires Windows Media Player 9 or later. Find out more about this real-time collaboration option on the Office Live Meeting home page, http://office.microsoft.com/en-us/livemeeting/default.aspx.*

One nice thing about Live Meeting is it's been a Microsoft product for a number of years and has an abundance of online help, publications, and training related to the product. You can download Live Meeting and use it for a 14-day trial period. After that, you need to pay a license fee to keep the software. The fee depends on the number of copies you need for your office. Complete the form at http://main.placeware.com/about_us/contact_sales/reg.cfm to get a quote.

Before you download or purchase Live Meeting, try Windows Live Messenger first. Live Meeting is suitable for corporate environments. But if you only need to talk to one or two others in your company, you can download and start using Windows Live Messenger right within the Office Live interface. See the upcoming section "Instant Messaging."

Office Live Communicator

Live Meeting gives workgroup members a way to connect in real-time using their respective computers. These days, computers are hardly considered mobile communications tools. To be mobile, you need to integrate your schedule on your palm device with your desktop, and you need to send text and instant messages (IM). *Office Communicator 2007* is software that integrates workers' address books and directories. It even has the capability to share "presence information" from your calendaring software to tell people if you are available. It can help members of a workgroup communicate not only using Live Meeting, but also IM and video.

Communicator is built in to the Microsoft Office Professional Plus and Microsoft Office Enterprise packages. You can find out more about Office Communicator at http://office.microsoft.com/en-us/communicator/HA102037151033.aspx.

Scheduling and Communications Tools in Office Live

As an Office Live user, you don't necessarily want to go looking for special software to schedule meetings and communicate with your coworkers and business partners. You want to explore the options available in the service itself. The following sections describe some built-in options that can help you reach out and connect with important business contacts.

Scheduling Utilities

Office Live gives you several calendars that can help you get organized and be on the same page with your coworkers when it comes to meetings and appointments. The *Office Live Mail* application, which comes with all three Office live subscription levels, includes a Personal Calendar. Click Go To Calendar on the Office Live Mail toolbar to open it. Click on dates to record appointments and invite others in your office who have Office live e-mail accounts to attend.

Like other personal calendars offered by Yahoo! and Google, the Office Live personal calendar can also be shared with family and friends. Click Sharing to identify those who have access to your schedule (see Figure 16-2).

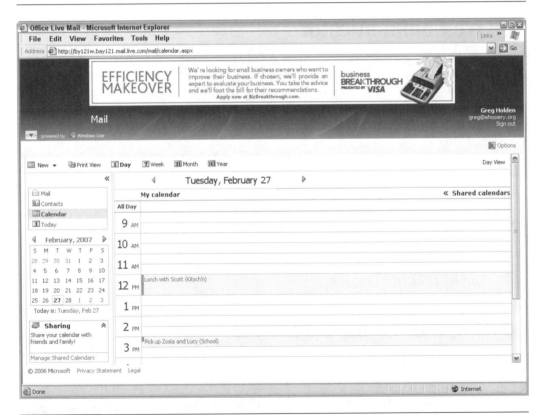

FIGURE 16-2   You can share your free personal calendar with friends and coworkers.

If you subscribe to Office Live Premium, you have access to the *Time Manager application,* which provides you with a Schedule and Reservations section similar to, but somewhat more sophisticated than, the personal calendar in Office Live Mail. Time Manager's calendar, shown in Figure 16-3, lets you view events for a single person for a selected week or for an entire workgroup for a week. It lets you identify office resources that need to be used for meetings and other events.

You notice the real sophistication of Time Manager when you set up appointments. Not only do you get to specify which workgroup members and which resources need to be set aside, but the bottom-half of the form you complete to list meetings also tells you who is available or busy in the office at the time, and it checks for double bookings of the facilities you want to use (see Figure 16-4).

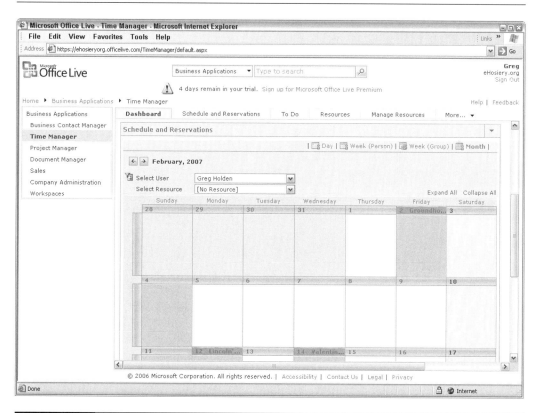

FIGURE 16-3 Time Manager can display appointments for an individual or everyone in a group.

16

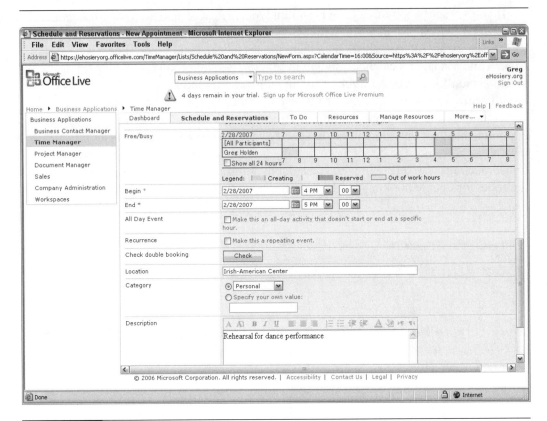

Instant Messaging

Instant messaging (IM-ing) isn't just for teenagers or preteens. If you're in a hurry and you can't talk on the phone because you're in a public place, you can send a quick text message to someone in your workgroup. You download and make use of *Windows Live Messenger,* the IM client integrated with Office Live. The service works with Basic, Essentials, or Premium through the E-Mail application. What's more, it enables you to make phone calls over your PC, conduct videoconferences, or send text messages to your colleagues' phones. Follow these steps to install Windows Live Messenger:

1. Sign on to Office Live and connect to your home page.

2. Click E-Mail.

3. Under the heading Instant Message, click Download Now!

4. When the Windows Live Messenger page appears, click Get it free.

5. When the File Download dialog box appears, click Run, and then follow the steps on subsequent screens to install the software.

You don't have to log into the Office Live site to download Windows Live Messenger. You also find a link to it on the MSN home page (http://www .msn.com).

Once the Windows Live Messenger window, shown in Figure 16-5, opens, you sign in with your Office Live ID and password. You add contacts from your workgroup, which lets you know who is online at any given time.

Marketing Your Office Live Business with adManager

Search marketing is an exciting and relatively new way to market yourself or your business using search engines. Millions of people go to Google, Yahoo!, or Windows Live search every day to find content on the Web. They enter a word or phrase in a search engine's search box, and then they submit this query to the service's server. The search results that follow contain links related to the fact, product, or service they're looking for. The links in the main body of a search results page are the natural results. The paid search results are ads you and other advertisers display around the edges of a search results page. The ads appear only when someone performs a search for keywords that match ones you (the advertiser) already associated with the ad you create.

One significant advantage of search engine marketing is that you don't pay a fee to the search service every time your ad is displayed. You only pay a fee when someone clicks it. You determine the amount you are going to pay: you place a bid on each click. The higher your bid is in relation to other advertisers who specified the same keywords you have, the higher and more prominently your ad appears on a page full of search results. (Presumably, ads near the top of a given page are most likely to be clicked by someone who is searching for a similar product or service. But, it's also important to write your ad in a compelling way.)

If you want to market your Office Live business or web site, search marketing is a great way to do it. Office Live users have access to a tool called *adManager* to create and place ads. The ads appear on Microsoft's search services, MSN Search and Windows Live Search.

16

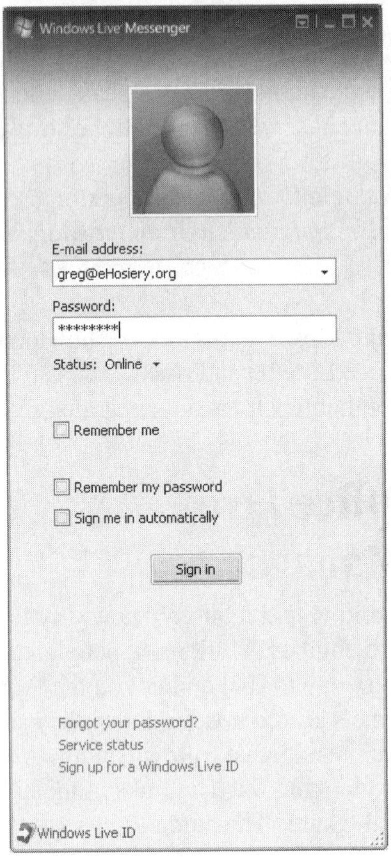

FIGURE 16-5   Add your Office Live workgroup members to your Windows Live Messenger list of contacts.

adManager is part of Office Live at all subscription levels. And, adManager is free: no matter what the limitations, trying it is worthwhile. The big limitation of adManager program is, at press time, it only works with Windows Live Search. As you and the rest of the online world know, Google is the "big dog" in search services, and it's also the leader in search marketing. If you want to take out a pay-per-click ad to market your new business on Google, you need to sign up for Google AdWords.

To start using adManager, click Sales and Marketing in the links on the left side of the Office Live window. The Microsoft Office Live adManager screen appears.

Read about the program to see how it works. As you learn from the instructions, you are charged a $5 setup fee to create your account. Click Start to initiate the process of creating that account, and then follow the Setup Wizard through the steps involved.

A utility called Wordtracker *(http://www.wordtracker.com) helps search marketers select keywords that can maximize their exposure while keeping their ads targeted to customers who are looking for what they have to offer. Creating search marketing ads, and then "refining" and improving them is a skill beyond the scope of this book. See* How to Do Everything with Google, *written by Fritz Schneider, Nancy Blachman, Eric Fredri, and published by McGraw-Hill, for more information.*

Where to Find It

Microsoft Office Live Groove	http://office.microsoft.com/en-us/groove/default.aspx
Microsoft Office Live Groove blog	http://blogs.msdn.com/marco/archive/2006/02/23/538047.aspx
Microsoft Office Live Meeting	http://office.microsoft.com/en-us/livemeeting/default.aspx
Microsoft Office Communicator	http://office.microsoft.com/en-us/communicator/HA102037151033.aspx
adManager	https://admanager.officelive.com

16

Part VI

Appendixes

Appendix A

Resources for Running a Business Web Site

Office Live provides you with an impressive set of business tools. They are the sorts of shared applications usually found in Office Enterprise and other far-more expensive resources. But, some gaps are in Office Live's feature set. For small businesses that need to conduct sales transactions online, some add-on services are a necessity. This appendix examines the must-haves, as well as some optional accounting and backup services that can strengthen your Office Live business presence.

Accounting Resources

As you learned in Chapter 15, both Office Live and Microsoft Office Accounting can help you keep track of your company's financial records. Once you have those records, you can file your taxes and perform other functions with the help of these useful online resources.

QuickBooks

http://quickbooks.intuit.com

Several well-known accounting software packages exist for home and business use (such as Quicken, www.quicken.com), but I mention this one because it has a QuickBooks for the web service that lets you keep your books online in a fashion similar to Office Live.

Owl Small Business Accounting

http://www.owlsoftware.com

I like the Owl Software accounting programs because they're exceptionally easy to use and economical as well.

Morebusiness.com

http://www.morebusiness.com

This isn't a site about bookkeeping or accounting per se, but it does provide visitors with software programs, as well as useful financial and legal documents, including a calculator, sample business agreements, and business plans you can adapt to your own needs.

Payment Services

Office Live can help you set up a free web site and create a sales catalog. But, when it comes to processing payments, you need to either accept paper checks or money orders, or sign up with a payment service. The following describes several options.

Merchant Accounts

A *merchant account* is an account provided by a bank, savings and loan, or credit card service to a business that needs to process payments from customers.

Wells Fargo Merchant Services

https://www.wellsfargo.com/biz/merchant/options/gateways/ima/   Many banks and financial institutions provide merchant accounts to Internet businesspeople. But, Wells Fargo Bank has been in the Internet merchant account space longer than nearly anyone. Their features include an Address Verification Service designed to reduce fraud.

1st American Card Service

http://www.1stamericancardservice.com   *1st American Card Service* isn't a traditional bank, instead, it's a service that specializes in merchant services for online businesses that want to accept credit card payments. Many such services are on the Internet, but this is one of the best known and most reputable.

Online Escrow Services

An *escrow service* is a company that acts as a go-between, transferring funds from one person or business to another to complete payments conducted on the Internet.

PayPal

https://www.paypal.com

PayPal, a service owned by eBay, is the big player in the electronic payment field these days. That's due, in part, to its integration with eBay, but also because PayPal so easy to use and so secure.

A

Moneybookers.com

http://www.moneybookers.com

A service based in Europe, Moneybookers.com is primarily intended for online merchants and customers who deal in Euros. However, U.S. e-commerce individuals can sign up, which is especially useful if they have customers who come from Europe.

Shopping Carts and Catalog Services

Office Live does not include two utilities that help shoppers make selections and "check out" their items, as well as totaling them and calculating sales tax. To help your customers shop the way they do on Amazon.com or other e-commerce sites, you need to provide an online catalog and a shopping cart application.

Freemerchant

http://www.freemerchant.com

You can set up a free web site with Office Live, but when your visitors want to make catalog purchases, you can send them to this site. *Freemerchant* provides store builders, catalogs, and a shopping cart utility, among other tools. Despite its name, Freemerchant isn't free. Hosting packages start at an economical $9.95 per month, however.

osCommerce

http://www.oscommerce.com

This open source software solution claims that nearly 12,000 stores around the world use its shopping cart solution. "Open source" means the source code is open for development and improvement.

Backups and Security

When you are working with customer information, security is a big concern. You have to protect your valuable clients' credit cards, addresses, or other data. And, if you store a substantial number of business files on your Office Live site, it's important to back them up so you don't lose any critical data.

FilesAnywhere

http://www.filesanywhere.com

FilesAnywhere gives you 100MB of server space for a mere $3.95 per month. Other packages are available that provide even more space. The site conducts automatic daily backups for its customers. So, if you use it as a backup area for your Office Live files, you'll also get backups of your backups.

IBackup

http://www.ibackup.com

IBackup doesn't provide quite as much storage space as FilesAnywhere (packages between at $3 per month or $30 per year for 50MB of storage space), but files are protected with Secure Sockets Layer (SSL) encryption and you gain the capability to map your IBackup storage directly, so it appears to be a drive on your local file system.

A

Appendix B

Office Live, SharePoint, and Related Resources

You're not operating in a vacuum when it comes to learning how to use Microsoft Office Live. Microsoft itself has put out a good deal of information on the subject in the interest of making the topic less intimidating for users who are creating their first web site or shared site. At the same time, some of these sites provide you with "inside" information about new features or developments pertaining to Office Live. Both types of sites can help you work smarter and make better use of the service.

Blogs and Community Resources

When it comes to getting focused information on a particular topic, such as Office Live, community forums are often the best place to turn. That's particularly true in the case of Microsoft products, because support isn't always quick or convenient. The Office Live blogs and the community forums mentioned in the following sections are good places to connect with Microsoft experts, as well as other users who are in the same situation as you.

Office Live Community

http://officelivecommunity.com/default.aspx

Go here to access the Office Live message boards as well as the Office Live team blog. The message boards are broken into separate topics: Announcements, Getting Started, Customer Gallery, Design Tips, Customizing Business Applications, and more.

The Office Live Blog

http://officeliveblog.spaces.live.com

This is the official blog that developers of Office Live maintain. Go here for announcements and developments pertaining to the service. Blogs created by the developers of a product or service are especially useful because, if you have comments or questions, they give you the chance to talk directly to the development team.

Chris's Unofficial Office Live Developer Blog

http://blogs.msdn.com/cbeiter

This is a blog created by Chris Beiter of the Office Live developer team. The emphasis here is on customizing Office Live by using SharePoint Designer and other tools. However, Beiter also discusses issues related to creating a successful web site, such as ways to keep users on your site.

Instructional Web Sites and Presentations

Books like this one are good starting points for learning about aspects of working with software and computer equipment. But online presentations are sometimes more up-to-date. The following ones were also created by Microsoft staff, who are involved with developing Office Live or related software, such as SharePoint.

Presentations on Office Live/SharePoint Designer

http://channel9.msdn.com/Showforum.aspx?forumid=38&tagid=114

Albert Shen of Microsoft presents a variety of presentations showing how to customize Office Live applications by opening your Office Live site in SharePoint Designer and customizing business applications. The presentations are entitled Office Live Workflows, Using the Data Form Web Part in Office Live, and Office Live with SharePoint Designer. The last presentation is the place to start.

About Office Live Business Applications

http://msdn2.microsoft.com/en-us/library/aa973400.aspx

This page from the Microsoft Developer Network site examines the creation of business applications from templates. There is a link to a how-to page on customizing Office Live applications with SharePoint Designer.

Programs and Products Related to Office Live

You can learn about a computer application in many ways. In the case of an online service such as Office Live, many web sites can help you perform different functions related to collaboration and productivity.

SharePoint Designer Home Page

http://office.microsoft.com/en-us/sharepointdesigner/FX100487631033.aspx

Learn more about SharePoint Designer here and download a demo version of the program you can try out with your Office Live site.

B

Office Live Advisor

Go to the Office Live home page and click Sign up for a free newsletter.

This online newsletter covers a variety of Windows Live products, including Office Live.

Microsoft Small Business Center

http://smallbusiness.microsoft.com

This site is dedicated to giving small business owners support using Microsoft products. If you have a Windows Live ID (the same ID you use for Office Live), you can log in to a level of service called "Small Business Center+" and start typing chat messages to a Microsoft Help desk.

Index